Inside
Looking Out

More Rock'n'Roll tales from inside the British music business

THE ANIMALS – Inside Looking Out
February 1966 reached #12 in the British Charts

Inside
Looking Out

More Rock'n'Roll tales from inside the
British music business

by

Mark Rye

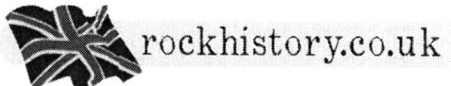 rockhistory.co.uk

Inside Looking Out
A RockHistory Book
www.RockHistory.co.uk

1

Published and printed in the United Kingdom and the United States of
America by RockHistory Ltd.

RockHistory Ltd
PO Box 509A, Surrey KT7 0WQ

Cover: Raven Design
Book Design: Velin@Perseus-Design.com

PAPERBACK ISBN   978-0-9576881-5-5
EBOOK ISBN   978-0-9576881-6-2

For Ash, this is what Grandpa did for a living

Dedicated to Anthea Joseph and Steve O'Rourke for
inadvertently starting all this.

Many thanks to Pete Brown, Roger Dopson, Stephen
Gammond, Kate Highfield, Malcolm Hill, Sarah Knapp,
Rupert Perry, The Professor, Greg Smith, Steve Waters & that
very White Crow.

Huge thanks to all the interviewees in the never-ending
RockHistory project, a selection of which appear within these
pages. For their time, their memories and for the music.

This book is planned to be like one of those Larry Parnes Sixties package tours. You have bought a ticket and now you will get to enjoy a whole variety of acts on the bill, each doing a few numbers and then on to the next. If you don't enjoy this one, well there is another one along in a minute or two, so stay on-board. It does not matter if you have no idea who the turn is, they will either please you or they won't – and then it is time for you to move on again. But they will all try really, really hard to entertain you and I am absolutely sure some will succeed with these stories about the growth of British music, how it was, and how it came into being. Most of these people you have probably never heard of – but for every artist and there are quite a few here, there was a host of backroom people of various levels of ability and competence all working to try and get the record to be a 'hit'. This is nearly fifty years of the British music scene in action, what used to happen and how it all sort of worked itself into greatness.

Of course, our job was to make Hit records. It was all about Hits.
If you didn't get a Hit record, there was no point in continuing.
JOHN SCHROEDER

This book has stories from so many people, both artists and backroom staff, who witnessed the phenomenal growth of pop music and the monumental social changes that it both caused and mirrored, and boy has this country changed. Popular music in Britain used to be a largely working class thing in the days when we were still a completely class-ridden country after World War II and this is why so many exceptional Jewish people were drawn to the entertainment business where that sort of complete class divide did not operate as strongly. Hit songs were what mattered, your accent or what school you went to, did not. Having success and making money was what it was all about in those early days for the business. In the Fifties, popular music in Britain was mainly pop, jazz and folk: with folk music then being heavily supported by the post-war communist countries. They believed this was the way to reach our youngsters' hearts and minds and hence their politics, while jazz was a New Orleans American invention or then again even Afro-European in its origins, it all depends how far down the roots you want to go. Pop is Pop, is Popular where all that matters is if you can hum it, sing it or whistle it, while all the time it whirls round in your head and makes you go out and buy a copy. I use the term 'pop' as an all encompassing genre for our music. So some jazz could become pop, some folk could also be pop, let alone consider the simple pop plea of 'Love Me Do' to all those besotted teenage girls.

Lonnie Donegan kick-started a unique time in British music with what became known by that fine old English word 'skiffle', which originally meant 'to make a mess of any business'. Well he certainly did that when he kick-started the change in how everything worked in Denmark Street, London W1, the home of our very own Tin Pan Alley and the music centre of Britain. His version of American jug band music, folk and blues, largely copped (but not credited) from Lead Belly, became mandatory for almost every young musician in the isle. Then not that long after skiffle, we got to be swept along with a wave of American rock'n'roll when this was grabbed and added to the mix as well. This healthy aural collision fuelled the motivation of most of that era of British youth to become musicians, not least of all The Beatles who became our very own boy band styled by their Svengali from Liverpool and boy did they 'happen', not only in Britain but everywhere else on this planet. This fascinating musical period became the time where the split between 'Variety' and Rock starts to occur. The Beatles in the early days were still expected to do Variety, to appear on the bill with *Morcambe and Wise* or play *Sunday Night At the London Palladium* and be all-round entertainers like everyone before them. But when it came to The Stones, they famously would not even stand and wave at the end of the show, cue more public outrage. Musically the world was tilting and nothing would ever be the same again.

The British Invasion swept across America shipping new versions of their own music back to these cousins across the pond where they all thought it was newer than new and grabbed it with both hands. We all shook our heads from side to side and lapped up all this fabulous music, it was the swinging soundtrack for the country's new rampant teenagers. The business side of things started to change rapidly as the other classes got involved because it looked so much fun to the music-hungry baby boomers, and all the cool male students wanted to be the Social Secretaries of their Universities and Colleges and to put on the best bands in the land and get the most girls. After all, to start with you could book Roxy Music for £15, The Who for £50, David Bowie for £40, or maybe £25 for Free, in the Sixties and the halls were rammed with partying teenage students out enjoying their young lives. Many of the kids that got bitten by the music bug charged into this newly changing British music business and many will tell you to this day that they have had the time of their lives. Just read their stories.

Such was the massive social impact of pop music, that most people can still remember which shop they bought that record in and even the colour of the record shop's bag as well. You belonged to a new movement and identified yourself with it and by it. Record shops moved from the side streets to the High Streets, one shop became two, soon becoming a whole chain of them such was the demand for records. There were all these glorious happening groups you could go and see and so large distances were travelled by fans around this small country on a still basic transport system, by bus or train or rammed into an over-full old car with all your mates going to gigs and following your favourite group wherever they played.

Pop music is popular music and the adoration of the fans has been timeless. The village maids had always made a beeline for the travelling minstrel in days of yore and thus it proved with Frank Sinatra or Johnny Mathis in the Fifties where this timeless trend was continued. So we had Beatlemania of the Sixties, Bolan and Bowie in the Seventies and an endless procession of wannabe pop stars in every subsequent decade. Here in Britain in the Sixties, radio washed from the limited Reithian output of the BBC and crackly Radio Luxembourg through to the swashbuckling pirate radio stations and their unlimited music, our music, recorded just for our generation.

These pirate radio DJs were largely locked on their boats but their huge success led to Labour's Tony Benn's stamping on their cavalier and unlegislated money-making activities, which all led the BBC grudgingly to the birth of pop radio's own Radio One in 1967. This gave us a new set of national disc jockey stars who relentlessly promoted themselves at every opportunity, using the music and with the connivance of wunderful Radio One. The BBC were able to pay them a pittance and let them make up their salary by doing public appearances, thus also promoting this BBC brand in person all over the country. DJ Annie Nightingale once raised a point about why Radio One DJs became so ab-fab in the UK but not anywhere else – the answer was that Radio One needed huge listening figures to succeed as the rest of BBC Radio absolutely hated them and were jealous of their popularity, with their tiny budgets and huge success, how very dare they? Of course the maleness of it all meant that some were able to get away with almost whatever they wished in those days. It was the behaviour of the time and our authorities joined in and exploited it all just as much, but then powerful figures always have.

> *John Peel was obviously the main guy at the time, who had one of those religious conversion kind of things. He'd been playing long progressive rock tracks on his Radio One show up until 1976, and then suddenly he played the Sex Pistols and said I'm not going to play that other stuff any more, and just abandoned the old music and whatever audience was listening to that, and moved on to the new, two-minute wonders. So John was the unique figure in British radio for as long as he was there. Curiously he was very uncertain of his position; he never felt the management at Radio One valued him in the way that he knew the audience and the outside world did. So he was forever expecting to be fired and in the end they just shuffled him into a terrible late night slot.*
> ### *CHARLIE GILLETT*

In this golden era of great British music we grew and idolised guitar players on this new-to-Britain instrument. Legends like Bert Weedon, Hank Marvin, Johnny Kidd, Big Jim Sullivan, Eric Clapton, Jeff Beck, Jimmy Page, Pete Townshend, George Harrison, David Gilmour, Ritchie Blackmore, Peter Green, Phil Manzanera, Steve Howe, Alvin Lee, Steve Hackett, Tony Iommi, Steve Hillage, Andy Summers, Albert Lee, John McLaughlin, Peter Frampton, Ray Fenwick, Peter Green and so many more. Make your own list up as I am sure you will, we can start a wall for you to write on as I am sure I must have left some legends out. But it is interesting to reflect that prior to skiffle the guitar was not an instrument taught in British schools, it was the violin or the piano that ruled the roost in those days. Post-skiffle the guitar became the coolest instrument of them all, well apart from the saxophone that is, oh and there are sparkly drum kits as well. But you get my drift I hope.

In those days we had almost no knowledge of what people in any other country actually did.
CHRIS BARBER

The development of the British music scene is a fascinating little island story that swept around the world. We were blessed with some of the best song-writers and musicians ever heard and the technicians to make it audible and loud enough for the masses. We started off, post-war, suspicious of, and isolated from, all these other countries around us. Yet we accepted modified American versions of our own music with a rapacious enthusiasm and then modified it again and shipped it back to them all over again. What the Americans call the British Invasion opened up the British music business to wealth on a scale that was unheard of and our new more professional music business grabbed the opportunity to tour our groups and bands around the world, vacuuming up the cash with extraordinary diligence. The musicians and their back room staff were full of characters the like of which we will probably never see again, deals were made and plots hatched but most important of all, the music was made and has survived intact. It is just how you get to listen to it now that keeps changing.

When the music business first got up and running you to had to be a maverick, you had to be an entrepreneur and you had to be a risk taker to get anywhere. Most of those nefarious people I met had a very large and colourful character and you could not help but like them.
ROD DUNCOMBE

The changes to once powerful record companies caused by the internet now have been seismic and this in turn means that touring support and recording budgets for artists have been torn to shreds. No longer will the record company fund a band to spend forty-eight hours or forty-eight months in the studio perfecting their art, and anyway now, with these same changes in technology, you can record music in your very own home studio or lap-top when the muse strikes. So those record companies and studios have merged or closed, the staff have gone and now all the money is back in performing live again, not in record sales. So look out for the 'human jukebox' appearing in a town near you soon, playing all their hits and more and please support them with your pocket money or your pensions. Not Arf.

The RockHistory project is about collecting first-hand as many as we can of the people and their stories and therefore recording the social history of a business that has now largely gone forever. Some of these people themselves may have gone to the great gig in the sky, yet most remain. But their fabulous stories and great memories of the golden years, like the extraordinary music, can still be enjoyed again and again.

Mark Rye

STUART EPPS, Studio Engineer

Elton John was making an album at The Mill studios, the *Single Man* album, and Elton is easy to work with but he has got a short temper and things have to keep going and you don't want to mess around when he is around or he will soon lose his temper. Anyway all day we had been working away and he said, I've written this instrumental and I want to put it down at some point, and we forgot about it and then at the end of the day we were quite knackered really it was just about eleven o'clock, maybe midnight and Elton says, Oh, I just want to put down this instrumental. Well if he wants to put down an instrumental, fine. So I put a bit of tape on, he goes out there and starts playing this thing – 'Song For Guy' – we did not know what it was called at the time, anyway it was a bit unusual, I had not really heard Elton play an instrumental before, I did not really know what was going on.

It was kind of complicated and he would get about fifteen seconds in and he would make a mistake. Alright rewind the tape, start again. Clive and I were in the control room and he keeps making mistakes and it is now one o'clock, one-thirty in the morning and he is getting annoyed now and pissed off with himself and he knows he is keeping us behind. It was only going to take ten minutes, usual story, anyway this time he is two and a half minutes in and no mistakes and I look round and I had not put a full reel of tape on by any means, just a bit of spare, and I'm thinking it can only be a couple of minutes long. Then I'm thinking, I wonder how long this is because this is the first time he has got this far with this song. So now I am getting a bit hot and I am saying to Clive look how much tape there is left, oh he'll be finished, how long can it be?

Now we are getting into a serious situation because there is not much tape and you cannot even judge on a multi-track when it is that low and we are just thinking we cannot run out of tape now, because this is the master, it is going extremely well, it does not sound like a bad tune and obviously this is the one, we cannot run out of tape, but he does not look like he is going to stop and now we are looking

1

like we are running on air, the take up spool is really going, sweating now, does it look like he is going to stop soon? Well no word of a lie, as he finishes the last chord, and as it dies away the tape comes off the spool and we more or less fall to the floor. Never told him. Did you get it? Yes of course we got it, come in have a listen. Because we were so relieved we did not mind staying around for another one, so he started adding another piano and another piano and it started to build up into this track and they are still playing it on the radio today.

BOB MERCER, MD, EMI Records

Queen were going on tour, the first album had been out, we'd had close hits with 'Seven Seas of Rhye' and another track, I can't remember what it was, and they were going to open for Mott the Hoople. You used to pay to get your band on an opening slot in those days, and I paid for them to get on this slot. Freddie comes in to see me. I met with Queen pretty much every other week, always with all four of them; we worked very, very closely. So Freddie comes in, he's not on his own, he's got this woman with him, Zandra Rhodes, who was a frock designer, an outrageous frock designer, and he introduces me to Zandra Rhodes, I knew exactly who she is and I'm kind of puzzled. And he goes, I've asked Zandra to make our costumes; I said, what costumes? This was a jeans and t-shirt band. He said, for the shows, for our opening of Mott the Hoople; we're going to get dressed up. I said, that's wonderful. He said, well she needs £10,000. I said Freddy, I've already paid to get you on the bill, I can't pay for costumes. Oh my dear fellow, and he starts to throw a wobbly, so I said alright, alright. I said to Zandra Rhodes, do it for as little money as you can and disguise the invoice so that accounting don't come up to me and say what's this – frocks for the boys?

I didn't think any more of it; hadn't been to any rehearsals. But I go up to the opening night in Manchester – an old theatre with a

2

fire curtain. The place is packed, and up comes the fire curtain and there's Queen in what we then became used to seeing them in, the outfits – Brian with the cape, Freddie with some kind of frou-frou leotard – and I think they were set to do a thirty-minute show. This was Queen in, I guess, 1974; so ten years before Live Aid, but if you'll remember, at Live Aid they turned that thing around with a twenty-five-minute set, because like everybody else they'd paid attention to what they were going to do; they'd programmed it, they'd rehearsed it, it went from beginning to end; they just turned the whole thing around. They did exactly the same ten years earlier opening for Mott the Hoople. They just hit it; they were just so impressive. When they finished, the audience went nuts and they came on to do an encore, which was strictly forbidden under the deal that I'd made with Jack Nelson who was managing Mott the Hoople at the time; strictly forbidden that they did an encore. But back they came; Freddie had now changed into tight shorts with the Union Jack on the front and the Stars & Stripes on his ass, and they did 'Big Spender', that old Broadway song, I suppose. That was it.

So I'm going backstage, half-time, to congratulate the boys and take them out for something to eat. I get backstage and Jack Nelson grabs hold of me, pushes me up against the wall and says, they're off the tour. I go, what are you fucking talking about, they were great. He says, exactly; my band can't follow that; we've got twenty-one days, Mott the Hoople will be dead by the end of that. And it was the best news I heard all night and I said, well, tough; I paid my money, they're staying on the show. No fucking way are they off the show, off the tour. And that tour really took them in; they were *NME*'s darling. And Mott the Hoople hardly worked after that; they really destroyed them. And of course Jack Nelson ended up managing Queen very shortly afterwards.

STUART WATSON,
EMI Special Promotions

Queen was the band I rated, the band I worked with and the band I loved best. The first demo tape was brought into EMI and the deputy managing director, Roy Featherstone, ran into my office and said Stuart, Stuart you have got to listen to this, there are only two people in the company that like it and I think it is amazing, you have got to tell me what you think. The big man who was Dutch did not like it even though his Dutch A&R man did. There were three tracks on this cassette, 'Liar', 'Keep Yourself Alive' and the other was I think 'Seven Seas Of Rhye'. The voice was amazing, the guitar amazing and I said wow what's this? There were three of us rushed into the Dutchman's office and we said we have got to sign this band, so eventually they got signed, we paid the money. The first show was April 1973 at the Marquee and I had already met them as I had been going up to Kensington Market where Roger and Freddie had a stall and Freddie's girlfriend at the time, Mary, was working in Biba so they were all hanging around that area. After the Marquee we all went to a pub up the road and there were not many EMI people around then. Next there was a support slot on a Mott the Hoople tour and I remember going on all those dates as a special promotion sort of thing and then one freezing cold night in Southend and Queen all got up on stage to sing backing to 'All the Young Dudes', well apart from John, and it was amazing and all the press were there and it all sort of started that night.

JOHN BAGNALL,
EMI Artist Development

In the early days of Queen, Freddie and Mary used to live in Holland Road which was five minutes round the corner so my wife and I used to go round and feed Freddie's cats. And also just drop in to make sure Mary was OK and I remember being there one evening when she dug out a couple of cassettes and she said please don't ever tell Freddie I played you this and it was 'Killer Queen', the original piano demo and one or two other things, and it was just fantastic. With Queen you always felt it was going to be when, not if, they would make it but it was very hard work to get them away, they were perceived as being a bit of a glam throwback and television in particular wasn't that sure about them. My recollection is being in Ronnie Fowler's office one evening as we often were and racking our brains as to what we could try next to get Queen away and the phone rang. It was *Top Of The Pops* and Heathrow was closed by fog and an American band that had been set for TOTP had been delayed. So the question to Ronnie was can you get this band of yours, Queen or whatever they are called, to the studio to record the backing track within two hours? Ronnie said: Yeah, yeah of course. Put the phone down and prayed that Freddie was in. That would have been 'Seven Seas Of Rhye'.

MIKE APPLETON, Producer, *OGWT*

Because I was sent all the records that were coming out at the time, it was very difficult, and it's still difficult, for me to know exactly what my musical taste would have been. I got access to things that I know I would never have found if they hadn't ended up on my desk. One of the records that ended up on my desk one day, I was out at lunch, and when I got back, there was a white label sitting on the desk. White labels, for those who don't know, are the first pressing that the record companies have of an album. They're usually very high quality in reproduction, and very low quality on information. Normally, a promotional guy would write on it Fred Bloggs and the name of the album, but nothing had been written on this at all. I thought: I'll have a listen to it, see what it is. I put it on, and it was brilliant. It was one of those things that grabs you straight away. I didn't know what it was.

I rang Phil Jenkinson, who used to do our videos. I said, look, I've got a record here. It's been dumped on the desk. It's obviously about to come out, and I don't know what it is, but it's really good. Would you do me a video for it? I sent it over to him. He found a great piece of black and white film. It was an express train going across America. On the front of the express train was Roosevelt's face. The whole thing was a promotional thing for a whistle-stop tour for an election or something. Anyway, I sent it over, he sent it back. Then that evening, I put it in the programme, but I still didn't know what it was, so I had to preface the introduction saying: This arrived on the desk in the office this week. I've no idea who it is. I've no idea which record company it is. I think it's fabulous, but I can't credit it with anybody. It sounds like it's called 'Keep Yourself Alive', from the repetition of the words. Would somebody, if they recognise it, please let us know. Phone in and let us know who it is and what the album is called.

Nobody did during the programme, but the next day, a red-faced plugger came in and said: It's a new band called Queen, and it's their new album. I gave the information out the next week. It's the only time

I've ever done anything like that. There was something that indicated something to do with taste, because it was just based entirely on no knowledge whatsoever, just a gut reaction.

DAVID MUNNS,
EMI Marketing Manager

The Queen stuff was probably the most exciting because it worked so well. 'Bohemian Rhapsody' was a record that nobody thought was do-able. I remember getting the bill for that video. That was when I almost lost my job, because the bill came in and it was £9,000 or something. LG Wood found out about it and I nearly... Ron White, Roy Featherstone were always the guys who claimed to know nothing about it. How the hell did that happen? And Bob Mercer was going, I think this is great. And I got the royal rollicking of my life, because they'd never spent more than £1,000 on a video before. I think it was just under £10,000, £9,000 and change. Stupid bloody record, it's too long. And we set that record up just perfectly, and one play on the radio, bang, that was it.

NICK MOBBS,
EMI A&R Manager

On 'Bohemian Rhapsody', the famous EMI meetings would be Tuesday morning or whatever, where all the marketing people and the A&R people would get together, and they would discuss upcoming releases, whether to release them or not. This was for third-party acts as well as directly signed ones. Queen were a third-party act, they weren't signed directly, they were licensed. I well remember it was that fourteen people, or whatever, that used to attend this meeting, Eric Hall being one of them as the plugger, and me being one as A&R. Out of those fourteen people, only Eric and I thought that 'Bohemian Rhapsody' should even be released. Again, it's one of those classic things, where this is what you're up against in the rock'n'roll/pop industry when you're trying to be a paradigm shifter.

One of the first connections I had with Don Arden was when he rang up to say that Roy Wood had made a new single, and that, between him and us, it was a disaster, something called 'California Man'. Could I go round and persuade Roy that this was in no way a single? Inevitably, I went round there, and I heard 'California Man' and thought: That sounds really commercial to me. I said to Don: I think it is commercial. He said: Oh no, no. It's crap. Just tell him it's rubbish. I said: I can't, because I think it's really good. I said to Don: Let's release it. Of course, it was a pretty decent sized hit.

£££

ARTHUR SHARP,
Don Arden Management

Roy Wood's Wizzard were on EMI. The old man figured Warner Brothers should have this, they're going to pay more than EMI. To hell with your contracts – he didn't agree with contracts – throw them out the door. I'm going over there. By now, Roy had recorded this wonderful record called 'I Wish It Could Be Christmas Every Day'. We're now at the beginning of December. I actually had a copy of 'I Wish It Could Be Christmas Every Day' on Warner Brothers. I haven't got it now. EMI threw an injunction in, knowing full well that come the 27th of December, that record was as dead as a dodo. The old man's in Los Angeles. Sharon's crying her eyes out in London: We've got to do something. Otherwise this record's dead. He said: OK, let EMI have what they want. Of course, the thing went off like a rocket. In three weeks, sold over 800,000 records. But they had us, because they knew it was going to be dead by the 26th/27th of December

NICK MOBBS,
EMI A&R Manager

Don Arden was always a pussycat with me. I went to see him on one occasion when I got wind that they were trying to take Roy, in particular, away from EMI and Harvest. In fact, it got to a point, I'd been on winter holiday, and 'I Wish It Could Be Christmas Every Day' was about to come out in the Wizzard phase. I came back to find that it had been printed up on Warner Brothers label. I was saying to people: What's gone on here? They're signed to EMI/Harvest. The EMI label's legal department was going: Yeah, don't worry about it. Don Arden's gone crazy. They can't possibly release it. Which they didn't. They printed up I don't know how many thousand on Warner's, but of course, it did come out on Harvest. At this point, as Don was trying to take them away to Warner's, I went to see him one memorable evening, when he was sitting in a sort of *Godfather's* office, with a very low light, just him on the beautiful leather recliner, and desk surrounded with papers. I went there with the express mission of saving EMI and keeping the act with EMI. I probably spent a good forty minutes making this unbelievably persuasive case as to why they should stick with EMI and what we could do for them. He listened to it very patiently, and he said: Nick, I really appreciate you coming here today and telling me all this. I do hear what you're saying. Warner Brothers will be ringing you tomorrow with a very, very attractive job offer. Sure enough, they did. It was extraordinary.

£££

ARTHUR SHARP,
Don Arden Management

After the Nashville Teens I joined Don Arden in his management company. At least I was going to get paid every week. He was managing the Electric Light Orchestra. This is pure Don Arden, and Sharon, this is early Sharon as well. He'd got ELO, which were originally on EMI Harvest label, but now they were starting to get a bit of a name for themselves, so let's move them over, and he wanted them to go to Warner Brothers. Joan Collins's husband – he's dead now – he was the head of Warner Brothers. Anyway, this deal was in the air. We had the offices on Wimbledon Common. It's in a house: number 44 Parkside. Sharon, bless her, Mrs Osbourne by then, she was on the telephone board, massive great things. This guy kept ringing in: I want to speak to Don. Don always told Sharon: Tell him I'm in New York. What he was trying to do was keep him on the hook. Don't tell him anything. Of course, those days, you had to book a call to New York, do it at ten o'clock in the morning.

Hopefully, at five o'clock in the afternoon someone would ring you and got you through.

It came the time when he said: Right, Sharon. Let's do the trick. You phone up from here, but you're not really, you're in New York. Put your accent on, and tell him that I want to speak to him. They'd kept him on the hook now for four or five days. Sharon, with headphones and that horn thing: Oh, hi. Can I speak to so and so? Anyway, Sharon says: Oh, hi. I have a Mr Don Arden for you. Of course, bang, bang, bang, it went straight through. Now she puts it through to Don, who's sitting there on Wimbledon Common. The old man says: Yeah, how are you doing over there? He said: This is not a very good line, is it. Well of course not. Sharon's got a handkerchief going (imitates static) – because there's no satellites, it's all by cable under the Atlantic – to make it all look and sound genuine. Got away with it. They were all in London. He thought it was in New York. That's why he could hang him on for five days. Of course, the deal was done. He signed the deal. I think he upped the ante on it. The money was there. He didn't want to agree now. Let's keep them worried that we might go elsewhere, pure Don Arden. Of course, four or five days later, from Wimbledon Common to somewhere in the West End of London, he fell for it. He was still in New York. The deal was struck for the price that Don Arden wanted, not what Warner Brothers wanted.

ERIC HALL,
Record Plugger

I left school at fifteen as you did in those days. Never had no qualifications. A real schmuck really. Always wanted to be in the record business or the music business, because just pre that, I went to acting school for a little while – Italia Conti, for literally a little while. I had a friend of the family, a man called Tony Hiller, songwriter and would work for Mills Music, Denmark Street, the famous Tin Pan Alley. My lovely mum, Eva, rest her soul,

11

said: Tony, my son's left school. Wants to leave school at Christmas. Because my birthday's in November, and you could leave at Christmas time then. I don't know what the shtick is now. He got me a job as a tea boy at Mills Music in Denmark Street. Another tea boy there started the same kind of week as me was a boy called Reg Dwight, who became Elton John. Over the road, I think Southern Music in Denmark Street, London, was Davy Jones, who then became David Bowie. Just up the road, I think in Campbell Connelly, or one of the others in that same street, was Steve Marriott. We were all sort of about similar ages, and all kind of started. They went onto become monster, monster, hit records and things: Small Faces, and David Bowie, and of course, Elton John. I went on to do what I did.

You used to go to Judy's Caff in Denmark Street, Tin Pan Alley. Three/four o'clock in the afternoon, or eleven o'clock in the morning, you'd go round and do all your staff. Tea. I'll have a coffee, Eric. Give me a tea. I'll have a coffee. Ham sandwich. I don't know if they're asking for chicken or ham sandwiches, being a nice Jewish boy. You did all that. You got them a cake. I got used to going to Denmark Street. In those days, tailors, there were songwriters, publishers. You saw these stars. If Perry Como was over from America, he'd go to Denmark Street, or Sinatra, only because they needed songs. I started at 20 Denmark Street, Mills Music, we did the rounds, us tea boys, in those days. Next door to 21 Denmark Street, Lawrence Wright. Eric Winston used to come in there to get to the top lines. I use to be in promotion then. I wasn't a tea boy any more. I'd just sell sheet music. Because that's when you sold sheet music. Even in the Sixties, people were still buying sheet music, and top lines, and orchestrations. You'd have all these Ted Heath, and Eric Winston, lovely, lovely Joe Loss.

I used to go to a club even before I was working in Denmark Street. By thirteen or fourteen, when I was still at school, I used to work at a club called the El Toro in St. John's Wood, with Marc Bolan. Because I knew Marc when I was twelve, from Clapton in London. I was a monster, monster fan again. Many, many, many years later, I was promoting his label, the T-Rex label, which was at one time distributed by EMI, and I was the promotion manager. It's like Elton John. I once said to Elton John when I was the chairman of Rocket Records, I looked at him one day and said, did we realise when we were both fifteen-ish, we're similar ages, very similar, a couple of months older than me, who would have thought? Here I am, chairman of your record company, and you're Elton John, who's the biggest. Amazing how life is strange and things.

I worked for Don Arden, just pre-EMI, my last job before EMI. Very notorious. They call him the Al Capone of the pop business. The pussycat, really. They started this EMI label. The beigey browny thing. They still kept Harvest and they kept on or two other little labels. Everybody was going to be on this new little shtick, beigey, sort of reddy beigey label. I get a call from a man called Roy Featherstone, he said: We've started this new label. We'd like you, and a man called Ronnie Fowler, to be head of promotion. He said: He won't be your boss, you're not his boss. Together. We think we've got there the two best pluggers in the business. Great. Company car. Expense account. Whatever you want to spend. He didn't realise what I was going to spend at the end of the day. Wonderful.

Don Arden, bless him. Love him, rest his soul. You didn't know if you got paid next week. He just was ducking and diving every week. His daughter is now the famous Sharon Osbourne. I knew Sharon, she used to do that old fashioned switchboard in Hay Hill in Berkeley Square. I think we moved to Parkside, Wimbledon. I remember the day I went to tell Don I'm going to leave, I'm going to put my notice in. We'd just come from a monster hit, play-wise, with a group called Judas Jump 'The Feeling We Feel'. A lot of plays, every man. They were happy with the record. A lot of plays.

I get a call that night, after I've talked terms with Roy Featherstone. I'm at home, my Loughton address, Essex. Like I say monster, monster, he had an expression: Frightening, Frightening. Roy rang up and said: We've got a problem. I said: What's that? He said: Frightening, frightening. It's frightening. What's frightening for Roy? I don't really know the man that well then. He said: I had a visit from your boss today, Don Arden. You told him you're leaving, did you? I said: Yes. Well, I've got to tell him. I can't just have two jobs. He said: He came to the office about four o'clock with a rifle and a man called Wilf Pine and Reg King – two heavies, side by side, and a rifle. Was going to shoot me for poaching his staff, and says that there's no way that you are going to join, and then he's going to kill me. If you join my company, he's going to kill me. I said: I love Don. He can't stop me, and I'm sure, at the end of the day, he won't. I would like to join the company and have a go at this new shtick you do.

MICK UNDERWOOD,
Musician

I don't think Don Arden mucked about to be honest with you but Peter Grant, I had all the time in the world for Peter really did you know, he was a funny man. He came out with some really funny things. I mean he actually used to lumber me sometimes to look after Gene Vincent. If Pete couldn't do it, and I'm nineteen. He said: Could you take the Finger, that's what his nickname for Gene was, the Finger, he said: Can you take Gene? We had one, we flew out to Belfast and two nights in this club, this is with The Outlaws and that, Kenny Lynch was on that and all. And Gene had just had a new thing on his leg and it was hurting him 'cause the block at the bottom was too big and we got out there and there's me and then Kenny Lynch came in as well, managed to get hold of a saw and we were sawing a big lump off this block, he's got his foot up here and I'm cutting his, you know, Be-bop-a-lula. I'm cutting this off, and I think we did the first night, but not the second night. And I've got his ticket. And he's saying to me: Man I've gotta go home. What? I said: Come on, we've got another show to do. And he kept on and on. I thought: Well what can I do? He's gonna go, he ain't gonna be here tomorrow anyway. So I gave him his ticket. And I got hell from Granty on that one, he phoned me up in the day I got home and he went absolutely garrity down the phone at me. I can't even say what he said. I go: What are you talking, oh God. And then he started laughing and said: You never know what happened do you? Well he got home 'cause he was having a bit of trouble with his wife. I don't know what it was, no idea what it was. And he pulled a gun on her and got arrested. OK. So, we're going: Alright, OK. We've got a broadcast that week to do for the BBC, a session. And the studio was that one under the Embankment, under the railway arches there. It was this theatre-type thing, so we're in there all set up ready to go with Gene and he walked in and I think he had her with him, and he's looking a bit sheepish you know, little bit sheepy. Anyway we did the session and it all got blown over then, but I mean it was such fun, just a laugh with Peter Grant, he's going potty at me. Calling me every name and a few that I'd not heard of before because I wasn't very old and then started laughing and told me the tale and I loved that. That was just brilliant. Brilliant.

NEIL CHRISTIAN, Musician

Don Arden brought over Gene Vincent and Eddie Cochran. I went along to the Kingston Granada. He was standing in the doorway, an exit near the front of the stage where I was sitting, standing there. I think it was Jimmy, Jimmy Page was with us, he said: That's the manager bloke, Don Arden, who brought him over. I said: Oh. I got out my seat, and I went over to him. I said: Excuse me, Sir. Could I have a word? I said: Would there be any chance at all that I went up and could meet Gene Vincent? He said: Oh yeah. I told him, he said: Yeah, go on then. I called over to Jimmy, he didn't come, but Jumbo the bass player came, and we went up these stairs, backstage, and we saw this door, Gene Vincent on it. He says: Go on, you knock. I said: Alright. I knocked on the door, and the door opened, there was this handsome blond-haired guy standing there. It's Eddie Cochran. I didn't know what to say. I said: It's great to see you, Eddie, but I've come to see Gene. You know what I mean? I really didn't know what to say. I was completely flabbergasted that I saw these two guys together. Cochran says: Come in, come in. We go in. Sits us down. Supplies us with drinks. We're sitting down, and Cochran started playing. He said: What did you think of this song? He started playing 'Sittin' on the Balcony'. He said: I've not recorded it yet. What do you think? I said: Not bad, not bad.

That's how I first met Don. Whenever he had a big show on anywhere around that area, I used to go to see him, and says: Yeah, go backstage. Then when I started going myself doing the rounds, I just went up to see him one night, or one afternoon, and says: Do you reckon you can get us any work? He said: Yeah, sure. That was it. That was the relationship with Don. He never stalled with any payments. Always paid whenever he said he would. Never a bit of trouble at all. I found the man most charming. Half these stories you hear about him, I mean, he could be hard, don't get me wrong. He could be a bit of a hard sod. If people messed him around, then it needed it. If you played ball with him, he was a lovely man. I liked him.

When Jimmy was in the band it was all rock'n'roll. Absolutely anything. He used to tell me what to sing. He used to say: Right, we're going to do this tonight. That night finished, he'd say: Right, learn these four numbers, because we'll be putting them in next night. All rock'n'roll. Anything. Vincent stuff. Anything. Anything that was popular. Cochran gear, anything. He could play it all as well. Note for note, he'd come out there. We used to open with 'What I'd Say'. I came on, and he went wah, wah, wah, wah. I thought: What's he playing? He started laughing. Then he broke out and started doing the thing. Afterwards I said: What was all that about? He said: I don't know. I've got this thing about music. It was Led Zeppelin, wasn't it? It was already being formed in his head. Yeah, funny that, never forgot that. He was always on the case, Jimmy, always. He said: I want to do a bit with The Yardbirds and that. I said: OK. He started doing The Yardbirds. Who got him into the job was Jeff Beck, because Jeff Beck was playing lead. Jeff had got Jimmy in as rhythm. I don't know if you know the full story, but they sacked Jeff and kept Jimmy. Jeff was never pleased about that. There was always conflict between the pair of them. You know what one of my biggest things is, is that I never ever had a tape recorder on the stage all that time he played for me. Can you imagine? Some of

16

those solos were blistering really. Same with Ritchie Blackmore he was the same. Ritchie loved rock'n'roll, it's all he liked. They were all rock'n'roll fanatics that played for me.

TERRY SLATER, Musician

I used to play the local working men's clubs around Hanwell, and Ealing, and all that type of stuff, Acton and Chiswick. One day I saw this advert for a lead guitarist. It was a Sunday morning. I went along to the audition and I was accepted. It was a group with another guitarist, and three saxophonists – a baritone, two tenors – myself on lead guitar, a rhythm guitarist, and drummer. I got the job. They were called the Flintstones. That was pretty cool, I liked that. We got picked up by an agent called Roy Tempest, of the day, who was a lovely guy. Crooked as hell, as one found out later. Anyway, he got us working on all the American bases: Brize Norton, this that and the other, Fairford. Then we got the Top Rank ballroom circuit and we got the Mecca ballroom circuit. Things were pretty good. I became leader of the band. I made the guys an offer. I said: Do you want to work and be paid as it comes in, or I will pay you, guarantee you £30 a week for whatever work we do? They went for the £30 a week, which was a big load on my shoulder, because I had to find enough money to raise £200 a week every week, but that was possible. We did work five or six, seven days a week all over England. All the Mecca ballroom circuit, and Top Rank, etc., etc. Then, fortunately, the whole Beatles thing was happening, and we all ended up going to the Star Club and the Top Ten Club in Germany, things were really cool.

That's really how I started. My first time abroad was Hamburg, went by train. Don Arden got us dodgy tickets, because none of us had work permits. He used to buy all the groups tickets to Denmark, and you'd get off at Hamburg and then try and hope the police didn't pick you up. The police used to come in the clubs: Top Ten Club, Star Club, whatever club. You never knew when they were coming, but between ten o'clock, midnight, one o'clock, they'd come in. Didn't have your permit, your arse was out. That was a great experience, because that's when you met everybody. I'd never met any Liverpudlians before, and most of the Liverpudlians vice versa, they hadn't met Londoners. My best buddy became Gerry Marsden. It was great. We were really fighting buddies. We used to get into fist-fights out there. We were both guitarists. We used to learn from each other and admired each other. That was a wonderful period for people like me. Being in that whole Top Ten Club and the Star Club, with The Beatles, and Roy Young, Kingsize Taylor, so on and so forth. That was just really wonderful. We all lived in one room, usually above the club, one sink, one loo. But we got £20 a week in cash. Amazing. The club that opened at six in the evening closed at six in the morning. If you were at the Star Club, The Beatles would do six to seven, and then Gerry would do seven to eight, I would do nine to ten, Kingsize Taylor would do ten to eleven, and then The Beatles might play eleven to twelve. Then Ricky Barnes would do midnight to one o'clock. That's how it worked, seven days a week. It was dangerous. We saw terrible beatings. On our amplifiers, we used to have dusters. Under the dusters, we usually had slip coshes. In some cases, we would have pistols, because when shit used to break out in the club, it was very dangerous.

£££

LARRY PAGE,
Manager

The Kinks were then The Ravens but they were just walking up and down Denmark Street trying to get a deal and they finished up at my door. But the idea was, Robert Wace really wanted to be their singer. There was no singer in the band. Well I started doing demos with them in Regent Sounds, and then

Talmy & Stone had come over from America because everything was hot. That was why Bert Berns was there, because Bert Berns was Bert Russell, he was over recording Them at the time for Phil Solomon. So Talmy & Stone had come over to this country because Americans were hot and they had done a deal with every record company to produce three acts for them. They had to produce three for Pye, three for EMI, three for Philips, three for... they done a block deal, right. So I took the demos to see Louis Benjamin and you know Benji, you could play anything to him, he wouldn't have a bloody clue. But if you ask for six and he gave you four then he figured musically they must be good. He's done a good deal. He was great. And I managed to go in there and I would sit there and he'd have two people, one either side of me, and then they'd move back a little bit and you knew that he was going: So what do you want? And you knew they were nodding yes or no at the back of you. So I then got into the habit of moving the chair back you know which was quite funny. But he said: Look, we can do the deal but I've got these American producers, I've gotta give them three acts, so if we throw them in there will be no problem. Which is what we did. So that's when they started recording with Talmy & Stone which basically was a disaster and their version of 'You Really Got Me' was a disaster and never saw the light of day because I, as the publisher, was the only person that could stop the record, we blocked the record until the other version came out which was basically the demo.

I used people like Jimmy Page and Clem Cattini and Bobby Graham because they were session players who we used for the sessions. They knew how to work the studio. If you took raw players in, you were teaching them. It's a bit like as we said me going into a studio and expecting to have microphone technique. It's not that easy. I used all the best players. I mean really, really did. And I would use people like Ronnie Verrell who, you know, Ted Heath and his orchestra, just great, great players. I recorded the Riot Squad, Mitch Mitchell and Carl Palmer. I loved good drummers and I loved good musos. Well it was standard that you'd go in to get two tracks done. An A side and a B side but when I was singing, going back to that, when I was singing we used to play the Rialto, York, and the guy who owned it, Jack Prendergast would say: I'm booking you for Sunday, but you have to use my son's band. His son was John Barry. So that was who we used. And I finished up doing about eight tracks with John which is out there, Larry Page and the Saga Satellites, and it's John Barry, Les Reed, Vic Flick, I mean all in that one band. How bloody talented was that? Brilliant. Well, you used them because their drums were used to that studio. They were used to that studio. And nine times out of ten their drums stayed in that studio, or the guitars. I used to book Clem Cattini, I'd book him for ten o'clock thinking he'd be fresh, and he'd, yeah I did a jingle spot and I was up to see this club, and you'd go: Bloody hell. So he was knackered before we started. And then of course when you're talking about that, I mean all the trouble we have with Musician's Union where they wouldn't allow overdubbing and you couldn't put the voice on after, and so many people then were recording overseas. I used Olympic, the old Olympic off Baker Street, and then the new ones in Barnes, Lansdowne a lot, Abbey Road of course.

CHRIS BRIGGS,
Ewell Tech

In 1968, I'm guessing. I'm not good at dates, before Led Zeppelin's Marquee residency, and before they went to Germany. I think they went to Germany and did some shows. Mike Dolan at Marquee Marketing was the booking agent for Ewell Tech. Paul Conroy had found him. Paul did all the donkey work, it has to be said. Paul Conroy did all the grafting at Ewell Tech. We just posed about, tried to talk to the groups, tried to attract girls' attention, that kind of thing. Paul did all the work. We booked The Yardbirds through Johnny Toogood, who was also part of Marquee. Then a few weeks before the gig, we'd had Dave Arnott print up very nice looking silk screen posters. We had The Yardbirds booked. Paul had the posters printed. Bit of a problem: band had broken up. Remember that band you had last term, Robert Plant and the Band of Joy? The guitarist, Jimmy Page, is doing something with them. It's probably called the New Yardbirds. It's like: Should we have some 'new' printed up and put on the posters? I can't remember if we ever did or not, because that's something Paul would have done. I'd have been too busy cleaning my car. I can't remember who turned up with them. Certain people stick in your mind. The Led Zeppelin evening really sticks in my mind, the New Yardbirds, two weeks before the show, with the posters up – became Led Zeppelin. Paul gets another phone call from Johnny Toogood: They've changed their name. We've got the fucking posters up now, you twat.

I'll never forget Bill Clark coming out of the audience at me that night, because they were astonishingly good, and it was one of those gigs where you watch with your mouth open. They were astonishingly good. It wasn't a particularly well attended gig. From our point of view, it was probably the important gig that, by some accident, we ended up putting on. There was a bit of a fuck, you know. People were turning up expecting … We're explaining. There's a lot of that: What do you mean it's not The Yardbirds? Well you can have your money back. I seem to remember Jimmy Page telling us that he'd sunk a lot of his own money into this from all his session work. If it didn't work, it was back on his head, you know, play on. They were unbelievable. I don't know whether it was conscious, but they were so good. It was like another level. Obviously, this was a warm-up. From their point of view, they left it in, rather than pull it. Seeing it now from the side of having done this myself for a living for a few years, they've probably gone: Oh shit, we've got all these gigs in as The Yardbirds. Oh, we'll use them as warm-ups. Why not? It's around the corner. He's got Ewell, he's got Epsom around the corner: I can go and see my parents.

DAVID STOPPS,
Promoter, Friars Aylesbury

The band I was managing, Smokey Rice, supported Led Zeppelin in Southall, I think it was the third gig Led Zeppelin had ever done and a tiny little gig called the Northcote Arms in Southall, it was a very different town in those days than it is now. I think the Northcote Arms is still there actually and it's got a plaque on it or something saying: Led Zeppelin played here, but it was an amazing gig. Smokey Rice were a blues band, it was that blues era, and basically a tiny little stage like a little triangular stage in the back of this pub and we played, you know, and that was fine. Quite a few people were there. Led Zeppelin came on and I had never seen anything like it you know. It was like they were a blues band, but they were a lot more than a blues band. It was like rock'n'roll meets blues, and this sort of incredible exciting sound and I just remember just looking at them thinking: This is something else. I've never seen anything quite like this. Particularly the drummer, John Bonham, was absolutely incredible, I remember thinking at the time. Then we started Friars, two months after that 1969, June 1969 or three months after that, and if we'd started a few months earlier we probably would have put Zeppelin on as one of the first bands who got on but it caught fire with them so quickly they were playing like 2000 capacity venues within three months of that pub gig.

PAUL KING,
Social Secretary, Brunel

At Brunel University there was no local competition really, it was London and the Marquee club. It was not really competition because we only ran once a week whereas the Marquee would be running seven times a week, we were really using the local ten miles area as our captive audience. We were doing such big bands for what was relatively a small venue, we had no real problem economically. We were in a very fortunate position of being able to do what we wanted to do. The agents, I remember MAM was Rod Smallwood and Lindsey Brown. Rod subsequently went on to form Sanctuary through his management of Iron Maiden. Most of those agents are still agents today which is sad because it is a dreadful job. Part of the joy and fun of being a Social Secretary was talking to this music business that was there in London. The great thing was they would bribe you, they would take you out for lunch, give you records in return for agreeing to put one of their bands on as support and they would spend as much money on lunch as you would give them to pay the group. You were treated like royalty because if you had got that situation where it was quite an important gig, far enough away from London for them to treat it as separate from playing London. We became quite influential which meant that I was treated incredibly well, and I made the most of it. We would never have seen those London venues otherwise, we were students on grants.

We had recently had a new sports arena built at the university and the guy they had brought in to run it, well it was his baby and the last thing he wanted was filthy rock bands and dodgy punters from the neighbourhood soiling his sprung floor. It was a no-go zone, non-negotiable, piss off back to the canteen and keep squeezing your thousand punters into that little room. Strings were pulled with the Vice-Chancellor and sure enough one of the first bands we put on there was – The Sex Pistols. The guy never forgave me, there was no damage done, nothing went wrong, but that really did add insult to injury. I had actually left by then but I was determined to get one over this guy and behind the scenes I sorted it out with the guy who took over from me. They were popular enough to sell out fifteen hundred people and I still have the contract for them to play Guildford Civic Hall with Johnny Thunders Heartbreakers, the Clash and the Dammed actually signed by Malcolm McLaren. The fee was £500 for all four bands.

ROBIN BLACK,
Studio Engineer

Morgan Studios was in Willesden, North London, not a great place to get to. In fact when I was a young engineer they were openly collecting for the IRA on the corner of the street. It was a very Irish place, so you got out straight into your car going home, did not mention anything about the Irish. It is a funny place to have a studio but it got this reputation for being a great place to go, it was terrific. Cat Stevens, I worked with him there, Black Sabbath used the place. When Cat Stevens came in Paul Samwell Smith was producing, really good producer because he was one of The Yardbirds, great musicians, everything had to be absolutely perfect so it was great training for an engineer watching the producer get everyone to get every single note spot on. Steve himself as he was known then, not Usef, was absolutely so particular at getting everything right. The slightest phrase that should not be there was stopped, do it again. Just terrific. You listen to those albums today and they sound lovely, really nice, and I am very pleased about the work I did on those songs for *Tea For The Tillerman*, *Teaser And The Firecat* and a couple of others.

In Morgan Studios I also worked with Mickie Most and I remember the day he walked in the first day I started working with him, he just walked in the control room and said, my name is Mickie Most, I produce HIT records. I said I am Robin Black, nice to meet you. I should have said, I engineer Hit records but I didn't, I was too in awe of the man. Everything we did there was a hit record, Hot Chocolate and people like Suzi Quatro. Mickie Most was very much a man who had to be in charge, God bless his soul. I remember once when Suzi was not pleasing him with her vocal performance and he just said, right I am going home now. She said, well you gave me a lift here and he said, Robin will give you a lift home and just left the building. So I was thinking crikey, I am going to be driving Suzi Quatro, how fantastic. So I drove her miles wherever she lived and then sort of got home about three o'clock in the morning completely exhausted. He knew in his mind exactly what he wanted, he really did know the charts. He believed he knew what people wanted to hear, so every session he did, the arranger, the musicians, they did exactly what Mickie wanted and if you didn't, well that was that. They would have several arguments but the bottom line was Mickie would say, I am the hit producer, you do as I say. And he was usually right.

CHRIS SPEDDING,
Musician

I worked with Mickie Most with Donovan. *The Cosmic Wheels* album, he produced it and he had me on the sessions. He was a very interesting guy to work with because he was very, very hip about what was going on. I remember I used to come up with all these ideas, you know sort of: Why don't we try this? Why don't we try that? And he took me aside, Mickie, and he said: Listen, Spedding. Shut up, he says. It's not a Spedding record, it's a Donovan record. I know you've got a lot of good ideas but it's just not appropriate, just play the songs. So I thought this is very interesting so I would like somebody to do that for me on my record. And the other thing was that when we'd finished the backing tracks Mickie came up to me and he said: Have you ever written any string arrangements? So I said: No. And he said: OK, well you're doing the string arrangements on this, because I know that you have ideas and I wanna use them. So I thought this guy uses

25

what he can get and he's very hip and he knows what's going on and he doesn't miss anything. So I had a lot of respect for him and I think every time I've been in the situation where I've produced anybody later on I'm always thinking: What would Mickie have done here? What would he have said you know? So he's been a good model for me for very hip sort of production. And of course yeah, he's a pop music producer and that's my kind of interest.

JOHN LECKIE,
Studio Engineer

In the Seventies you did a lot of sessions with session musicians who would come in, like Mickie Most sessions, which were always nerve-racking but always great fun in a sense of achievement in the end because in three hours you would do four songs with a twenty-minute tea break, musicians union tea break, in that three hours, and you'd do four songs. And it would be from ten till one, which meant that at ten in the morning, you had to be ready to record at ten; you didn't walk in the studio and start plugging things in at ten; you were ready to record at ten. And the session musicians and the line up might be bass drums, acoustic guitar, electric guitar, Hammond organ, piano, congas, two trumpets, sax, trombone and a string quartet, and The Ladybirds, three girls singing in a booth, and Ken Dodd doing his vocals. And you'd have to do four songs in three hours, and be ready to record. Not only has everything got to work but you have to create a balance that sounds like a finished product almost. You'd have a bit of reverb going; for the producer to ascertain whether he was getting a good performance or a take it, would have to sound close to the record, and that's what the balance engineer did. But those high pace sessions had to work. By half-past ten you've got to get your first track down. That's maybe with twenty four musicians, and they've maybe done a take, listened to it, done take two, if take two is not happening and it's half-past then Mickie Most is going to be freaking out; it's going to be bad vibes. You won't work with him again. He'd go straight and see Ken Townsend and say, I don't want that boy on my session. I never had that with him, we always got on great, Mickie, but other people did it, because it was pretty full on. And you'd do a session like that and then you'd have to clear it down – at half-past two Pink Floyd would come in, and you'd then be there till four in the morning with Floyd. And then do the same the next day – set up for Ken Dodd, Floyd in the afternoon in Studio 2.

ROB DAVIS, Musician

The great thing about the era was we all gave up our jobs and went professional for a month as we had got offered a Swedish tour and I think a Swedish band came over here. We were about nineteen or twenty and we thought, right we want to do this, and from that tour onwards we managed to get agents in the UK and would be touring all over the place. A lot of bands thought we came from Manchester but we didn't, we was always up in Manchester, Newcastle, Scotland, everywhere. Made a really good living before we were even known you know, there were loads of gigs out there then. I think it was a northern agent who said to Mickie Most, this band is amazing live because we used to muck around live, and Mickie came to see us and Chinn and Chapman and that was it from there on really. They said, we are going to write you a hit and they came up with 'Crazy'. The first two singles were session musicians but we had to play everything ourselves for *Top Of The Pops* and then from the next one, which was 'Dyna-mite', we played on everything. We had spent a whole day on 'Tiger Feet' and we were allowed to write our B sides so then at the end of the day Nicky Chinn said, right you have got fifteen minutes to write this B side.

CHRIS THOMAS, Producer

The Pretenders started by the fact that with Chris Spedding he wanted girls who'd dyed their hair black and wore leather to be his backing vocalists, so we had Judy Nylon, Pat Palladin and Chrissie Hynde. Of which Chrissie was the only one that could sing, so I pulled her back the next day and got her to replace the parts of the other two, and so that's how I got to know Chrissie and she said: Can you help me with, you know in terms of, obviously she wanted to get somewhere with her career, and I said: Well. I said: You're going to have to write your own songs and you're going to have to form a band 'cause I don't do this thing of going out and finding songs for artists and I like to work with writers, I don't want to work with, can't work just with singers, that doesn't really mean anything to me. And we stayed in contact, I used to see her around a lot. You know, I'd see her at the Nashville or somewhere like that so we were good pals. And then she did 'Stop the Sobbing' and I heard it on the radio and immediately knew the voice and I went like: She's cracked it, that's fantastic.

Then she phoned up and said, would I, you know, would I do their next single? And I'd just come off a Wings project that had gone on for about ten months and I just don't want to see another studio for the rest of my life, I said. I've really had it. And she was: Oh come on, why don't you come down and see the band and the rest of it. Anyway she sent me a demo – four songs – and of those four songs one was 'Brass in Pocket', one was 'Private Lives', I think another one was something like 'Tattooed Love Boys'. I mean it was just like: Whoa! You know, the sort of breadth of stuff there, so I definitely went to see them. I thought they sounded great. And so we went in to do 'Kid', that was the first thing that we did. And then three albums, you know, worked with her for the next four years, and working on that first album was probably the most exciting thing that I'd ever worked on because the songs were so amazing. I twigged something just towards the end, 'cause you can really, in those days you're making an album so it's really quite important that you have a flow to the album. It's not a question of just shoving the songs on there. And I twigged that all these, this was her diary. It was autobiographical. The first song 'Precious' is about when she leaves Akron and she goes to work in Cleveland, you know, and the last song is 'Mystery Achievement', it's like: Where is all this going, you know? So that gave me the bookends and that's how I worked out the running order for the album.

CHRIS SPEDDING, Musician

I had a hit, my own hit. 'Motor Bikin''. After my experience with Mickie Most and Donovan and the fact that he saw that I had some ideas and he asked me to write these strings when I'd never written strings before, I sort of thought this is a guy I think I can work with in the future. But then I started two years with the Sharks, I didn't do a single session. But when I came out of the Sharks after the Sharks had been a dismal failure you know commercially, I had to sort of get myself back in the swing of things and I was driving round central London with this idea for a song, 'Motor Bikin'', and I just stopped by Mickie's office, it was near Berkeley Square at the time, and it was almost like a scene from a movie you know. I got an acoustic guitar, barged into his office, sat down and played him the song and Mickie said: It's gonna be a hit. It's like a scene from a bad rock'n'roll movie, but it was actually what happened. He got on the phone, he got me out of my contract with Island because he knew Chris Blackwell of course, about all record company bosses. Called the studio up, by the end of that week we were in the studio cutting the record. It took a while to get to be a hit. Oh, yeah I'd written it because I'd looked at the Top Ten and instead of like what most people do when they write for the pop market, they don't write what's popular. I wrote something that was missing. The retro angle. The groove that was missing, the one thing that I'd missed. I thought the Top Ten was a load of rubbish so

I said: I'm gonna write something that I like. And so I applied that ethic to it and it worked that once, it's not worked since but anyway, the interesting thing about being the pop star for fifteen minutes was I was on *Top of the Pops* singing 'Motor Bikin'' and I was touring with John Cale. Now, there's something about how fragmented the music scene was then, the people that would have bought 'Motor Bikin'' would never go to a John Cale concert. The people that would go to a John Cale concert would never have listened to *Top of the Pops*. so this weird thing's going on here. I was this pop star who had the record in the charts. John Cale's record wasn't in the charts, he wasn't a pop star. So there's this weird sort of thing going on and that was very weird. That was very surreal you know. There was no people shouting for 'Motor Bikin'' in the John Cale show you know, not that I expected there to be, but there wasn't and then I kind of understood why, but it's kind of weird. Now it wouldn't happen I don't think. If I had a hit now and I was touring with somebody they'd all know about it. Oh he's the guy that got a hit, guitar player there. Didn't happen then. It was all totally watertight compartments, the different types of pop music.

STEVE JENKINS,
Record Shop Promotion

In the early days, it was a diary system. Most of it was operated out of independent record stores. If you knew where those independent record stores were, because some independent record stores were on the diary, some weren't, if you know the record stores that had the diary, it was more important for your records to sell through those stores than the ones that didn't have a diary. The focus was on the stores that had diaries. The dealer would then write down the number of the record in their diary, and quantity '1'. Then at the end of the week, this diary would go back to London, and they would add up all the numbers of all the records that have been sold that were registered in the diary. That would be the chart that was broadcast on a Sunday night on the radio.

That developed into a company called Record Sales. Record Sales contacted me and said they were thinking of starting a radio promotion company to go along with their sales basis, which operated on stores that had diaries. I went along, and they were just basically talking to me about setting up their radio arm, and I operated their radio arm for probably six or nine months. It was doing pretty well. I learnt about the way the chart worked, which I never knew before. I was not interested in how it was added up or what it was, it was just the chart. Now I started to understand the mechanics of how the chart worked. The mathematics of the chart is probably what I enjoyed. All of a sudden, being at Record Sales, it all made sense to me. That's how it works. You get the record on the radio, fantastic; you get the artist on TV, fantastic; then you put the records in the right stores. Out of explosion comes a chart position, and then if you get yourself high enough on the chart, you're on *Top of the Pops*. Once you're on *Top of the Pops*, cha-ching, you're in and at it. This is the record business. Record Sales really gave me a broad knowledge of how the record business worked. It was independent. Basically, at that point in time, they were cowboys. They were riding into town and shooting up the town, but they were doing it fantastic. The record companies loved it, because they couldn't work out: How does this company keep getting these records on the chart, and why isn't our chart position always higher? The record companies didn't really grasp what was happening. All they knew was, if they paid £2,000 to this company and delivered 2,000 records, all of a sudden, their chart position was good. They didn't want to know. They thought maybe it's a foul, maybe it's not a foul. It's far enough away from us that it doesn't affect us, so give them the money, give them the records, and let's go. I would say Record Sales probably operated for, in total, somewhere between three and four years. It was the first one, really. It was the first sales/marketing/promotion company that was independent, and that all the record labels used. At that point in time, there's still that clear definition of the reps that deal with the stores for record companies are not what Record

Sales is. Record Sales are perceived as these wild cowboys that are driving around the stores. Most of the people that work for Record Sales had not worked for record companies.

£££

DAVID ARDEN,
Manager

Chart fixing, the old man used to have all sorts of people who'd go out and do it for you. He had his own, you know, list of people up and down the country you know; wives and single mums; and they'd go out, he'd send them the dosh and they'd send us the records, and then there were other people that would set up business and were doing it as well. But of course, the one guy was Harvey Freed who was fixing all the charts with the *Melody Maker*, *NME* and *Record Mirror*. Now we'd, and this is one of my first things that I was in the business proper with the old man, we'd got 'Hi Ho Silver Lining', the publishing for it for England and Europe, and recorded it with a group called The Attack. Mickie Most was pissed off 'cause we'd got the publishing, 'cause we had a relationship with Scott English who wrote it with Larry Weiss, so he's done it with Jeff Beck so off we go, we're ahead with sales. We've got the sub-publishing so we're getting the sales figures for both records. We know The Attack is outselling Jeff Beck.

It's early days you know, we're up at thirty-eight, you know. Jeff Beck's down there and Harvey's getting his whatever it was each week. Now we want it to go up another five places next week. No, I don't want a do this too much. The old man was very careful, he always knew there's only so far you can push something, and then it's got to have its own legs and then he also didn't want people thinking it was being hyped, so he was always very careful with it so, anyway, the next week we were expecting to be at fifteen or twelve, somewhere like that, and we dropped and Jeff Beck's ran up. Mickie had obviously given Harvey... well that was the old man's interpretation, taken the money to put us down and put him up. So that was it. The old man, as far as he was concerned, that was playing dirty. He said: You don't mind paying to put records up, but not to put records down. And so of course he tore Harvey Freed a new arsehole and blew the wad so that was it.

JONATHAN KING, UK Records

I always got on really well with Mickie and Dave Most, his brother. The two of them decided to stop speaking for no good reason. There's so many people I know in this business, because I know everybody in the business, and always have done. I used to spend hours trying to persuade both Mickie and Dave to speak to each other: For God's sake, you're brothers. They never did. They died without speaking again. Tragedy, and I couldn't work out why. I had the same situations with Sharon Osbourne and her father, Don Arden. I knew Don, and I knew Sharon when she was Sharon Arden, when she was a little girl. I did manage to persuade her to start speaking to him again, which she did. By that time, he was beginning to get Alzheimer's, but the good thing was they were reconciled by the time he died. I can't work out people not speaking to each other.

No, Mickie was a brilliant producer. Producers are brilliant in different ways. Mickie was more of a good producer in getting the talent out of talented people, and getting it on tape and on record. I was more in the sort of Phil Spectre/Joe Meek area of making my own little works of art, although their works of art were much greater than my works of art. Mine were, in their own way, they were me projected into a record. I was better at that. I did produce people like Genesis and so on, but I wasn't very good at it, in encouraging others to bring it out, because that wasn't really my skill. That was very much Mickie's

33

skill. He would find the talent in people like Chinn and Chapman as producers, and Suzi Quatro, and various performers and so on. He'd bring it out of them. Hot Chocolate. He would bring the talent out of them that then came through, rather than exert his own talent into it. He was a different type of producer, but a very, very good one.

Fairly early on, I was at school, went down to Charterhouse, my old school, to visit all my old friends. I'd only left a year or two earlier. I was still at Cambridge, I think. 1967 we're talking. One kid came up to me and said: This is a school band, can you listen to it? A tape. They didn't have a name at all. Despite rumours to the contrary them being called the Garden Wall or something. They had no name at this point. I think they were in between being different groups. Anyway, I listened to the tape. The one thing I thought were: This guy has got a lovely voice, a lovely smoky gorgeous voice. In my little car I had already installed a cassette player, which was revolutionary, but more than that, a single record player, where you could push the centre out of the vinyl single. It had one of those stabilisers. It was in an Austin-Healey Sprite I was in. It meant that you could play these singles by popping them in, and it didn't skip. Anyway, I was listening to it on the cassette, and I listened to it and I thought: They're really good. When I got back, I phoned up the house and said: I'd really liked it, we'll have a meeting. We had a meeting. Peter Gabriel was lead singer, and just about the line up that remain: Mike Rutherford, Tony Banks, and Tony Phillips, who left fairly early on. They never really had a drummer. We went through a lot of drummers until they finally found Phil Collins after they'd left me. I really liked it, and I said: Let's make a couple of tracks. We did 'The Silent Sun', and it was a single, and then I made an album in the school holidays, and all that. That was essentially it. I think I taught them a bit how to write. I trimmed a lot of the things down. I gave them the name Genesis, because that was the start of my production career, that was how I was thinking of it. We put the album out, *From Genesis To Revelation*. Because actually, they didn't have a name. I wasn't going to give them a name. I just wanted to call the album *From Genesis To Revelation*. Terrible mistake. It got put in the religious bins in all the retail shops, and nobody could find it. Didn't really do much.

I then passed them on, because they needed someone who was going to look after them. I didn't want to be a manager. I didn't want to look after the group. I then gave them, eventually to Tony Stratton-Smith, who was a friend of mine, who was a journalist at the time on the *Daily Sketch*, writing about football. He was a nice man. I liked him a lot. He was moral, he was honest. He was gay, and I said to him: You're straight, not sexually, but you're straight morally. I don't want to hand these kids to somebody who's going to rip them off. I think, to this day, they've cherished the fact that I passed them on to him. He took them over. I knew Tony anyway, socially, but also, he had a group called the Koobas. One of whom, the drummer, Tony O'Reilly, had been the first drummer in a group that was trying to get themselves together that eventually became Yes. Anyway, the Koobas, I'd made a couple of tracks with them, but didn't do anything as a producer. That's how I got to know Tony. Tony, therefore, had become a friend. That's how I handed Genesis on to them, and they went on to bigger and better things. They're very nice. They remained really decent human beings.

10cc, similar thing. I'd started my label, UK Records. A lot of the tracks on it were me under other names. I wanted to find a band. I'd got friendly with Eric Stewart when he was in The Mindbenders. Eric rang me up and said: Could you listen to this? Sent it down. Again, they had no name or anything. I thought it sounded like a smash to me. I said: Oh yes, this is a hit. We can turn this into a hit. What's the name of the group? We haven't got a name. I said: Right, I'll let you know the name tomorrow. Had a dream that night that I had this band that were number one on the Billboard album charts called 10cc. I thought: Oh, that's not a bad name. I called them 10cc. Everyone's come up with lots of theories – usually involving sperm – since, which has absolutely no truth in any of it whatsoever. 10cc they became, signed them up, gave them the big hit. Then when it was a hit, I said: Right, I need an album in twenty-four hours. We can't do that. I said: Well all right, I'll give you a week. We can't. I said: Then write an album, produce an album, but make it in a week. They did. I went up there and said: Yeah, that's fucking fabulous. Trim this down, this solo's too long, cut that out, don't like that song, drop that song, do another song for there. Went and delivered it. That was the first album. It was, still to this day, one of the great albums of all time.

Then *Sheet Music* came, it's the second one. I said at the time, and I now say, this is almost *Sgt. Pepper*. It's full of tracks that are just brilliant. To this day, I listen to quite a lot of the stuff and think: This is absolute magic. However, of course, the problem was all artists are cunts. Sure enough, at that time, money offers came in from all the big record companies. I'd already had to renegotiate. I'd given them something like a 2% royalty. Mickie Most and I used to vie on who could give our artists the lowest royalty. I'd only been on that when I was an artist, so you know, why not? In those days, artists got small royalties. So they should have done. We spent all the money, did all the bloody work turning the record into a hit. That's what they'd done with me and Decca with 'Everyone's Gone To The Moon'. That's how I treated other people. I'd realised very early on being behind the scenes. I upped it to 4%. They actually recorded, one of the B sides of one of their hits was called '4% Of Something', dedicated to it. Of course, these other record companies were offering them double that, three times that. Huge advances, lots of money. Of course, all of it goes to their heads. Easily explainable. I'd said to them: We do not have any more negotiations. I've doubled your percentage. That's it. I've got a five-year deal with you. I'm going to be losing a fortune in the first and second years. In the third year, I'm going to break even. I will make my money in the fourth and fifth year, where I intend to make a fortune. At the end the fifth year, you're quite entitled to hit me for as much as you can possibly hit me, and I will then have to battle against the equivalent of Universal, as they now are: But of course, it wasn't fair enough. Come the end of the second year, when I'm breaking even, and I'd managed to get them a hit in America, and all that, it's all beginning to go. I'm making no money at all, but spending a fortune. They then come back, want to renegotiate. Anyway, to cut a long story short, I sold them to Phonogram, I got a percentage. Funnily enough, I got 4% override on all their future records. I got a large sum of money. I got to keep all the tracks I'd made and they went and did their own thing. I'm very sad, because a lot of the tracks that they had hits with, they'd recorded under my aegis. Things like 'I'm Not in Love', and so on, 'I'm Mandy, Fly Me'. All that next album had been done while they were technically under contract to me, but I didn't lay claim, I said: Take it.

NIGEL GRAINGE,
Phonogram Records

10cc, through their manager, had an association with the company when it was Philips and then Phonogram when Eric Stewart had been part of the Mindbenders and they were managed out of Manchester by Rick Dixon who also managed the Sid Lawrence Orchestra signed to Philips. He had a great relationship with our very straight MD Tony Morris. When there were some royalty issues with Jonathan King, Rick came to Tony Morris and said, my boys have made the best album you will ever hear and I want a huge deal. So Tony Morris came in and he said, I want you to go to Manchester and tell me if I am going to spend a million pounds on 10cc. I thought, great, there's not too much heat in that then. Well they sat me down in the Strawberry Studio and the first track was bloody 'I'm Not In Love' in wide screen monstrous sound and I thought it's a done deal. I went back to London with the tapes and said it is a done deal, but I remember the shock with the Promotion Department when I said BUT we are not going to put out 'I'm Not In Love' as the first single. We are going to go with 'Love Is A Minestrone', WHAT ! It hasn't got a chance. I said we are going to open the doors with 'Minestrone' and have a top five record with that, then we are going to go with the big one. And that was exactly what happened because otherwise you start with a blitz and then there is only one way and that is down.

JOHN SCHROEDER,
Pye Records

One day, a guy called Ronnie Scott, who worked at a music publisher, brought me a demo of a group called Spectres. They wrote their own material, and he believed in them. They made a demo, funnily enough, of a Shirley Bassey song, 'I Who Have Nothing'. Can you believe that? Status Quo – well, not Status Quo, but that group – doing 'I Who Have Nothing'. They did. It was a very extraordinary arrangement of that song. It really impressed me actually at the time. I thought: I think they've got something. I don't know what it is, but there's something there. I went into it deeper and deeper, and then finally I signed them. I looked around for material for them and couldn't find anything really strong enough, other than to release 'I Who Have Nothing'. We released 'I Who Have Nothing' – well, it's 'We Who Had Nothing' – really didn't do anything. We had to think very seriously about a follow-up record. Then, of course, Ronnie said: Well they do write themselves. They had two, Joe Bunce handled all the purse strings, the money side, and the other guy Pat, he was a plumber, and he came up to see me in his boiler suit with a spanner in his pocket. It was hilarious actually. It's Pat Barlow who was the main character. They believed implicitly in this group, and they put all their effort, and time, and finance behind it. We tried to come up with a hit record. That's what it's all about. We were into making hit records, this time with a self-contained group. Of course, at that time, they weren't performing or doing really anything great promotion-wise to support anything. It all came down to one thing: it's the song, trying to find the right song, the song that's got the magic.

Pye's policy was that after three singles, out the window. With Status Quo, it was another story. I nearly lost my job over that band, because I believed in them so implicitly. I think by that time, Lou Benjamin was getting very difficult. He said: You can't go on. They were getting very uptight that I was wanting to continue to record this group. He said: You know, John, you've made four records now. We can't continue. You can't go on like this. Even if we had a selling record now, it wouldn't make up for the money you've spent in recording them. I said: You've got to continue with them. They are going to make it. I tell you, they are going to. Anyway, for the band and for me, it was terribly disheartening that every record we put out, nearly made it then didn't. Somehow, the titles of the song had a funny sort of omen: 'I Who Have Nothing', 'We Ain't Got Nothing Yet', 'Almost But Not Quite There'. There was a sort of hidden message behind the titles of those songs.

Then we had a serious meeting, and I said: You know, guys, you know what we need to make a hit, you know what the ingredients are. We need a song that is immediately identifiable right from the start to the end of it. It's got to have a very strong intro, it's got to happen straight away. It's got to have a strong hook, it's got to have lots of little guitar riffs and things we need. We went into the ingredients of what we needed to come up with to have the hit song. I said: I believe that you've got it in you to find it, but I'm going to lose my job over this. They won't have me. They're going to tell me to drop you as an artist. Pat Barlow said: Well I'll talk to Rossi. We know full well the seriousness of this situation, and all the rest of it. Anyway, they went away, I didn't hear from them for about three weeks. Then I got a call from Pat Barlow, he said: Francis has come up with a fantastic hook. It's the bestest thing I've ever heard anyone do. This is the nucleus of something really good. They would like you to come round and hear it, and hear the bones of it. I went down to one of their houses. I can't remember which one it was. We were down in the basement, and I was sitting on an orange box. I heard the rough skeleton of 'Pictures of Matchstick Men'. I said: That is the strongest thing they've come out with. That riff is really good. Can you embellish it and work on it? They did. It became a song, and it's called 'Pictures of Matchstick Men'. They started out as the Spectres, then we changed their name to Traffic Jam, and then Stevie Winwood had Traffic, and we couldn't use that.

Then came the idea of the Status Quo, which came from a suggestion of Quo Vadis, that's where it came from. Who thought of Quo Vadis, I don't know, but anyway, they thought of the name of Status Quo. I think it was Pat Barlow who actually thought of it. We all agreed that they should be called Status Quo. I thought: How am

I going to deal with Lou Benjamin in this. It's the fifth record. He's not going to wear it. Then I thought: I know, with changing their name, it's a new group called Status Quo. I caught Benji at a time, the timing of catching him at the right moment. It was at the end of the day and beginning of the evening, and there he is in his office with all his mates, and they were discussing what they were going to do that evening, socially. I knocked on his office door, and I said: Benji, could I have a word? He said: Oh no, what do you want? I said: I seriously want to discuss this thing with you. He said: All right. Come in. I said: I want to make another record with you know who. He said: You can't. We're not making any more records. I said: We're going to change the name. The new group is going to be called Status Quo. We've got one hell of a song called 'Pictures of Matchstick Men'. He said: No. His assistant, Les Cox, looked me and he said: I'll tell you what, Benji. He looked at me, at how uptight I was about it. He said: Now listen, what would happen? Consider this: supposing we turned this down, they've got a new name. We've turned the group down, we've turned the song down, and they go to another record company and have a number one with it. What would you say then? Oh, he said, well I don't think they'll do that. He said: Well they could do that. Say that they've got a fantastic song, John believes in it, they believe in it. They change the name of the group. They're new artists. Oh, all right then. He conceded, and he let me produce 'Pictures of Matchstick Men'. Well, you know what happened to 'Pictures of Matchstick Men'. It was not only a hit in this country, it was a hit in America as well.

The worst thing that we didn't have that was necessary was an image. We had no image. They were just a pop group, and it relied every time on finding the right song to create the hit. The follow-up record's already proved it's all failed, and then we've got to start again and look for another one, and do the same thing again. If we had an image, and the group went out with an image, and could start to perform with an image that was different from all this type of material, this is what bugged them and me a great deal. More them than me, because as long as we got hits, I was quite happy, I was doing my job. But for them, they were fed up, pissed off with middle-of-the-road poppy songs. They decided they wanted to go heavy. They wanted to get into jeans, that sort of stuff. Change the image completely, totally.

The looks, the hair, everything. Everything became really heavy. At the same time, to be able to support that change of image, they needed the hit record as well. Now I had to start looking for material in a different shape or form. They went away and changed their image. The first time that Ronnie Scott saw them, it blew his mind. He said: They're a totally different group. They're just something totally different. The first time I saw them they were amazing. He said: I've got a song. It's an Australian song, as matter of fact, that would suit this change of image, that we could do possibly as a single to support it. Lo and behold it was, it was 'Down The Dustpipe'. It was fantastic, because the song was so right for what they were trying to do. We got a hit with it. I'll never forget, it went to Tony Blackburn, this single, he played it – not on air – he played it, and his comment was: Oh well, Status Quo, it's called 'Down The Dustpipe'. It's down the dustbin as far as I'm concerned. He didn't dig it at all. He didn't support it at all. Of course, you could eat his words now. Of course, it became a hit, and it was the start of the Status Quo proper, as a real mind-blowing stage band, the whole of the image and all of the things. Fantastic.

NICK SIMPER,
Musician

In 1967 I was touring then with a band call the Flowerpot Men, which was a studio made up band. We were doing one of the very last theatre tours, where you'd have about ten acts who all got five minutes each. That was where we saw the Vanilla Fudge. They were on the bill, but they only did the one night, because try and tell American bands that they've only got a ten minute slot. They wouldn't even get half a number done in those days. I was so amazed when I saw Vanilla Fudge. I didn't even want to go out and see them. The drummer with the Flowerpot Men, Carlo Little, he said: You've got to come and see the American guys. You must come out and watch the American guys. The whole style of what they were doing, and the way they were playing. How can you describe it? The way they were set about it, everybody just came out and watched these guys. Of course, they got thrown off the tour that same night, because they went over too long. Somebody pulled the tabs, and there was almost a punch up. The crowd were booing, because they wanted more. I never forgot this. I thought: Vanilla Fudge. That's the sort of stuff I want to do.

It got to that strange time in music when everything was starting to change, nobody was quite sure what it was changing to. Different types of bands. Everybody had been a group up to then. We were all groups, and all classed as pop groups really. Then you had people, blues bands started to appear, and the whole music scene started to diverse. It was fragmented into different tangents really. I knew I didn't want to stick out this Flowerpot Men stuff. Carlo Little and I had tentatively been planning to form a band with Ritchie Blackmore, because, as you know, Ritchie and Carlo Little worked with Screaming Lord Sutch for years. Ritchie had stayed in Germany. I'd played with Sutch, and I knew Ritchie just to say hello to really. We met him over in Germany when we were on the road, and we decided we'd do something. Then when the Flowerpot Men came along, the Flowerpot Men situation was making so much money, because there was a hit record with it, so it was creating a lot of money. We forgot all about Richard Blackmore. But after doing it for about a year, we got fed up with playing this harmony. Carlo kept on reminding: We've got to get back with Richard. We've got to do this. We've got to do that.

We started introducing a few numbers before the four singers in the Flowerpot Men came on. There was a line-up of four vocalists. The band would do some before they came on. It started going down very well. It was usually something culled from Graham Bond's catalogue. They hadn't invented the term then, but it really was the start of heavy metal as we know it today, hard rock, when you listen to the Graham Bond Organisation. It was going down very well. The singers didn't like it. They said: Well, we'd rather you didn't do all these song before we come on. Just do one instrumental before we come on. There was a bit of friction growing.

On that tour, the keyboard player took sick. They kept sending different deps in. One of these guys was Jon Lord. He was with the

Artwoods, who were in their death throes then. He started filling in for our keyboard player and we said to Jon: Do you want to stay as a permanent fixture? He said: Yeah, yeah. We got quite close, he would stay at my parent's place. Of course, he knew of Ritchie Blackmore, so he got him involved as well. I think Ritchie flew over to talk to Chris Curtis, and when he heard his ideas, he flew back as fast as he could. Because Chris, God bless him, his ideas were completely off the wall. Nobody could grasp what he was on about. The whole thing fizzled out. One day, while we were on tour with the Flowerpot Men, there was a telegram for Jon Lord from some businessmen. I was there when he showed me this telegram. It just said: If you're interested in doing it without Chris, call us. They more or less passed the ball over to Jon Lord: You get the band together. If you don't want to do it with Chris, we'll do it with you.

He obviously had me in his sights. He didn't say anything at the time. Early 1968, or the very end of 1967, I can't remember which, we had a tour of Holland. Jon was very mysterious. He said to me: When we get to the hotel, I'd like you to room with me. I thought: Well that's a bit difficult, because I'd always roomed with Carlo Little. We'd been on the road for years, always rooming together. There had to be something buzzing here, so I said to Carlo: I'm going to room with Jon. Poor old Carlo looked at me all sort of hurt: Why is that then? I said: Well, I'm not sure, but he wants to talk to me about something. As soon as we got in the hotel room, he furtively pulled the curtains, looked around the door, made sure no one's listening. He said: Would you give this up, all this money we're making? It was very good money. He said: Would you give this money up for a basic wage of, say, £25 a week? Which is about a quarter of what we were getting. I said: To do what? He said: To do our own music. I said: You've got it. Include me in.

He said: Well I've got these businessmen. They're going to finance the whole thing. He said: I've got Ritchie Blackmore on board. I said: Oh great. I know Ritchie, yeah, fabulous. As it happened, it was the perfect timing, because the flower power scene was just completely starting to collapse. All this love, and bells, and kaftans, and beads and stuff, it just reached the end of the cycle. It was all changing. Music was getting tougher and harder. The managers got the four of us, and they rented a place for us. It was a big old Georgian manor house, out near South Mimms. It was called Deeves Hall, and it was in a little village called Ridge. There were no neighbours, nobody around. I think the nearest neighbour was Graham Hill, the racing driver, who lived a couple of miles away. Jon had also seen Vanilla Fudge, so he had the same kind of ambition as I had to do something really loud and lairy like they did. They were a big inspiration with us. We moved into Deeves Hall and I said: We must go to Marshall's and get some mega equipment, which we did. Instead of my little 50 watt, I was buying 200 watt tops with two stacks. These guys put the money up for all this stuff, and a road crew as well. We got all this stuff into Deeves Hall and we started to rehearse. We got about four gigs and a TV show lined up in Denmark, and off we went. We had no name still.

Every time we talked about names: What about this? What about that? Oh no, somebody's got that. Or the managers would check it out and say: That name's been registered by somebody, you can't have that. Ritchie Blackmore kept saying: What about Deep Purple? Deep Purple? That is the most un-rock'n'roll name you could have. The song 'Deep Purple' comes from the Thirties: When the deep purple falls. I said: People will laugh at that. He said: Yeah, but it's got a kind of sound to it, and it was my old granny's favourite. I said: Well, it was one of my favourites, but it's not rock'n'roll.

We went to Denmark, by then we were getting desperate. We didn't have a name. Ritchie and I were talking to a guy on the boat across to Denmark, he was a journalist. He was asking us who our influences were and all this. Ritchie was giving him all the usual verbal about: I've always rated the Wally Thud Trio, and the Ted Babbage Folk Four, and all that. This guy's writing it all down. Ritchie was always winding people up like that. Then finally the guy said: What is the name of your band? We looked at one another. I don't know which one of us said Deep Purple, but it came out. The guy said: Deep Purple. He wrote it down. Ritchie and I were a bit pink around the gills. We kind of decided there and then: That's it, we're going to use it.

MICK UNDERWOOD, Musician

I played locally with Ritchie Blackmore and bands and various other people as I'd left school at sixteen but that was just about the cusp really. I was seventeen when I started playing with Jet Harris; my first pro gig. He'd just left the Shadows and he put a band together. I was on the road with Little Richard and Sam Cooke and all the rest of it. It was wonderful, that was a great learning curve. And it lasted four months I suppose, and then it was decided you know, that they had a change in the band and I was one that went, and I think they thought I was too much of a kid, you know in amongst these old jazzers, and I was a bit at a loose end then and I thought: Oh, what do I do now? I saw Screaming Lord Sutch and his band, they were friends of mine you know. They were playing Hounslow locally to where I lived and one of them said: Why don't you give Joe Meek a call? Well, I knew who he was 'cause I was quite a fan of The Outlaws funnily enough from before then, and they said: Well, he's always got sessions going, you know, recording sessions and he's always looking for people to play on them so I said: Yeah, OK and I called him up. He said: Come on up, I do actually have a band that I need a drummer for. I went up to the studio, and he introduced me to two of the band who was Chas Hodges and Ken Lundgren and it was The Outlaws, funnily enough, which I was very pleased about that.

In the meantime I have a couple of other offers which were fairly good set-ups, but it meant me moving away to North of England and I was sort of: Sod that, I'm not going to do that. Who's gonna do the ironing? So I didn't go for those but I did go for the Joe Meek one, had a little play, they said: Yeah, fine, lovely, and we need a guitarist. I didn't know that at the time that they were looking for two, you know and I said: Well, I've got a friend who's pretty good, and that was Ritchie Blackmore. So Ritchie came, so we both joined. It was a bit: Well, if I join if you do it I'll do it, bla bla you know. And we both joined and that was the beginning of working with Joe which was excellent for me, for everybody I guess. They were the house band,

45

the recording studio band you know, we did most of the sessions. Not all of them but most of them, and particularly at that time, because The Tornados were another one that was kind of a house band and they were out pumping around doing 'Telstar' here and there so we just basically got all the work. It was great learning how to play in studios. Joe had his moments. I mean it was not uncommon for him to come into the studio and we were doing a session, you know, and him not be very happy with what was going on. He'd chuck us all out: Go on! Off, off, go on! The first time it happens you go: Christ, what's happening here, you know. But Chas and Ken they'd been with him for a while and they knew the form so we used to just bugger off, go and get a cup of tea somewhere and after about an hour he'd turn up, looking for us to carry on you know. And he'd go: Can we get on with the session then? and we'd go: Oh, yeah, OK Joe, and we shoot there and bang it out and carry on doing it. But we were working hard in those studios, it was a great learning curve for me.

RICHARD BROWN, Musician

I was fourteen / fifteen. I was still at school in Lyon Park School, Wembley, where we used to practise. One day, Bert Weedon came and took a look at us there. I don't think he was very impressed. I think the reason he came was he lived down my road, Sudbury Court Road. I pestered him to come have a look. He just took a look and he left. We also used to rehearse in the Swan pub, round the back. They had a small hall down in Sudbury. We were rehearsing in there one day. I think it was next to a caff called the Cannibal Pot. I think that's how Dave Sutch got to know us. He used to go in the Cannibal Pot. He was fascinated by rock'n'roll, and he knew we were rehearsing around the back. He was round the back one day listening to us rehearsing. He got so excited by what we were playing that he started jogging up and down. He had a hat with all his hair underneath it, and his hat flew off, and his hair came down all over the place, right down to his shoulders. Carl said: Wow, that's good. You ought to do a stage act and do that on stage.

That is how Sutch started. In those days, nobody had anything other than short back and sides, so it was a real oddity to see. Apart from his hair, he didn't have much in the way of musical talent or anything, but that's how Sutch started off. The early promoters, I think, it was people who had an eye for the main charts, and they could see young kids wanted to spend money, and this rock'n'roll drew them in, and they loved it. They put on these dances in any hall they could get their hands on. That's all it was really, just any old hall. Church hall, drill hall. They charged the kids to get in on the door. They might be able to get a bottle of Coca Cola and a bag of crisps, and that was the lot. My impression, after we started touring all over the country, is some of these outlying places, these sorts of audiences, these kids have got nothing else in their life. It's a really big deal for them coming to one of the dances to see a band from London. Oh, you've come from London. Oh, wow!

Next guitarist in line was Ritchie Blackmore. He never mentioned it, but I suspect he was going for lessons with Big Jim Sullivan, because he had a bit of a sort of twinkle in his eye. He was just using it for experience, I think, our band. That was the time when we delved at the idea of the Savages wearing loincloths. At the same time as that, Sutch had bought a new, proper, bigger van by then, a Bedford Dormobile. We did a tour down the south coast, summer season down there. Sutch saw in a junk shop somewhere, he saw this enormous stuffed crocodile. One of those real ones. He had to buy it, and he had it on the roof of this van for weeks, this crocodile. That was in that picture that was taken on Torquay Beach of us in our loincloths, and Sutch with his bull loose horns, and we're all attacking this stuffed crocodile on the beach.

Anyway, with Sutch, when Ritchie was with us, we got the idea that we were the main attraction and we were better than Sutch, believe it or not. Carlo, of all people, he thought this. Carlo was the one that nurtured Sutch and actually made him what he was. We decided to leave and branch out on our own. By that time, I had gotten my driving licence. I bought an old decommissioned taxi cab. We got our first and only gig as the Savages on our own, with this leopard skins on, up in Atherstone Memorial Hall. I think the audience was about two people and a dog. It was a complete failure. That was the end of that little enterprise. Sutch, of course, got a new band straight away.

BOB SOLLY, Musician

We were playing all the main ones – Marquee, Flamingo, Eel Pie Island, the Scene. I can't remember; all over the Home Counties and London. We were quite a popular band in London and the Home Counties. And of course in Kent we did quite a bit of stuff still, because we started from there.

I loved Eel Pie Island. It was always sunny when we went there fortunately. We had a sort of a residency there at one time. It wasn't an official residency, we were there a lot. I remember Rod Stewart was with Long John Baldry then and everyone shared the same dressing room. So if the Stones were there, for example, you'd be in with the Stones; there was no separation at all. It was a long dressing room with a glass front – you could see into it from the audience – above the stage. I remember Rod Stewart very well; Long John Baldry; although Long John Baldry was mostly in the bar I think, drinking. It was difficult to park, obviously it was on the Thames, it was an island. It was an old hotel built on an island in the Thames. It was a fairly, from memory, a derelict sort of place, more like a barn than a hotel, but it had something about it. It's like these things you see in Louisiana, in the swamplands; it's like an oasis in the middle of the Thames. You had a bridge to go over, so the problem was of course you had to hump all your heavy equipment piece by piece over this bridge to get into the hotel in the first place. But it was a great venue; it was just an empty ballroom I think really. But I always remember that as one of the most memorable places to play. You had people like the Downliners Sect, Long John Baldry, Rod Stewart, the Stones used to play there. I think virtually everyone who did R&B and jazz. It was very good; excellent.

We recorded for Joe Meek; did a couple of recordings at two different times. I couldn't stand him, couldn't wait to get out of there; couldn't bear him. He was just someone who I couldn't take to. Didn't know him; just someone you instantly thought, oh God, this is going to be a problem here. He was never constructive about anything; non-committal, totally non-committal over his little machines. He'd come out and he'd say, you're dragging the bass, and the bass player would say, what? you're dragging. And the bass player would look at all of us and say... so things like that, or the saxes are out of tune; something of that nature; always contradictory things, there was never any constructive... he could never actually make a constructive opinion on something. I'm sure if you got to know him he was OK. But I'm sure he kept them actually because he was someone who didn't throw things away. Now, in retrospect, I consider him to be a total musical innovator. But at the time he just didn't gel with me. Your livelihood's at stake, you're always hustling around and you really want to get favourable things going on; you don't want to be knocked back at all, because you're boosting yourself up and you want people to at least, even if it's forced, try and boost you up all the time. In those days it was a hustling job; if you didn't hustle you didn't get anywhere.

MIKE BERRY,
Musician

I just got a skiffle group together and then had a band with three Italians, the drum kit was a drum as opposed to a washboard but it was still one drum and we became Kenny Lord and the Statesmen and we used to rehearse in the Mazzini Garibaldi club in Holborn as they were members. I had an apprenticeship in the print, opposite St Pauls, and there was a guy there who was also in a skiffle group who told me there was a place in South London you could make a demo because he had done one too. Being North Londoners it was all a bit worrying but we did it and we made this 4-track demo. We met this guy Peter Raymond whose real name was Iaquinandi, came to see us because he heard this demo and he liked what we were doing and he sent the demo to Jack Good who was God in those days when it came to rock'n'roll with *Oh Boy!* And *Six Five Special*. I just took it all with a pinch of salt, I thought this was my destiny to be a star and thought well they will be lucky if they get me and Joe Meek got it as well. Jack Good did not like the band but liked what he heard and I went to see him and he said we will go in the studio on Tuesday week and do this song that Johnny Worth has written 'Not Guilty' and you are going to be the next Adam Faith. Oh alright. What do you know at seventeen?

Then I went to see Joe Meek before I had made this record with Jack Good at his little flat above the leather shop at 304 Holloway Road, the famous studio and he had his office there and I went to see him with my Nan, she was my guardian. He was very nice, very polite, respectful of my Grandmother, it was amazing how people did respect older people then. He was telling me what he wanted me to do, I want you to be my Buddy Holly he said and there will be an LP with you and a ghostly picture of Buddy Holly in the background. I have got this album already planned. Oh that's for me I thought, you can stick Adam Faith.

Really of course it all went pear-shaped after that with Joe, it took nine months to get a record out, let alone a flop and it was a flop. We did a record called 'Set Me Free' that Peter Raymond had written, we all went with it and thought it was OK. It was sent to Decca and they said well we don't like the song but we do like the singer. Will you cover this record that we are sending you, an American record that is not coming out over here by this group called The Shirelles and it is called 'Will You Still Love Me Tomorrow?' This is history now, they got to number one and mine sunk without trace, and I had to face the guys in the print when I got back to work as my record was still being played on Radio Luxembourg in the Decca slot. Anybody in rock'n'roll that has had any success will always tell you it is the second or the third take or you are wasting your time. So we were on take twenty and I was straining, I said to Joe Meek and this shows you how naive I was, it's a bit high, can we take it down a bit? There were all these string players up and down the stairs, in the office, in the bathroom, girl singers all doing this big backing. Can we take it down a bit, it was all arranged, written out, huge arrangements, and he said in his Newent accent: Too high! You should have fucking thought of that before. I went away with my tail between my legs and carried on singing, consequently it was very strained and not a great rendition and it has taken me fifty years to learn how to sing the song.

CHARLIE WATKINS, WEM

I don't do electronics. I don't know a resistor from a capacitor. But I know a sound from a sound. I particularly know when a sound is not there when it should be there. When I saw blokes in bands with heavy-gauge strings trying to be heard over a poxy bloody alto-sax. I thought, well, this isn't right. I knew that the music the nouveau guitarist was putting out was at least as good as the saxophonist with his music tuition; of all the other finesse he had the guitar was a very pleasant sound. And the glaring error was that you couldn't hear it.

But what that brought in was that they would get together and they would buy. I made an amplifier called a Watkins Westminster.

After my success with that amplifier, stories started permeating the trade about a band in Italy called Marino Marini Quintet, and I was still playing gigs and we used to play like them, because they had this lovely bu-bu-bu-bu-bu-bu, and I thought, I want that; and we didn't know what it was. So next was Bill Purkis, a really highly-trained electronics man, and when I put it to him that I wanted that bu-bu-bu-bu, he said that's an echo repeat of whatever the guitar is playing. I said that's what I want. He said, tape recorders, because that's how Marino Marini did it – great big expensive Ferrograph, or something like that. I said, no, I want it in a little box so you can take it to a gig and do it. Anyway, I gave him three months and he took me upstairs in their little shop one day and I heard bu-bu-bu-bu, this lovely, lovely sound, and he'd done the first Copicat. About 1956 I suppose it was. There I was, sat with a Copicat and an amplifier. Significantly the basics of what they term the Sixties Sound, although it wasn't really the Sixties yet, and the Copicat, when I made it – it was like when the skiffle started; I had a queue out my door. I had Johnny Kidd and the Pirates, The Shadows, all asking for my Copicat. Forewarned is forewarned I know, but I wasn't forearmed; I thought, well I can score on this; so in three months of selling that Copicat, I had enough money to go and buy a factory, a 10,000 square foot factory down in Offley Road, Brixton.

BIG JIM SULLIVAN, Musician

I used a little Watkins for the heavy sound. If I wanted a real grunty sound the little Watkins was great for that. I think Hank Marvin had the first Watkins Copicat and I had the second. I got my Copicat nicked. We went for a tour of Ireland with Marty Wilde and it got nicked off the train; so that was that.

CHARLIE WATKINS, WEM

Dave Bowie was one of mine. He liked what I was doing but I didn't like what he was doing because I didn't understand it, but he knew what I was doing because he wanted to buy it, a bit cheap; he was broke. Over a month he'd be around about every other day. He used to sit in the office and he had a little recorder. I used to wish to Christ he'd go away and let me do my work. And he'd say, can I get a bit more bass if I do that? Anyway I made him a sound system and I was advised, customer after all. What was that song? 'Major Tom'. He composed that on my desk, with his little whistle. Amazing bloke. Never did a gig with him though.

The best memories I had was of Marc Bolan. In the old days of the Roundhouse – where the underground was – the Roundhouse in Camden, that's where another stanza of the picture took place. You wouldn't get the Stones there or anybody like that; you would get the Pink Floyd, almost weekly, people like that. Elton John was there. They all came. The Roundhouse was like the Marquee. The Marquee was for people who wanted to get on the commercial scene but the

Roundhouse was for dedicated nouveau music people, and that's where we developed a lot of our sound systems in there. Manfred Mann, done him, yeah, done him a lot. He wouldn't talk to me because I was old. No, I know why he didn't talk to me, because we did a gig with him and when they finished he ordered a PA system; I thought, I better say something complimentary about his music. I said, I quite like this rhythm & blues scene; and he looked at me with such contempt, complete with curled lip, I crept away. I never said another word to him, ever. Paul Jones was alright, he was cool. I was only about forty-five then, but that was old to them.

I remember when Jimi Hendrix came here, Chas Chandler was going to send him back home because he had not proved his worth. And he came on that show with us and he was broke; he didn't have a bean in his pocket. When he was hungry, him and me used to go round the fish and chip shop and I'd get him fish and chips. We'd sit on the side of the stage and eat our fish and chips, me and Jimi Hendrix. I liked talking to him, he was alright. This was before he got too difficult. And I said to him one night, Jim, who pays for those guitars that you're setting on fire? Oh, he says, it's taken out of my fee. I said, how much are they? Oh, about £100. It was a good one – Gibson; and of course he'd play it first and then he'd burn it. I said, well, instead of you paying £100 for a guitar for two shows a night, seven nights a week, why don't you get a cheap old guitar, a Watkins Rapier, or something like that, and when it comes to the point you throw the mains, destroy the mains lighting, change your guitar, and burn the Watkins Rapier; it's cheaper. Plus of course I could sell you a couple. And that's what he did. He thought I was a genius.

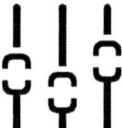

PETER WHITEHEAD,
Film Maker

So I get a phone call one day. Hi, my name is Mike Jeffery. You know who I am, don't you? I said yeah, everything going well? He said, I've got another guy, I've just brought him over from America. Oh, he said, he's amazing. This is the biggest, the best, the most amazing thing that's ever happened. This young black guy from Chicago. I said, what's so great about him? Oh, you can't believe it, he plays the guitar with his teeth. So I thought, OK; this one is going to be a bit difficult. Anyway I get roped into this bloody thing, and I think the first one I did was Jimi. So he comes back and I have to listen to this song called 'Hey Joe'. This is his first single, he's arriving in England, he's going to be big, and all this kind of stuff. And, the good news is his first UK concert is going to be in Shaftesbury Avenue theatre, and it was on the Sunday night I remember and I could go along there and film it live, see; clever stuff. End up with a little film of the thing live, so that would be as good as being on *Top of the Pops*, because *Top of the Pops* probably wouldn't have accepted him anyway. So he says, right, come down to the Shaftesbury Theatre; the concert starts at whatever, eight o'clock; come an hour before maybe.

So I arrived there and I'm dragged down to the basement I remember, where all the dressing rooms were. Mike Jeffery was there, he was the manager of quite a bunch of guys who went on to be a great success. Introduced to Jimi, sat in his corner surrounded by a few groupies and goodness knows what else. So I sat in the corner and thought I might as well do a bit of filming. I'm famous for my dressing room scenes. What else can you film? There's nothing else happening. Then I said, what do you want me to do Mike – any ideas on this? Oh no, great, just film 'Hey Joe', OK. I'll let you know. I said, I need to know. He said of course, I'll let you know. Because I said I didn't want to film the whole bloody concert. In the meantime I can go up there and film some of the audience. He said of course; it's all in your hands; 'Hey Joe'. So I end up behind the curtain, and there I was just peeping out and the guys come and they start bang,

bang, bang, crash, crash, crash. Mike had said of course he smashes all his guitars, and blows up all his Marshall amps and things at the end of the concert. So keep a bit of film for that. This was the first time I'd heard that people smash their guitars. It seemed to me to be a waste of a good guitar.

Anyway I'm watching the audience and watching the drummer on the side of the thing, and thinking, oh my God, is this really my forte? The things I do for money and then suddenly I think, hold on. I can hear this guy going 'Hey Joe'. This is the bloody song! I'm looking for Mike. And of course I bloody start. He'd completely forgotten to warn me. So I start filming and he's already a third of the way through the song. I manage to film him doing this and that, playing with his teeth, and I do a few other occasions, by which time I lost too much enthusiasm; wasn't going to spend too much film on it. So I end up going back with a scene of him smoking a joint in the dressing room surrounded by girls, going down onto the stage, which is always a good shot, and two thirds of the song; and then a shot at the end of him coming out of the bloody theatre and getting into a car, and all the kids throwing themselves on the car. That was cute. And looking through the window – I happened to be on the right side of the car to be able to film it; had I been on the other side of the car I wouldn't have got him. I didn't know which side of the car he was going to get into. Police everywhere; kids flinging themselves around.

So I managed to get back, get the record, which I'd had already transferred to 16mm sound on film for my editing machine, and he was singing a totally different song. Well he wasn't, but completely different speed, different words, different this and that; everything. So I ring up Mike and say, listen – we talked about the fact that he hadn't told me and warned me – and he said, oh can't you lip sync and get some bits? I said, well yeah, I'll do my best. That was one film I had, and it was a mess; there's no doubt about it; but it was the first film of Jimi Hendrix. I did at some point try to re-sync a bit of it, but bits that were sync-able were at a different speed and you couldn't change speeds or anything like that.

GLORIA BRISTOW, PR, Philips Records

Helmut Gordon, really was an incredible character. He seemed to come out of nowhere. He wasn't linked to the music business officially, in any way. Nobody seemed to have heard of him. He ran a sweat-shop near where the old BBC studios were and for whatever reason he was interested in groups and well, I think making money. He saw himself you know finding another Beatles like everybody did at the time. And he haunted Philips Records and the other major companies, and of course there weren't that many then. So you had Philips and Pye actually located quite close to each other at Marble Arch and then you had EMI which was also very close by and then Decca just down over the river. So he went round and I think that virtually everybody just sent him away; they threw him out. He didn't get much past the front door, and I don't know how he inveigled his way past our concierge at Philips but he did. He managed to get into Stanhope House. And he also managed to find his way into my office, much against the better judgement of the girl who was my PA at the time who was absolutely furious but couldn't stop him. He came in the door, funny little man, strange little man. I mean not only was he small of stature but he was strange. There was something about him and you thought: He can't be anything to do with music. He just doesn't fit. But anyway, he came in and he started talking about this group he had. And he said: If you would come and see them. His English was very bad and his accent was very thick. And he said, and he kept saying: Could I come and see them. If I would just come and see them he was sure that I would recommend them to Philips's A&R men and he'd get a deal. And I kept telling him: No, No, No, No, No. Anyway he drove everybody around me mad and in the end a couple of the girls said to me: Please can you go and see what he's on about, 'cause then at least you've been and we can tell him: Look, she came, she's seen, she doesn't like them, she's not going to be able to help. Go away.

So eventually I went to see this group Episode Six and I think I took a couple of people from the Philips offices with me. Couple of the guys, actually from the sales department, and we went to look at them and we thought: They're good, actually. Much to our surprise. They're good. And we saw them in a hall in South London somewhere and the lead singer was Ian Gillan. And the first thing I thought when I saw them was: Wow, what a voice. What an ability. You know, he belongs somewhere else. He doesn't belong here grubbing about at this level, you know he's really got talent. Well then the girl singer I thought was good as well. They sort of were already into the business of being careful how they dressed and how they presented themselves on stage so they were a bit different from most of the stuff that was happening at the time because they took time over their appearance and their stage presentation which was impressive in itself. Anyway, I thought: Yeah, they're very good.

MICK UNDERWOOD,
Musician

The Ian Gillan Band was a bit sort of progressive jazz rock area. Ian eventually decided to shelve that, to stop that, and he formed the band Gillan. At this time I was using Kingsway Studios a lot with Strapps, we recorded quite a lot of stuff there. So I sort of could see what was going on a little bit with them, I didn't take that much notice 'cause we had our own stuff to do. But I'd see Ian and they were going great guns. They'd got an album out but I think they'd only got a release in Japan. I think it was the same stuff I'd been going through you know. Then I got a phone call one morning and he said to me: We're having some changes in the band, and I need a drummer Mick and would you be interested in coming to have a look? I'd heard one track that they'd recorded, I didn't hear all of it, and I didn't like it at all, what I heard you know. It was only because I was up the studio and he wanted a bit of our studio time to put a vocal on it, that's where I heard it. I wasn't in the box with it,

I just heard it. I said: Well, yeah, yeah, of course I'll come and have a play, you know. He said: We've got a guitarist. I mean Colin I knew quite well anyway, he was keyboard player, he was great. I said: Yeah, OK. So I shot up there, I mean like it wasn't then I took my gear there, we were mixing it. I met John McCoy who's at first hit is quite a guy to meet. We had met before somewhere and I didn't know that. Bernie Torme was the guitarist who I'd not met, didn't know anything about at all. So we set up and we just basically wanged away, bashed it out to see what came out and you know it very quickly it was feeling good. I felt: This is alright, you know? The players were excellent, absolutely excellent. It was great fun. And Ian's you know, let's go up the pub. We wore out the stairs going to the pub because we were there for so long. It turned out they said: So yeah, let's do it. Do you want to do it, Mick? And I said: Actually, I said: I do. I really would like to do this. I said: That is great, absolutely brilliant, and I think it was the next day or the day after we started recording the *Mr Universe* album and just carried on from there you know, which is a nice way of doing it actually. And you know it was one of those things where everyone contributed, it just came out. It was all the way through the band it was like that. It was great fun to do. And good band, you know, great people. Nice to work with Ian again.

Ian couldn't get arrested. He tried to get deals, he couldn't, no one was interested and we signed to Acrobat and they did some somersaults. The *Mr Universe* album came out, and it went almost immediately to number eleven, bang first week out wallop, and the record company collapsed. It broke the record company. No money to get the pressings or anything. Which we weren't pleased about, we were doing our first tour at that time. It was like: Great, you know, the album's out, we haven't got a record company. I wasn't involved in any of the dealing with this but the story basically was by that time other record companies had seen that happening and, sort of: Can we have you? There's a bit of action. Anyway, eventually it was Virgin, yeah, it was Virgin, the band signed to Virgin. We were to be honest absolutely honest and frank we were so busy at those times, I mean, if we weren't writing or recording in the studio we were touring and that's exactly what it was. And if we weren't doing an album and we weren't touring we were back in doing singles. Our feet never touched the ground. Which is good in some respects, and our touring was not only here it was all over the world, you know, it was really hot to trot stuff really that way. It was great to do it.

£££

JOHN GAYDON, Manager

We're sitting in our mews house, David Enthoven and I've a joint in my hand, Marc Bolan and June, his wife, and seven plain-clothes policemen break down our door and come in and bust us. It was because we'd been playing Frisbee outside in the mews at night and keeping the neighbours awake, and they knew something was going on. Anyway we got busted, they let Marc and June go, which was quite reasonable of them, and we went to the Hammersmith thing, and the Beak said, your parents have spent a fortune on your education, it's ridiculous that you should... blah blah. So I got fined £50. But funnily enough, much later I applied for a green card to live in America with my American wife at the time, and because John Lennon had fought a court case for his marijuana bust and he managed to get his green card to stay in America because there was a difference between the American Dangerous Drugs Act and the British Misuse of Drugs Act. The British Act, if you were guilty, you could be guilty if it was in the house you were in; but under the American Act it had to be on your person. So John Lennon went to court, won that on the technicality that he was busted under the UK Law, which meant it wasn't on his person, so he couldn't have been convicted under the American Law. So when I applied for my green card I had to go back to my police records and prove that I had less dope on me when we were busted in the house than John Lennon had, and I got my green card. So thanks to him.

JEFF DEXTER,
Disc Jockey

The first person I knew that got busted in a really bad way out of that scene was a guy called Guy Stevens who was a fellow disc jockey who worked with Chris Blackwell importing records and turning lots of people on to R&B and in the spring of 1967 he jumped right into the psychedelic thing big time. He was involved with the Granny Takes a Trip crowd, Hapshash and the Coloured Coat, and had started to develop new sounds from within a newly emerging Island record label. He created a couple of bands and he came up with this concept of a band that would be doing something that would reflect Bob Dylan, à-la *Blonde on Blonde*, related to a classical piece and put together a band called Procol Harum. Not many people know this but he actually helped create 'Whiter Shade of Pale' which became the Summer of Love anthem. That was the most successful hit of that period outside of *Sgt. Pepper* but a singular record 'Whiter Shade of Pale', but he got busted just after he got that whole thing together. He went to jail so he missed out on the whole success of that. Guy was a mover and shaker long before many other people and was involved in all the creative side, the art-work, he generated loads of energy. He was the first person I saw to suffer at the hands of the authorities and of course they were looking at bigger targets as well and of course they wanted to look at the Rolling Stones.

MOLLY DUNCAN, Musician

We were recording in Atlantic Studios in New York and in the other studio were the Stones, and this was when people hadn't really cleaned up their act. Atlantic Records was being run at that time by the Ertegun brothers. So we were all in the studio, situation completely normal, there were a few joints going round, Ahmet rushed in the door suddenly, the cops are on their way up, give me all your drugs, everything you've got and get this place cleaned up. All the people who didn't take things were suddenly producing little bits of this and that from here and there. Ash trays were emptied, people were spraying the air you know, put up the air conditioning, polishing things. Of course he had gone into the Stones as well.

So we were all waiting for the cops to come rushing in. Nothing happened. I thought I will have a look out in the hall so I go out and I looked through this little glass panel into the hall and there is the receptionist guy sitting there reading the paper, completely normal. Completely calm so I opened the door looked round, nothing, nobody. I went hey, Mac, that was his name, I said, are the cops coming up? Cops he said, what cops? I said Ahmet came in and told us the police were on their way up. Where is Ahmet? He said: Oh he has gone to a party in Long Island. True story, he went off, God know, what he got from the Stones studio.

£££

DOUG SMITH,
Clearwater Management

Clearwater was based in my mews flat, which was one great open room and a sort of balcony that came out. I lived in the balcony, and everybody sat downstairs at desks. That's where we all worked from. We ran gigs at All Saints hall.

Even got Bowie to play, actually. Wayne got that together as a favour, because High Tide had done the Beckenham Arts Lab, so Bowie said he'd do it. He came and did it and was harassed by a young girl in the audience that must have been about that big only. He actually handled it with great finesse, and she handled it with great finesse as well, but she had the last word. I think we couldn't sell any alcohol, and I think we could only sell Coca-Cola and orange juice, we charged 2/6d, and that was it. Paul Fenn booked the acts, and we put the money up and put the gigs on. To be honest with you, the amount of money we put out was like peanuts. We relied on the fact that people would come. We found that by running All Saints, and smoking a little of the weed, and staying high, and saying peace love man, and all the rest of it, we could accept this form of life, even though it was a disaster from day to day.

Because of the fact that Hawkwind had this reputation of drugs, they were always being busted. You'd get to a venue and you'd be raided backstage the whole time. They became very adept at taking care of their dope. As soon as they got to the gig, they knew the best place to put it, if it was a good gig and it had a fly bar, all the dope would be strapped to the fly bar and they'd just shifted it to the ceiling, and just left up there till the end of the gig. They'd have the old puff around or whatever. I mean, some very weird things happened. We were coming into Bournemouth with them on the bus and were hailed by all these fans on a roundabout to slow down. We slowed down, and they said the police are turning the place over. The band emptied out all their drugs, and buried it in the middle of the roundabout, and steamed off to the gig. The busts were just phenomenal, so many.

BRIAN BERG,
EMI Records

EMI was one of the major companies and had a bit of a dip in the Eighties before the CD revolution. We were the only area that was making a profit and we had about six MDs in eighteen months. The latest appointment worked for one of the companies which we had bought but he had a drink problem, great in the mornings and not in the afternoon. The marketing director had arranged for him to meet Kate Bush and the MD was about an hour late, then two hours late for the meeting. Kate said he must be busy so I will go, and in the stairwell they tripped over someone absolutely pissed lying there and the Marketing Manager said, Kate, this is our new MD. That is what it was like then.

There was a pub over the road where people used to go for drinks after work but the barman refused to serve our MD as he was pissed, so he grabbed his keys and wrote off twelve cars going down the road, but left his number plate. By the time he got to his own house there was a road block, he just got a fine. Nowadays you they would throw away your keys.

MUFF WINWOOD,
Musician

While I was still at Island, so this would have been about 1973, 1974 – I was taking Joe Cocker across America and we were doing... we were doing really well with Joe. He's done 'A Little Help From My Friends' which was a Beatles cover and that's why the Americans loved it. But he was a bizarre act and they loved that, too. And we were doing fantastic business all over America and I was taking him over there, looking after him, and we were on the road with the band. It was my birthday, so it was in June, and the manager of Traffic and Joe Cocker threw a birthday party for me in Manhattan when we were in town. And somebody in this birthday party absolutely slammed me with LSD and I was in a serious bad way. I always remember the drummer of Joe Cocker walking me through New York all night long, all night long. I was in a complete... and it didn't really go away very much the next couple of days and I felt really bad. Oh, they'd taken me to a doctor and they'd poured all kinds of downers down me and stuff and I'd gotta go to this, with Joe, this whacky rock festival up in Woodstock which was some new festival they were having. And in town and at the party was John Glover and John Glover was our ex-road manager of Spencer Davis Group who had since become the road manager of Traffic for Chris Blackwell, so was working for Island Records. He had come over with Spooky Tooth who we were trying to break in America and I said to him: I feel sick. He was going home, he'd finished his tour and they were going home the next day and I said to him: Oh God I feel so bad. I said: I've just had it. I've just gotta go home. And I said: I've gotta go up to this place, Woodstock. And he said: Look. He said: I'll tell you what. He said: If you like, you take Spooky Tooth home right and I'll take Joe up to this thing in Woodstock. Of course, he went to Woodstock and I missed it. The amazing story of Woodstock. There you go, how these things how, see just how a little thing in the day changes and there you go; and he got the history of Woodstock and I completely missed it. I was on the flight home.

CLIVE SELWOOD,
MD, Elektra Records

We were more successful in England with *Forever Changes* than Elektra was in America. We made it I think a Top Twenty album, and one of my proudest achievements was I edited 'Alone Again Or', for a single; and that's the one that's still played on the radio. That was in the old days when you had to do it with a razor blade. I remember sitting in the studio cutting bits of tape out with a razor blade and sticking them together with super glue. But it did come out and it was a relatively successful turntable hit; never really cracked it but it is released every now and again. During that time I also released Judy Collins 'Amazing Grace' against huge opposition from Jac Holzman, in fact, and lots of people thought I was crazy. I remember telling Jac I wanted to release it and he said, an acapella version of a hymn? Well I just think it's got it. He said OK, if you crazy Limeys want to do it, go ahead. So I did. I remember it was a public domain song but, because it said 'arranged by' on it, David Platz the publisher got the publishing rights; he also thought I was stupid to release it but he didn't object, and following Judy's success with it, I think it made the top three or something like that and in the charts for many weeks, the Coldstream Guards or someone like that recorded it, which also made it to number one, and David Platz scored all the publishing money off all that. He never even sent me a Christmas card. I was a bit ticked off about that; must have made him a great deal of money.

I went to Woodstock with Jac Holzman and Judy Collins; spent the night in Judy Collins bedroom, but so did several of us at the time because there was no room at the inn. It was a disaster. The approach to it was extraordinary because cars were just littering the road. People just stopped their cars in the middle of the highway and walked the rest of the way. It was extraordinary; it looked like a bomb had hit the place. And when we got there of course it poured with rain and nobody to get to or from the site, so the locals were charging $5 for a loaf of bread and $5 for a pint of milk, which is fairly extortionate. The bands could only get in by helicopter and there was no room at the inn; we had virtually the only rooms. And in this time of peace and love and brotherhood, I watched members of two of the biggest bands at the time scrapping it out, duking it out on the floor because they'd both been booked into the same room, so they just took to fisticuffs.

Everybody hated Woodstock, absolutely hated it; absolutely. And then when the movie came out a year or so later those same people were saying, hey man, what a trip. And I'd say to them, but you hated it; well no man. Just propaganda; but it was awful. I remember, because I was reporting also for Radio One at the time with a Uher tape recorder and wrote for the Melody Maker, and reported it as being a disaster. One of the things I remember, there was a terrible smell there too; an absolutely awful smell. I was standing some way from the site, because you couldn't get close to it, looking over a barred country gate, and Jac Holzman came up behind me with his big patrician nose, did a loud sniff and said, sounds like the Lord's laid a fart. Which is a unique expression, but fairly apposite at the time; it did smell really bad. So as I said, we spent the night with Judy watching old Marlene Dietrich movies on telly. Not very glamorous.

JOHN GAYDON, Manager

We went on tour in America with King Crimson. We played Filmore East, and Filmore West; I remember I was on the first bit of the tour and we played Miami; we played a big festival in – I don't know where it was but we had to get there by helicopter, and we stayed in this big hotel in Miami Beach. I remember sitting next door to Janis Joplin, with her bottle of Southern Comfort in her hand; we were flying in with The Byrds; all those acts of those days; it was incredible. The thing that struck me, and I don't remember a great deal about it, I just remember them having caravans on the site at the festival with the judge in it. So if you were found with marijuana on you, they would fine you there and then on the festival site. Anyway by the time we get to LA, Mike Giles and Ian McDonald, who were two members of Crimson were moaning, oh I don't want to be on the road, I want to go home or whatever it was. So at the end of that tour they broke up and Greg Lake said, OK, I'm going to try put another band together. He says he spoke to Jimi Hendrix to try and persuade him to join the band. Eventually persuaded Keith Emerson to leave The Nice and Carl Palmer from Atomic Rooster. Carl Palmer was represented by Robert Stigwood, Atomic Rooster was I guess, so we had to do a deal with Stiggy and David and I used to go up to his house in Stanmore, where he had go-carts. We beat him at table tennis, which really pissed him off. I think he just really wanted to go to bed with us both probably. But he was a real character. So we did a deal with him; basically a third, a third, a third – he got a third and we got two-thirds. And ELP was formed. I think in between ELP happening and Crimson reforming, Chris Blackwell called us up one day and said, Tyrannosaurus Rex, and they've got one gig in their book; at least just meet with them. We're saying we can't, we're out of our heads every weekend. We're in the Kings Road on our motorbikes, and the coolest people on the block and all that. OK, so we sort of meet Marc, this little elfin chap, and June his wife, and Mickey.

So Mark Fenwick joins us and Caroline Christie looked after Tyrannosaurus Rex; they had literally one gig in their book, and we kept saying you need to go electric; you've got to stand up Marc. Because it was a time of Zeppelin, it was the time of big music and rock, and he was playing acoustic warbling. So one day he came in and said, I've got a great idea; I'm going to get a drum and bass player; which is the way these things go. So we auditioned for drummers and bass players, and he brought in 'Ride a White Swan', which actually was the B side of the record; I think it was on Track Records – Kit Lambert and Chris Stamp, and we were very close to David Platz of Essex Music, who was our publisher for Crimson; he was very much a great guy. So we got them to flip the record, he went electric, we said you can't be called Tyrannosaurus Rex, it's a ridiculous name. T-Rex came out of that; then he came in with 'Hot Love', which obviously was a number one record. By this time we were taking him a little bit more seriously, so I started looking after him and got very, very close and very fond of Marc. We used to record at Trident Studios; we would drop in because Tony Visconti was the producer. In fact Bowie came to us to ask us to represent him, in between 'Space Odyssey' and when he really took off and we also turned down Yes. But we had all the madness of King Crimson, Emerson, Lake and Palmer, and everybody freaking out, and then T-Rex. And before that I'd looked after Joan Armatrading for her first album; we represented The Strawbs for a time and Julie Felix; a lot of stuff going on.

ALAN FITTER,
Salesman,
Transatlantic Records

In 1972 I was unemployed after Transatlantic Records and applied for a few jobs and got *Music Week* as you did and there was an advert for Field Promotion Officer for A&M Records. I thought, what is a Field Promotion Officer, but I liked A&M and I liked the product, a guy called Robin Blanchflower was running it and they had temporary offices just off Bond Street, so I went for the interview with Robin. Because they were temporary offices they were only partly partitioned, not up to the ceiling, so I sat there waiting while the person before me was being interviewed. Robin asked him if he knew what a Field Promotion Officer was and the guy said, no, so Robin began to tell him, we have them in America. The reason they were setting all this up was because commercial radio was coming and there was already local BBC stations. They were basically pluggers in the field who would go to local radio, colleges, record shops, anywhere where you could promote the records. So by I went in and Robin asked me, I replied I have done a bit of research... I could see Robin go, wow, and he went out to his boss John Deacon and said John, John, we have found our first guy. So we sorted out a car and he gave me a stack of albums because they were very into their product. My wife was working in town so I went to meet her with this huge stack of albums and she almost went apoplectic as I had been out of work for three or four months, you have been out buying albums. So I went to A&M and I loved it, helped train all the other guys.

A&M had The Strawbs and the single was called 'Lay Down', well one day Robin called me into his office and said take these singles, go to these shops and give them to them. Why? I asked. I cannot tell you, I mustn't tell you, but have a think about it. That was how hyping worked then, you went in and said here is a box of twenty-five copies, charge what you like, and unbeknown to me they were employing college students to go in within days to buy the single. The other way of hyping was you got friendly with the record shop and in those days there was a book in which, especially on a busy Saturday, the shop was supposed to write in the catalogue numbers of everything they sold. So you used to say give us the book and you would write in the catalogue numbers you wanted in different pens all clever like. Well 'Lay Down' was a minor hit and they followed it up with a very un-Strawbs like song 'Part Of The Union' which went to number one in the *NME* or two in *Music Week*.

DAVID ARDEN,
Management

I used to run around London paying for Radio London and Radio Caroline to keep playing the records. I'll always remember Phil Solomon, my Uncle Phil, I called him up, it was late, the old man was late paying. I said: Phil, I'm getting the money, I think it was £250 and I said: I'll be round to the apartment, it's alright if I bring it round to your apartment tomorrow being a Saturday? He said: All right David, you know. I call him up next morning, I said: Phil, got the money and I'll be round in about two hours. He said: Oh, he said, I won't be there. I went: Oh, OK, what's that? He said: Look, I'll tell you what to do, now there's a race on this afternoon.

I'll never forget it, it's the god's honest truth, I can't remember the race; I thought it was the St Leger but I got it wrong 'cause I looked it up. I remember the name of the horse 'Pieces of Eight' ridden by Lester Piggott. He said: I tell you what you do, he said, now you take a hundred of that £250 and you put it on 'Pieces of Eight' in the whatever at Doncaster. I mean, really? Do what I tell you, son. Well, fucking thing pissed it at like five to one, took him the money, he went: See! I mean, Phil Solomon was, great. You don't get characters like that anymore.

PHIL CLIFT, RCA Records, Regional Sales

I deferred university for a year and took a gap year ending up working in a local record shop and, six months on, the new owner said would I run it for him? I had just met Jane, my wife to be, so I thought I am not going to university, I like this business too much and I am in love as well. We were selling singles by Slade and Wizzard and album-wise I can remember being there when *Dark Side Of The Moon* came out. I got fifty copies off a Red Star wagon on a Friday for some reason and sold them straight through the weekend. All gone.

But after a couple of years I got irked by constantly seeing these reps coming in in their nice cars and I thought I would quite like to do that. The particular company that really appealed to me was Island Records, their reps always had the latest Ford Capri and they had a lovely slim-line catalogue. I thought it would be really easy to get into, but it wasn't, anyhow after numerous knock-backs I got some freelance work to do window displays, funnily enough for Island Records, travelling around in a beat up old Beetle mainly in the West Country. I soon discovered that it was a question of it was a bit of an old boys' network in the sense that it was a question of who you knew. If you were just applying off the street then it was very difficult. I just kept knocking at the door and eventually in 1976 I got a salaried position at RCA Records, they had decided to put together a field display team to do window and in-store displays and doing the displays at the entrance to venues for particular bands. I got a fantastic new Cortina Mk4 which I remember driving to play a football match one weekend and the guy saying, you are going to sleep in that tonight aren't you? All things were going well until the beginning of 1977 and we were invited to our first sales conference in West Bromwich and the following day they made us all redundant. Well within months Presley died and they had so much work we were then taken back on, on a freelance basis to cover all the re-released catalogue.

MARTIN NELSON,
EMI Records,
Regional Promotions

Regional promotion seemed to work very well but one of the problems was that I had people going to the same area that the singles sales force were going to so we came up with the great idea of actually combining the two forces so that the singles sales person would also become the promotion person for one area which of course doubled the workforce at a stroke. So I took over a singles sales promotion team and those same people worked both radio stations and a small number of local stores in the area so when they went into the stores they knew what was happening on the radio in their area, when they went into radio stations they knew what were selling in their area, so it worked extremely well. Displays was a separate team which I also controlled as well at that time and they went round to record stores only and they put displays up in record stores. And the early phase of regional promotion at EMI, the regional promotion team had to do it before there was a display team, so for example, I would follow a band like Pink Floyd and get to the place they were playing in the morning, put up displays in the record stores around the area and then for the evening show go and put up a display in the foyer which never used to last very long 'cause it was just stapled sleeves on a board but it was good when the manager arrived; it looked good then. And then of course watched the show. So I ended up watching Pink Floyd twenty-seven times when they were routining *Dark Side of the Moon* and working through it and getting it right before they actually went to record it. Steve O'Rourke was managing so I spent you know most of the early evening in the bar talking to him and then I had my place at the side of the stage each night which the band organised for me on top of a flight case where I'd go for the performance.

One day I get called in by the product manager and told that Pink Floyd are finishing off *Dark Side of the Moon* at Abbey Road and can I have a volunteer to go down and wait at Abbey Road until they finish recording it to then take a copy master and send it off to Capitol Records in Los Angeles because the Americans wanted to hear it as soon as possible, they weren't absolutely sure about this strange recording where it's just one track basically. So a concept album; one of the originals. They wanted to hear it first before they made a decision so I went down to Abbey Road studios at about midnight and I sat in reception for two and a half hours and at about half-past two in the morning the engineer came out and said: What are you doing here? I said: Well here's my packaging, I've gotta send the copy master off to America when you've finished and I'll wait until you are ready. So he said: Well, come and sit in the studio. So I went into the studio and there was just the engineer and Pink Floyd and me and that was it and they're busy working out how much of the swearing they're gonna keep in by the commissionaire. As you know, *Dark Side of the Moon* has a bit of swearing on it. And so they finally decided how much they were gonna keep in and at four o'clock in the morning they turned the lights down in the studio and they played back *Dark Side of the Moon* finished for the very first time. I sat on the floor of the studio, just me, the band and the engineer, absolutely entranced by this incredible music which was going through my head and got my copy master, drove out to Heathrow as dawn was breaking and an amazing experience. I thought I was being lumbered and wasn't too happy about having to do it and stay up all night to do it but looking back on it, fantastic experience. First person to hear *Dark Side of the Moon* finished apart from the band.

STUART WATSON, EMI Promotions

My Harvest Records memory was the launch of *Dark Side Of the Moon* at the Planetarium where, contrary to Nick Mason's wonderful book, I remember that one member of the group turned up. I went back to my 1974 programme and one of the questions in cartoon style with questions and answers was 'Which member of the Pink Floyd turned up at the Planetarium?' and you turned it upside down and the answer was Richard Wright. So at the Planetarium on that particular night I was responsible for assembling cardboard cut-outs in darkened seats in front of a long table in the Planetarium for Rick to sit beside. Rick comes in, sits down and the playback happens. The reason the guys refused to appear was that there was no Quadraphonic sound, the record company would not pay for the Quad system then. We then nominate Rick as the spokesman for the band to the press, he answers them then walks out. We dimmed the lights right down and we assumed that the cardboard cut-outs walked out behind him and the press all clap and everyone is finished.

NICK MOBBS, Harvest Records Label Manager

The reception or the press launch for *Dark Side of the Moon* was at the London Planetarium. Obviously, the band were all invited. They were at that stage where they wouldn't do anything. They were too sniffy, and were like: Oh no, no. We don't do that kind of thing. But we still went ahead with the press reception. It was a phenomenal success, because the London Planetarium was the perfect venue for it. Everybody had to sit there for the whole forty-five minutes listening with the stars going on above, and they did a super display in the Planetarium. Because the band wouldn't come, we just got these life-size black and white cut-outs and stuck them in the main reception, so as every guest arrived they were just met by these four Pink Floyd cut-outs, which went down incredibly well with the people who came. Actually, the Floyd quite liked the idea. Then Roger Waters fitting in perfectly with this theme when it came to collecting gold discs, again he was being sniffy, he wouldn't come to any official presentation. We just wrapped it up in this old brown paper bag, tatty old brown paper bag, and just sent it round via messenger, which again, he appreciated.

I can't claim that I signed Kate Bush. I was A&R manager when she was signed. Dave Gilmore, of course, was the connection. He knew her and he'd found her. The Floyd road manager first came in to see me to play a tape of Kate very early on. I said: It sounds really interesting. I'd like to keep an eye on what she's doing. Nothing really happened. Then another tape came in, probably also from the road manager, maybe a couple of months later or something, or a few months later. I said that same thing: Really interesting. Keep an eye on it. A few months later, Bob Mercer said: I know you've been listening to a few tapes of Kate Bush. What do you think? I said: Yeah, really interesting. Really got to keep an eye on her, because obviously she doesn't sound like anybody I know. Unique. He said: I think I need to sign her. I said: OK. I see what you're thinking. He said: No, this is getting a bit political. Because obviously, I agree with you, I do think she's really, really interesting, and of course, Floyd being involved and everything. They don't want a lot of money. It's just if we sign her, then we can still keep an eye on her, but then we can just let her develop. As I say, I can't possibly claim credit for signing her, but I was always totally sympathetic to the talent.

MARK RYE, Harvest Records Label Manager

By 1976 I was really enjoying my time at Harvest and spent quite a lot of time trying to be friendly with the band at the Floyd's Britannia Row. This was the studio they had built with the huge amount of money that had come in from the success of *Dark Side Of The Moon*. The band seemed awfully confused I suppose as to how the hell you follow up an album like that, which had just become so ridiculously successful, well beyond anyone's expectations. I think I spent time up at Abbey Road listening to playbacks of things and then some time later at Brit. Row which had been built by then. But spending a day listening to the engineers trying to get a certain drum sound for hour after hour certainly tested my patience. So my abiding memory is of the snooker table on the top floor and trying to play snooker with any of the band or whoever was around, and Roger Waters telling me one day how alienated he felt with their audience and how he wanted to build a big wall between himself and the audience. Which of course, some time later he did, big time.

When *Animals* was coming up for release, I had the unenviable task of taking the sleeve proofs over to the somewhat unapproachable and aloof Roger Waters who was living somewhere off Clapham Common for him to approve them. Our reproduction department had been given a copy of the American sleeve proof and had spent a frantic forty-eight hours trying to make our sleeve proofs match their sleeve proofs. Different system, different printers, different results.

Regardless of what the Hipgnosis artwork had been we wanted to make our version look the same as the American version. So I went over to Roger Waters house and sat there while he spent half an hour or so out in another room looking at and examining the two versions. Then he came back in and said: Oh I like it, that's fine, I like it, it is different. Relief – and then I was thinking you B. We could have done you 'different' forty-eight hours ago. But there you are, this is the prerogative of the artist.

DAVID MUNNS, EMI Records

You remember those meetings – Kate Bush, you know. I drove her to a sales meeting in Manchester, Kate Bush; she'd never stayed in a hotel before; she was seventeen. I made her play to the sales force in the Post House Hotel in Manchester; she's in there with a piano in the sales meeting playing 'Wuthering Heights'. Four weeks later they were beaten away from the front door; a household name. A month – you think about it. Amazing. They're the moments when you think, yes.

Marc Bolan used to sit in my office every afternoon. You'd go out for lunch, three o'clock in he'd come, pissed as a rat, pass out on my couch; I'd have all my meetings with him unconscious on the couch, that one summer when he couldn't stay off it. The year he died he was completely out of control. But you could set a record up in a meeting, put it out the next week; you didn't need to angst over different versions and all that; you just listened to it and went, yeah, let's do that and that and that, and something to make it noticed, something to get radio to work, there was a lot of records; they were putting out twenty or thirty singles a week. You had to sieve through all this stuff and see which one was going to be the one.

ALLAN JAMES,
EMI House Photographer

I applied for a job at the *British Journal of Photography* as a photographer for EMI Records; and I got it at eighteen years old, as EMI's in-house photographer. The negatives were owned by EMI, and in those days we never knew a lot about what was going to go on, I mean, I did the first photo shoot of Gilmour joining Pink Floyd; and the first photo shoot of Deep Purple when Glover and Gillan joined them in 1968, when EMI launched Harvest. I'd only been there two days and I had to take photographs of Cliff Richard; and in 1967 he was the biggest rock star in the UK; and he was great. I still think he's the nicest man in the world; him and The Shadows. He signed one of my photographs for my mum; I said, to Lily; and he put it on – she was in a flat working as a tailoress – so her son took a photograph of Cliff Richard and Cliff signed it 'To Lily, with love Cliff'. So I was a hero; I was my mum's hero. Because of that I got to know everybody. EMI, while I was there Radio One started and EMI... well, all the DJ's used to come to EMI; I'm sure payola worked then because I didn't know what the hell was going on but all the DJ's, Blackburn's and all that, coming in. I did the first Radio One calendar, because they all talked to me, and that's how I got to know all the DJ's and the producers, Johnny Beerling and all that and so they asked me, and it was fun.

How did I end up in the promotion game? Well I left EMI because I got frustrated at what I was doing; they were outsourcing a lot of this good creative stuff in the end – a company called Hipgnosis was doing all the Floyd catalogue album covers and The Beatles had their own photographer and all this and that. And I bummed around Europe and ended up in Australia, made a lot of money but absolutely hated being in Australia; this was like 1971, 1972. It was the end of the world then; you only had a phone; you'd phone up people and talk at five o'clock in the morning to someone in London. So I came back to the UK and I went broke. Ended up doing photographs of bands at the Marquee or Speakeasy, for £30. I was just talking to people and a guy at the time who used to run *Music Week*, Philip Parker, turned round and said, you know everybody in the music industry; you'd be good at promotion. So he just put a little teaser in Dooley saying, ex-EMI photographer Allan James back from Australia looking for a job in the music industry. And I got offered two jobs overnight. One was for Polydor and they were offering me The Rubettes, The Osmonds and a few other bands like that; and the other one was for ABC with a new band called Steely Dan, and a guitarist called Joe Walsh; and an act called Rufus with a lead singer called Chaka Khan. Plus they had a catalogue of Three Dog Night and the Mamas and Papas and stuff, and I think I went with ABC. That was how I got in it, and the first record I plugged that I can talk about was 'Do It Again' by Steely Dan.

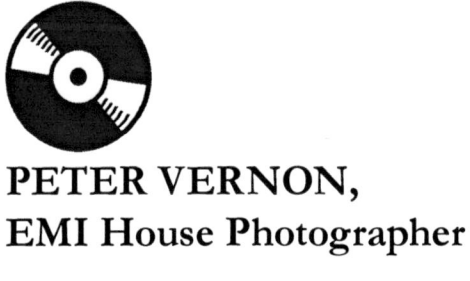

PETER VERNON, EMI House Photographer

Early 1971 March/April, something like that I got a phone call from Ron Dunton at my previous job, which was working at the art college where I was originally a student. I was assistant to the head of the photographic department. Ron said: We've heard you're a rather good photographer. Would you like to come up and bring us some of your work so we can look at it? I talked to Bob, I said: Look, this basically is EMI the record company. That's about as far as it went: EMI was a record company. I went up, had this interview. Then one of my pictures, I'd just got these lips, and I put red film across it. He went: I don't believe it. Wait there. He went out the room and came back, and he had a pull from the printers of some album, and there were these big red lips. I said: Well I didn't know anything about it. He said: No. Anyway, he really liked my work. It was completely different from anything he'd seen.

79

He said: Yes, you're the sort of person we want for the job. De, de, de, de, de, de, de, de, de. Then I started. That was it.

The first major artist I did was Cliff Richard. I'd been there about two or three weeks. I had him sitting on the floor in the studio. I felt bit: Ooh, this is Cliff Richard. I don't exactly like your work. That was some time in the past, not really liked it then. The Young Ones. I've nothing against Cliff. He's a nice guy. Was a nice guy to me, anyway. I can remember saying to him: Would you mind sitting on the floor, Cliff, or is that beneath you? Well, I know it's beneath you, and I was trying to get out this. Oh, shit! Ron White said that to me after about three weeks of being at EMI. He said: You'll meet a lot of famous people, stars and all that. Just treat them like anyone else. They are just human beings, just like you and me. I did then, and then people didn't want it. Fine. OK, you want to be like that? I'm here to do a job. If you don't want to do it, then up your proverbial. But generally, that worked. Most people were fine.

It was just photographing people that were booked in, for me to photograph sleeves, or publicity, or had to do a signing, or go to the Abbey Road, or any other studio, or any other place to do whatever it was that needed to be done. It was just what I did. People came in, I photographed them, they buggered off, and I went onto the next. It's like once I photographed someone called Kate, this young girl. She danced for me, and I videoed her, and I did stills and everything. Later, she was internationally famous. Kate Bush. Or I could be with Mrs Mills at some zoo in Twycross at lunchtime, photographing her with the apes or whatever. Then in the evening at a reception in Central London for Mickie Most. It could be anything. Doing gigs, after show bits. I would process the film. The colour film went to the lab, and I had to make sure that got there, and then I collected it. I was a one man band, so to speak.

PETER REICHARDT, Record Plugger

I had an aunt who worked for the BBC and via her I got the first job in Television Accounts processing invoices and thought I have got to get out of here. There were all sorts of different jobs advertised on the notice board and saw one for the Gramophone library and thought that is sort of exciting. I was based in Egton House and I would see all these guys turning up and all looking a bit flash with company cars. You very quickly learnt that Radio One was housed in the same building but two floors up, so I got to know all the Radio One producers. John Walters in particular who used to produce John Peel and they would just come down and chat, chat, chat. I would ask who are these guys that just seem to turn up outside? Record Pluggers. What do they do? They turn up because it is their job to get all the latest records played on Radio One. Oh, and I am thinking I like the look of that.

So I thought nothing ventured, nothing gained and I wrote to Warner Brothers or it might have been Kinney Records in those days, RCA and I cannot remember the other one. This is what I do, any chance of a job, and to my amazement I got a response from Warner Brothers, we are looking for a promotion man for Elektra Records, come on in and have a chat. I went in to this rather fearsome man who was Bill Fowler who was head of promotion and he said, what do you do at the BBC, so I told him and unintentionally name-dropped a few people like John Walters. He said so you know these people, you've got a fucking job my son, start next Monday. I went back to the BBC which in those days was a job for life, you never got the sack, it was pretty much the Civil Service. I went up to see John Walters and he said, look you seem a bright enough sort of lad, you are rotting away downstairs, give it a go. If it does not work, the BBC will take you back. So dear old John he pushed me into it.

Talk about a baptism of fire, I think to this day it is a great grounding being a plugger because you get shouted at you know. Well I turned up at Egton House on my first day with the records under my arm, swanning into to Roger Pusey's office. Oh hello Peter I haven't got time for you now. Get Out! Suddenly you were on the other side of the fence, I went and saw John Walters and he said, you look a bit dejected, and he said, you have got to understand, pluggers are good for a free lunch, otherwise you are just an annoyance.

RICHARD EVANS, Record Plugger

Tony Calder opened a record shop in the Kings Road and I got the job working there knowing nothing about the whole thing. You know when you first enter into the music business you realise just how little you know, you actually realise you know less than nothing because the bit of information you have got is a hindrance. So I worked in this shop for Tony Calder, need I say any more, and it went on for one summer and then I promise you, never in the history of the music business has this happened, but I opened a copy of *Record Retailer* and there was an advert in the job section for a junior plugger. Now I have never seen an advert for a promotion person since that day, and I doubt that there was one before. So I applied and got a job working for B&C Records and I was in really good company there and I am learning my craft with some really great people. But it literally was that they gave me a box of records and said: Go to Radio One, these are the people you go and see and their names are on the door. And I was just bloody terrified, the BBC for God's sake, it is like walking into Buckingham Palace, and I am walking in with a box of records under my arm and there are people called Johnny who I have got to call Johnny and I don't know them from Adam. I remember I was plugging a Lindisfarne record called 'Lady Eleanor' and I saw John Peel, and I liked John Peel and I thought he will be sympathetic, was he fuck! I said, John I have got this Lindisfarne record and he said, I have been playing that for six months, do your homework before you come and see me.

I phoned my wife and said, I cannot do this job. But then I did because I latched onto Nigel Molden I think it was, and he said I am going to Radio Two, so I went with him to Radio Two and he was writing all these plays down and I thought, what is he doing that for, these records are ten years old. So in the end I asked him, Nigel could you just explain and you are much more experienced than me, and he said I haven't got clue. I thought maybe I am not the only one wandering about aimlessly all day with nothing to do, because there were only fifteen people to see and I can do that in an afternoon, and in those days pluggers were not allowed back in the office. If you weren't plugging, you weren't working. So I just fell in amongst the crowd and we just had lunch. I went out for lunch in 1971 and got back in 1982. It was just the wildest time, we all used to go to each other's receptions, no-body knew who worked for what, it was a complete free-for-all and of course what I did not realise at the time was there weren't any rules because we were all making it up as we went along, so my skills were as good as anybody else's.

I had been at B&C about a month and they have just come off a number one, Atomic Rooster 'Devils Answer' and we had the Trojan catalogue but I did not really promote Trojan, but nevertheless Greyhound were doing *Top Of The Pops*, and I was sent down to meet Greyhound and I have never been to *Top Of The Pops* before. I don't know where it is, I have a vague idea it is at the TV Centre, I don't know anybody who works there, I don't know where the studio is so I get there early. I have little wander around and they are all strangers, so I think, shall I introduce myself now? No I will wait 'till the band get here and I'll introduce myself when the band get here and then I can start to meet people. So I go and have some tea. The call time was eleven o'clock, it came and went, eleven-thirty came and went, twelve came and went. I can hear all these people, where are Greyhound? Who has Greyhound? So I thought, probably not a good time to introduce myself, I will phone the office but there is nobody there interested in talking to me about this band. Anyway about half-past one a Dormobile van comes steaming round the corner literally with smoke pouring out of the window and out get these Rastas and they go into Television Centre. At this point I knew that I had a self-preservation instinct because I thought, let them do it on their own, we'll see how this goes. I spent the whole day at *Top Of The Pops* as the invisible man, I never met the group, I never met the *TOTP* people, I just wandered about pretending I was not there. I thought I will introduce myself next time we get somebody on.

STUART EPPS, Studio Engineer

I went from office boy at DJM, to disc cutter to studio assistant to engineer, and I was working with Steve Brown who more or less changed Elton's career from writing Songs For Europe to writing, and he produced the first album *Empty Sky* which was now serious Elton John music. I was working for Steve as his assistant and after the *Empty Sky* album he started doing the demos for the next album *Elton John* and Elton had written these incredible almost classical songs for this album and we had done piano and voice demos which were amazing songs. Steve attempted to do the album and thought I am not doing this justice, I must find a new producer and he found the arranger Paul Buckmaster who told Steve about Gus Dudgeon who he said had produced the Bowie single 'Space Oddity'. When Gus first met Elton and Bernie Taupin he walked in the room and Steve was there, he saw Bernie and started talking to him and Elton was, what is he talking to him for? Hello, he is just the lyricist, I am here, excuse me, HELLO. Gus had just assumed that Bernie was the singer because he had long hair and was the better looking one. Anyhow they started putting this album together and Gus being the complete perfectionist was going to get an orchestra in and Steve had to find a way to do this as I distinctly remember it was going to cost, £5,000 was going to be the bill from Trident Studios. Steve went to Dick to ask for the money and we were all thinking there is no way, £5,000 and Dick just went, yeah do it, fine. We could not believe it and that is the measure of Dick, he believed in Elton and he believed in what was going on and put everything behind it and had the whole company, forty people working to make Elton John into a big star really.

BOB FISHER, Journalist

Charlie Gillett used to write for a magazine called *Shout*. He had written *The Sound Of the City* and he started serialising it in *Shout* before it was published and one day he put in the editorial that people should interview musicians when you see them and talk to them. I thought well that is interesting, so I went to see Lowell Fulson one night at El Rondo, on my own I think, and he was just sitting around at the bar drinking. I just walked over to him and said, can I talk to you, can I ask you some questions? Yeah, sure, I'm drinking this. So I bought him a whisky and we sat and chatted, and then I wrote it up in *Shout* and Charlie thought this was rather good. Charlie eventually moved onto *Creem* and involved me there on the record reviewing team. Then he moved onto *Let It Rock* so I was enrolled with them too. Then some point around 1969 - 1970 the *NME* got rid of virtually everybody apart from Roy Carr and took almost the entire team of *Creem*. So as soon as the *Creem* guys arrived there of course they enrolled me there as well. So for a brief period I was writing for all three of them plus *International Times*.

I used to listen to Charlie Gillett's show most Sundays if I was around, and one particular Sunday he had this group that had found him and he played their acetate and it was this thing called 'Sultans Of Swing'. I thought, my God. So Monday morning I phone Charlie up and say who are this band, what's the deal here? He said, you are the third one, you are slightly too late, you should get in the office earlier. I will give them your details. Anyhow they came to my office

85

at EMI, nicked armfuls of Fantasy and Stax albums because they thought that was totally wonderful, loved the idea, and my boss Alan Kaupe's secretary actually knew Mark Knopfler. We had the demo, so I gave it to someone and never saw it again.

CHARLIE GILLETT,
Disc Jockey

Dave Robinson had called me again; Dave and I regularly spoke to each other. It would seem that we spoke more regularly than we actually did because each phone call seemed to have quite a lot of ramifications. So this one, he said, I've got some tapes I want to play. I said OK, I've only got a domestic tape recorder, so make sure you come down with five-inch spools, not those great big studio spools; which of course he forgot, so the first half-hour of the meeting was like, my mother used to do knitting and you kind of got skeins of wool and she's turning them into a ball; so in this case with pencils we managed to spool this tape onto smaller reels. And when we listened to them I just didn't like anything; they were all made by Ducks Deluxe and Brinsley Schwarz and whatever. And I was very well aware of Dave's disappointment; I was very dismissive of all of it. Eventually this thing starts and it's completely different. Opens feeling like a proper song, and it turned out to be Graham Parker, who at that time was completely unknown, and the song was 'Between You and Me'. And I said this is it Dave, this is great; I'll play this straight away next week. Good, he said, fine. And he didn't know that much about Graham Parker as it happened.

I played it the following Sunday and on Monday morning a guy called Nigel Grainge from Phonogram rang up and said, what was that? The guy sounded a bit like Van Morrison. I said, Dave Robinson is the man to talk to. So Dave instantly became the manager of this artist, signed him to Phonogram, and that rolled off into its own little story. Which among other things, Dave got so frustrated with Phonogram's pathetic attempts as far as he was concerned to market this guy, expecting him to gig up and down the colleges of Britain and somehow create his own audience that way; which was the way that rock was marketed by anybody in those days, and Dave felt they should be far more proactive, get the song onto the radio, into a proper hit so it could be a hit in America. And really it was the frustration of Phonogram's lack of energy in marketing Graham Parker that finally triggered Dave Robinson into deciding I'm going to start my own label here, and going off and setting up Stiff. And it was always his intention and hope that he would have got Graham Parker onto Stiff but Phonogram held onto Graham for too long for that to happen.

So then 1977, a woman writes a letter to me saying I'm going to start a shop in Kentish Town High Street called Honky Tonk Records, is that OK? So I rang her up and said, it's not my name; it's a name I've taken off a record. She said I know, but it's going to be a bit funny if I just start a shop up; people are going to assume there's a connection. I said go ahead, it's fine. After a while a guy introduced himself, he's working in the shop and he would call up on Monday and say, that song you played at half-past eleven, somebody's been in; can you fax a playlist. I didn't have a fax machine. So he regularly called me and one day he said, we're going to make a demo; I'm in a band and we're going to make a demo at Pathway Studios, can we bring you a tape? I said sure. I didn't think about it again, then one day there's a knock on the door upstairs here, and this big guy said I'm John, that's Mark, this is our tape. I said thank you; it was five-inch, perfect. And I said – it's Thursday, and I've just finished my play-list for that Sunday's show – I can't play it this week but I'll listen. Which was mainly a defensive measure; the proportion of demos you get that are of any interest is very small. So I put it on out of interest and the second song I thought, I've got to play this; I mean, it wasn't that the earth shook and trembled and I realised how good it was, but I definitely thought it was too good not to play. So I took something off the list and played it in between Bonnie Raitt and Squeeze, as it happens. And that was 'Sultans of Swing'.

While it was playing on the radio three A&R people called. I didn't know any A&R people ever listened to my show, really didn't.

And four more during the week: Chris Briggs, Nigel Grainge, and somebody from Virgin Music. I obviously told the group about it, and they were so dismayed – you told us you weren't going to play it so we didn't even listen; we were helping somebody move house. I said, don't worry, I'm going to play it again this Sunday. And I did; I played it and that was at the end of July; so all through August each week I played a different song from the tape until I'd basically played them all, and then I was going to start again. Despite every company being potentially interested in them and talking to them, only Phonogram, whose A&R man, Johnny Staines had just joined the company, and it is more or less true that when a record company brings in a new A&R man they kind of give him a lot of leeway on his first decision. It's a bit like a football manager, you're brought in and you've got to make it work or not. So he was so adamant and insistent that they decided to sign Dire Straits; and poor old Johnny never signed anybody else of any worth, and he didn't last very long there.

NIGEL GRAINGE,
Phonogram Records

Round about 1975 and I have had success with Thin Lizzy, 10cc, Steve Miller and I was a big fan of Charlie Gillett's radio show on Radio London on Sunday afternoon. He introduced a song as being by Graham Parker, so I called him on air and he said the guy who brought in the tape was a guy called Dave Robinson. He brought a tape in of this guy, Graham Parker, who happened to be a petrol pump attendant in Camberley. The demo tape was great but the one problem was that Dave had been squatting and obviously had not had a bath in I would say probably three months. The stench was horrible, but I fumigated the office and went to the Hope & Anchor to see the group that Dave had put together to back Graham and of course it was The Rumour and they were mind blowing and I signed Graham to a long term deal to Phonogram. Of course the first album was great and Nick Lowe produced that, the second album Mutt Langer produced. That was actually an interesting connection because Mutt had not had any success up to that time and there was a lot of resistance to an unknown producer. Graham was then supposed to be my first act on Ensign, but Dave Robinson and Jake Riviera who were working together felt that they did not want to be working with a third party label and would be better off staying with the main company. Big Mistake – Graham's career went down the toilet, he really should have come with me as I knew exactly what I was doing.

I am running Ensign and having a lot of success with the Boomtown Rats and in rapid succession I get a call from a guy from Ireland called Paul McGuiness and I knew him because he had tried before to get me to sign a band called Horslips who I hated. He was telling me about U2 and what he was going to do with them, and remember I had a staff of four people, and I have what is now one of the biggest bands in the country in the Rats. I went to see U2 at the Bridge House in Canning Town, there were four people and a dog had run in off the street and was running about in front of them. I found them bogus, I just did not get it and I passed on them, which to be honest I have never really regretted. Shortly after Charlie Gillett has still got his demo spot and the tune was 'Sultans Of Swing' fantastic demo. I am driving to a relative in South London and the signal was switching but I can just about make out the track he was playing and it sounds amazing. So I stopped the car and with no mobile phones in those days, I find a telephone box, phone the station and Charlie says I am the ninth person to call while the track has been playing. But Charlie says I'm going to get the bloke whose name is Mark to come in and see everybody. A couple of days later I get a phone call, we are coming in to see you Thursday at one o'clock. Thursday one o'clock no Mark, no Dire Straits, two o'clock, two-thirty, two-fifty-five and we are now pissed off. Finally the secretary says they are here and these guys walk in looking like death warmed up. The lead singer reaches out this hand which is like a soft wet kipper. I proceed to do my ebullient A&R man questions, what do you see you career going, how many songs have you got, yadda yadda yadda and every answer is monotone. I am nodding off and they play me the demo tape which has six songs on it and I only like 'Sultans Of Swing' so I finally decide 'thank you very much for coming in' don't call us, and we collapse on the floor in heaps of laughter and one of us, probably me, comes out with the immortal quote: Well if he is successful, I am a Chinaman. About a month later we hear from our friend John Staines at Phonogram, I just signed a band! What band? Dire Straits. You idiot, you have got to be crazy. And that was pretty much the reaction from the entire record business as John was pretty much a new A&R guy and everyone had passed on them. They definitely had the last laugh on that one.

TONY McGROGAN, RCA Artist Relations

First of all I went into Head Office Sales to help the guy there, and then I went into Marketing. There was a guy called Barry Bethell; I didn't even know the guy. Well Barry in those days was called Artists Relations, it's now Artists' Development but it was Artists Relations, limos and flowers and all that nonsense. We had just signed Bowie, and Dave was going to start his tour with Ziggy Stardust and the Spiders From Mars. He was going to start this tour, and Barry Bethell was the liaison guy between David and the record company, and so he went on tour with them as representative of the record company. Bethell always wanted to perform, and he was a good performer actually as it turns out, a good Elvis Presley impersonator. He used to start the show by coming on dressed as a Teddy Boy with all his hair slicked back and everything like that and do the announcement to start off David Bowie, all while still working for RCA. Well what happened was, David Bowie, then MainMan, the management company, Tony Defries, or Deep Freeze as we used to call him, said to Barry: Would you like to come work for MainMan? So with a stars in his eyes job, he said: Yeah.

It suited me lovely, because I'd done a little bit of helping him out and that, and they said: Would you like to do his job? I said: Oh yeah, I'll have a go at that! And that was it. That to me was whoop, I'm gone then. Suddenly I get an American Express card, I get a car. Yes please. But Barry Bethell then got the sack from MainMan. Defries got rid of him; and poor bugger was left out in the cold, but by now I was off and running. I never realised how good it was because then in Artists Relations we had mostly American acts. American acts used to come over to the UK and start off here, then go to Germany and things like that and do promotion. So then, what happened was, the Americans used to say: Can Tony come to France with us, or to Germany? RCA would say: Well, we have people over there doing his job; and the artists would say: I'd rather have him. In the end it was a good idea because it is better when they get comfortable with someone. I'd know that this artist doesn't want to get up at eight o'clock in the morning to do an interview and I'd always say to the record company in Germany: Look, there's no good putting interviews in at that time because he ain't going to get up. I never asked, it was always the artists who used to turn around and say they wanted me. I used to spend about eight months of the year on the road for the record company, which is quite a lot; I used to go on a lot of tours as well, not many record companies would let their personnel go from head office. But I used to go everywhere with them so it was great.

RUPERT PERRY, EMI Records

I suppose it was like, New York in 1982, roughly, 1982 or early 1983; we'd been in New York and the lawyers, Martin Haxby, Mark Levinson, they'd all been working away in the Eastman office, getting the David Bowie deal signed; and I remember walking over to the office, OK you can come over, you can sign the deal. I signed whatever I had to sign and then it was like, OK, you can now go to the studio and of course by this time we'd also passed over a cheque for – I can't remember what amount but a few million dollars probably as the advance. So we went down to the studio, and we had a mix of us at the time – there were those of us from the United States and people from Europe and the UK – and we walked into the studio and there was David, looking wonderful, beautifully dressed, immaculate. Good to meet you all; really looking forward to working with you all, and you know, my new record company after many, many years with BMG/RCA. And he said, OK, I'll play you the album and when it's done I'll come back in again. And he walked out of the studio, and there were about fifteen of us probably, and that was an album called *Let's Dance*. And we were bopping and we were so excited; we were elated. He'd been out of the market for several years; nobody quite knew what he was going to come back with; and it was like, wow. We can't wait to get this out. And of course I think even today it's still his best-selling album.

DAVID HOWELLS, Marketing Manager, CBS Records UK

When the company changed at the end of the Sixties and Clive Davis became the President, it became a very different company, and they focused much more on moving into the contemporary music scene. A lot of what they saw as side issues, i.e. the jazz/blues background, this amazing history, got pushed to one side and neglected. So there was this amazing man in America called Frank Driggs, and Frank for years had been in charge of the reissue programmes, reissuing and repackaging a lot of the stuff that Hammond had done in the Thirties and the Forties. There was an amazing sound engineer called Harvey Fein who was really good at reprocessing old lacquers and shellac and all that kind of material, because a lot of it was old masters before tape obviously. These guys got side-lined, so one of the things that we did was that we set up a line of funding from within CBS Records UK because we were enormously successful; and we employed them out of London without telling anyone; no-one knew about this. Well it was basically because of my knowledge by now of the catalogue and because of talking to everybody in there. I was one of those nerds that use to absorb discographies, and so I talked to the guys and say: Look, whatever happened to the rest of that Charles Christian stuff? Where are the other tracks?

I don't know if anybody knows this part of the story, I don't know if anybody's ever talked about it, but there was a point where an order came down through CBS, get rid of stuff, we need the space. So they started dumping old masters and the old lacquers, and literally putting them out in the alleyway. Well Frank Driggs and the others would go round in a truck and load up these dustbins and take the stuff home and then log it, file it, and save this resource. I mean, it's terrifying to think of what could have happened, but it was literally, this room is full of junk, get rid of the junk. This is a history of the company, get rid of the junk.

TONY WADSWORTH,
EMI Catalogue

Well, it was that whole thing of delving into this history that previously was unknown and hidden to you and finding that actually there were these living, breathing artists who were still going around the country doing their tours and things like this you know, I mean great sorts of stuff like getting a letter from Frank Sinatra thanking me for sending him a copy of the boxed set that I did and you know saying the sound quality was great and love, thank you for thinking of me. Frank. Thank you very much. That goes in a frame. And then let me see, and realising that maybe not all is all sweetness and light. I'm having this great time putting out all of these albums and isn't it all great? I'm over in Los Angeles at Capitol Records one particular day and I'd done Nellie Lutcher the Fifties R&B chanteuse who was going through a little bit of a trendy revival on the UK reissues that I'd done. I was at Capitol and they said, give her a call, she lives in Los Angeles, just call her. Tell her what you're doing. I thought: Oh, that's great, I'll call Nellie Lutcher and I phone her. Hello, I'm putting out your albums. What I wanna know is when do I get my money? And then: Ah, OK. Right. But, you know, it's great. That was that sort of frisson and I mean priceless moments. I was doing some Joe Loss reissues and he calls up and says, this legendary band leader, and says: Oh, I'll come over and give you a hand. In my office comes Joe, takes his jacket off, rolls his sleeves up, he's his braces on and sits down and we start compiling albums together. Compiling albums with Joe Loss who you know if you've grown up in the Fifties and Sixties is an absolute household name. It was tremendous and really funny things happen. I come back from lunch one day and Pippa in the office said: Oh, this guy came in to see you. I said: Did he have an appointment? Have I missed somebody? No. He said his name was Ronnie Ronalde. Really? I said: What did he say? He started whistling to us to prove who he was and this guy had just come in on the off-chance to see the back catalogue bloke asking why I didn't put enough whistling records out.

I could talk about it forever because it was such a rich time. I also put a lot of time into Blue Note as well, because nothing was released in the UK domestically on the best jazz label in the world possibly, owned by EMI, to the point where, Charly Records came in for a meeting to talk about licensing the label from us and the business affairs person at the time who will remain nameless thought: Oh, this is a back catalogue thing, better get Tony in, get him in you know and get me into the meeting and as the conversation's going on it became clear that this business affairs person thought that we were licensing this Blue Note label in from Charly Records. I put a whole load of Blue Note releases into the catalogue and actually met an eighteen-year-old kid from Switzerland called Gilles Peterson who'd got in touch with me and he said: I'm the man to compile the jazz records because I know what's being played in clubs this summer. I'm a DJ. And we got together and so that really sort of breathed life into that movement as well and we put out albums called *Blue Bossa* and *Blue...* God knows what, and it was infinite what we could do.

CHRIS BARBER,
Musician

Alexis Korner got his own band going in the end with the blues, he did have a number of strangely disparate individuals who you would wonder how they could be in the same band you know, Alexis loved the music, he really felt it, he could move a performance in his style, in a way that worked. He would play something and they would get the idea, of course you could not really hear his guitar much to be fair which was a shame. We encouraged him with his guitar and many years later he came along again with his guitar and amplifier and played with us for some months around 1963-1964 after we had had Muddy Waters tour with us when there was more of a chance that people would come and see us a bit more or book a band that did that. Alexis said that he really wanted to have his own band and play blues all the time, it sounded a reasonable thing.

We were by that time playing in the Marquee Club which, without rubbing it in, I happened to be co-owner of. Alexis said, I must get my own band with Cyril Davies on harmonica and the other guys were really good too. He did not get a complete band right away because the first few weeks he played and the first album he did, he had to borrow my drummer because he had not found a total blues man yet. He was a very thorough and sincere man about the blues, very good indeed. He could create an atmosphere without being a virtuoso and that is quite unusual. In most popular music the people who get things going are virtuosos, they may be the only one there, they may not want competition very much but they play things so accurately and so well. Anyone else plays them less well, they get shown up immediately you see so of course they either tend to leave or get better. He did ever so well in the end without being a consummate technician.

When Alexis Korner finally decided to have his own band and it so happened that I was the co-owner of the Marquee Club and playing Wednesday nights, so I said, look, do you want to have your own night at the Marquee? I believe we can give you Thursday night. So he said, obviously yes. He had not got a band yet just knew some guys who would play with him. He got his main thing which was Cyril Davies who would play the harmonica. He started this band up, one thing was he had been doing the last half hour of all of our concerts in my band at that time, so the band was playing everything from early New Orleans to sort of rhythm & blues more or less. So he started doing that with his own band and he discovered that he had to sing all the songs, he was the singer you see and that can be hard going you see, two sets, so he had to get a supporting act. There weren't many bands then, let alone supporting acts, but a young chap came along, he was a great devotee of Brownie McGee that marvellous guitar player and this young chap played his guitar and did his Brownie McGee songs on his own. It gave everyone a break you see and that of course was Jimmy Page.

BOB HARRIS,
TV & Radio Presenter

I met Alexis Korner in the early Seventies for the first time, we may have crossed paths a couple of times before that but it was really when I was arriving on the BBC, starting my radio programmes and then starting as the presenter of The *Old Grey Whistle Test.* I discovered that Alexis was fantastically supportive, we both shared the same management office, he was managed by Philip Roberge and eventually so was I. So I came across Alexis quite a lot, arriving as I was. Becoming famous, getting more and more involved in the epicentre of rock'n'roll and finding this was the whirlwind of my life happening around me. One of the absolute stability points was Alexis, he sort of took me under his wing, he was very much a mentor figure, he offered me fantastic advice. He had such a warm heart in that respect, that is one of the things that I so much remember. He was a fantastic example in terms of broadcasting skill because he had his radio programme, it was very eclectic, it was playing for its time right across rhythm & blues, blues, a little bit of rock, world music which I don't think anybody else was playing on the radio at that point. Sunday evening on Radio One is my memory of it and that rich voice of Alexis's. He used to come with me sometimes if I had a voice-over gig, the chances are that Alexis would come with me because he was the voice-over king in those days. I remember him saying to me when he was doing his voice-overs and stuff that the money he was earning was funding the rest of his life. So that he did not have to worry about making huge amounts of money as a travelling musician because that side of things was taken over by the voice-overs. That would release him to be him, do what he wanted to do, because he was the voice-over king. He had the richest voice, that chocolate voice that he had, honey and chocolate. In all these ways Alexis was a massive influence over me and a very positive force for good in my life.

GINGER BAKER, Musician

Yeah, Alexis was probably the first band that married blues and jazz players. What came out was something pretty extraordinary. Used to pack. I think it was a marked gig. It was like sardines, with solid people. It was really quite an experience. He wasn't a great wonder musician really, but his insight in what he got together, pulled something. I mean the beginning of everything was Alexis. I wouldn't say he was the most brilliant guitar player in the world, but his concept was quite extraordinary. He was absolutely charming. For instance, coming back from a gig, we were totally out of our boxes in this Bedford van with Alexis driving. Alexis had a bottle of champagne between his legs. We got pulled over by the police, and Alexis handed the bottle to me and I put it down on the floor. We were all so pissed, but you'd never believe Alexis was pissed: Oh, hello officer. Just talked his way out of it. After five minutes, we were on our way. Quite extraordinary.

The sound of the band changed when Graham Bond came on board quite enormously. I remember saying to Alexis: Blimey, Alex, he'll steal the band. Which is exactly what he did. We did a gig at the Twisted Wheel in Manchester, just Jack, me, and Graham playing organ and sax. It went down incredibly well. We were driving back in the Bedford, and Graham's going: That's it. We've won the pools. We've won the pools, man. This is it. We're made. We've got to leave Alexis and do this, he said. I tried to calm him down saying: Listen, Graham. We've just done one gig. We're doing great with Alexis, so why change it? The next day, we had a rehearsal at the Flamingo. I turned up a bit late, and Graham caught me as I walked in and said: That's it, I've left the band for us. He left Alexis for me and Jack as well. Extraordinary. In the Graham Bond, the second record, you'll notice that every song is written by John Group. I discovered, years ago, I just made an inquiry: What ever happened to the John Group payments? It turned out that Jack Bruce declared himself John Group and he got all the payments. Absolutely true.

JACK BRUCE,
Musician

When I was a child I was a fantastic singer, boy soprano, won all sort of medals and festivals so I started off as a singer and I wanted to learn how to sing with this new voice that I was trying to find because I could not find my range, so I managed to convince Graham that I could sing a couple of songs. He never said that was great or anything like that.

The Graham Bond Organisation was important to British music, nowadays people tend to forget about that, the band was important. The band was what was happening and there had never been anything like that before or since. The power of that band was something completely new and I think that influenced a lot of younger bands.

We knew what we were doing writing songs in our pomp, although we did not know that we knew what we were doing. I don't think anybody really is aware at the time, if you had told me that those songs would still be quite popular or that people would still listen to them and that there would be new versions of them now, I would have been very surprised, very pleased. The one thing that I felt at the time was timeless and that would last was the riff of 'Sunshine' when I came up with that I just felt that I had touched something or that something had touched me that was profound in a very, very simple but human way that I could not put into words. That was the only time that I ever felt anything like that.

NORMAN BEAKER,
Musician

I moved on to play with Jack Bruce from the Seventies right up until a couple of years before he sadly died. I would say he was my biggest influence out of everybody musically. He thought Alexis was the same for him, he inspired him so much he had great devotion. I worked with Graham Bond several times. Graham was into Holy Magick and all sorts of weird things, I was quite young, I was probably about eighteen the first time I met him and that was quite an eye-opener for me you know. He was walking round with a wand and cape and stuff, it was pre-Harry Potter, it was quite strange stuff. I knew Graham as a saxophonist initially with his quartet and we got to know him as a keyboard player with The Organisation when he had John McLaughlin on guitar and Dick Heckstall-Smith, Ginger Baker and Jack. I remember seeing them for the first time on a big stage doing one of the support spots with Chuck Berry in Manchester and I remember them saying, oh we are going to let the bass player sing a song now, and it was Jack which was fantastic. We just did not expect it but Graham was another one who was very influential. They were very close which cannot be said for the whole of the band, very, very close.

RICHARD JONES,
Musician

Eventually I was out of a job again. I went to South Harrow Memorial Hall to see Alexis Korner rhythm & blues band. There was Jack Bruce on double bass and Ginger Baker on drums, I think was there. Alexis Korner was just starting off this new thing called rhythm & blues. I don't know how it happened, but this chap just approached me. I don't know who on earth it was. It was Cyril Davies. He said he was with them, Alexis Korner, but he wanted to form his own band, and it was going to be the first band in the country with electric bass guitar rhythm & blues. Was I interested? I said: Yeah. Somebody must have pointed me out to him, because I didn't know who he was. Strangely enough, he lived in South Harrow as well, the same as Sutch. I joined up with Cyril, and immediately got Carlo in, and Nicky Hopkins and Bernard Watson. That was that first Cyril Davis Rhythm & Blues Band. He bought an old Dormobile van we used to go around in. He was trying to do rhythm & blues as authentically as he could. He said he'd been listening to Lead Belly, and all that sort of thing. It was at the first rehearsal we had, he said, I've studied Lead for twelve years. We didn't know what he was talking about. Studied Lead? Yeah, we had this old van, and we used to go all over. He had good contacts with a big jazz agency, and they got us a lot of work. It was promoted very well.

We had got a residency at the Marquee Jazz Club on Wednesday nights, I think. Cyril had heard about these Stones, he called them the Bones. He'd heard about them. They were just forming. They were struggling to form a band. They were very keen on rhythm & blues, but they hadn't got a complete band, they hadn't got a bass player. He booked them. He said: Alright, for our interval spot at our residency, we'll give them the interval spot, £10 between them. They turned up, and hadn't got a bass player. That's rather ambitious of them. Anyone, somebody said to me: They haven't got a bass player, you'd better help them out. That's how I got involved with them. I think, as far as I can remember, there was two or three other gigs they had, and they still hadn't settled with their own bass player, so they asked me to help them out and go along with that. It wasn't too difficult for me, because they were playing all the stuff which I already knew: Chuck Berry, and that sort of thing. Quite simple twelve-bar stuff. I enjoyed playing them. Brian Jones, he was the most friendly one to me, I think.

Cyril – double scotch in one hand and a small cigar in the other. And another image of him, we were driving up the motorway in this Dormobile, which he'd got from his day job, he was a car repairer, back street garage in Ealing. He got one of these Dormobiles. We were going up the motorway, and it overheated, so he had to stop. He was so angry with this van overheating, the van which he'd got, and probably repaired and thought it was OK, he just stood beside of this van, he was cursing and swearing, and he gave it a massive punch with his fist. I was horrified to see the power behind his first. I thought: If there's any trouble, we're safe with him. God, dear me. Did he hit it! With Cyril, we went all over the place, he was getting quite good money for his gigs. He was very, very popular. Very popular. We got some really decent gigs with Cyril. I don't know how I left. I don't know if I was sacked or if I just left.

NORMAN JOPLING,
Journalist

I had got a job as an office boy with *Record & Show Mirror* and had a few articles I had written published but they would not let me go out and interview anyone until I was eighteen. Then the first person they sent me out to see was Little Richard which was a real eye-opener. Well I went up to this little hotel room and there were just two single beds and Richard is sitting on one and Billy Preston was asleep in the other one. So I sat next to Richard and we are talking and obviously I realised straight away and I'm thinking, Little Richard you are a hero, and then he starts stroking my cheek and he says, you've got such soft cheeks. Of course, he said, nobody's cheeks are as soft as Elvis's.

I used to go to the Marquee and see Alexis Korner and these people but when you were listening to the American records they don't really sound OK. When you are young I was comparing Alexis Korner and Cyril Davies and Long John Baldry with Bo Diddley and it just was not the same, good though they were. The senior journalist on Record Mirror was Peter Jones and he used to go round to De Hems, an oyster bar in Macclesfield Street and kind of hold court there, and all the publicists would go there because Peter was an easy touch and one of his mates was Giorgio Gomelsky who kept pestering him to see this group. Peter went to the Station Hotel in Richmond to see this group and came back and said, you are the rhythm & blues expert, I think you should do this, I cannot really do it. And I said they are British, they cannot possibly be any good. Peter who was obviously being pestered by Giorgio was pestering me. It must have been a matter of a couple of weeks I suppose and I gave in.

I took my girlfriend there and a photographer and I remember we got there and you could hear this from outside and there was a crowd outside that could not get in and we pushed our way in, got in, stood there and I had never heard anything like it. I had been to a lot of gigs but that small club thing and the Rolling Stones when they started was a real epiphany and I remember thinking, white people can do this, they can make this sound, get this feel, make this sound. Anyway the gig finished and I had met Giorgio who introduced me to Brian Jones and Brian said, what can you do for us? and I said anything you want really because I was completely knocked out. We went with them to a party at some producer's flat and they were picking up instruments and playing, messing about, and I got to know them a little bit and Ian who was driving for them as well as playing with them, drove us back to north London. Then I had to write the article but the problem was they did not have a record deal and *New Record Mirror* was a record paper so I cleared it and wrote a fairly careful half-page article. Anyway Peter was round at De Hems and Andrew Loog Oldham was pestering him and Peter said, oh look Norman is writing this rave article on this group called the Rollin' Stones. They were the Rollin' Stones then with an apostrophe, I think you should check these out Andrew because apparently they had mentioned something about management to Peter. So of course Andrew went down there and grabbed them. My article appeared not the following week, but the week after and the day that it appeared three out of the four major record labels phoned me up and said where can we get hold of them?

JOHN SCHROEDER,
Oriole Records

The Motown story is part of Oriole Records, of course, because when I joined there, my brief was to establish the record label. I checked out the studios, very good little studio in Bond Street. Great engineer in Geoff Frost. They were raring to go. I looked at the artists they had on their books, and got rid of practically everybody, but retained Clinton Ford and retained Maureen Evans, both of who had hit records. Then I said to Morris Levy: If we're going to be a really amazing label, or we're going to compete with an amazing label, we need American product. We've got to have American product. We need a pop-oriented product. We need something that's really competitive. Oh, he said, I don't know. I said: Well, will you allow me to look for American product? See if I can find any avenues with American sources. He said: Yes, go ahead. I was an ardent reader of *Cashbox*. I mean, I loved whatever America was doing. When I was at EMI, even, I started looking at it and listening to American stuff. *Cashbox* became one of my bibles. I saw this company called Motown. About six or seven chart entries. All the time they appeared. I said to myself: They've got no distribution in this country. I don't hear any product coming out of this label. I went into it deeper and deeper, and I said to Morris Levy: Look, there is a label called Motown that's having huge success in America. They've got no representation here, no distribution and things. Why don't we go after it? He said: Who do we contact? I said: The president of the company is guy called Berry Gordy, who's a songwriter. He might like what we do, because I'm a songwriter too. He might like what we're trying to do here. At least make contact. Will you make contact with him? He said: Yes I will, and he did.

He contacted Berry Gordy and he came over to England. I wined and dined him. Whilst I wined and dined him, of which there is a photograph that I've been lynched for nearly, of me actually at the Talk of the Town with Berry Gordy, and the meal we had, and pictures taken of Berry Gordy, my wife at the time, Barney Ales and Esther Edwards. From that moment, I introduced him and told him the Oriole story. Morris Levy supported it, the whole company were with me, but it was a fantastic feeling, because it was my baby. I told him: Berry, we need American product. To do what we needed to do, we need to be important enough and we need to have American product. I said: You are doing incredible things over there. Would you let us have a chance with it over here? He said: Yeah. I like the way you talk, I like your enthusiasm, I like this music. I know you're small, I know you've got a small distribution and all of the rest of this, but at this stage of our career, in England – as far as he was concerned – we know that you are completely, totally committed to our product as a person. He said: I want to support that. That's what happened. We had Tamla Motown, for two years, and we lost the label after two years. I did all the work, and my team at Oriole, pushing and pushing that label, and no one wanted to know. No one would play it.

None of the BBC producers would play it. Alan Freeman, 'Fluff', said: John, I'd love to play this stuff. I believe in it. It's going to happen. But my producer will not allow me to. It stands out like a sore thumb. I can't play it. The only person in those two years that gave it substantial support was Peter Jones of the *Record Mirror*. He did a full page every week, full-page spread on Motown and what Oriole was doing. He was a gem. He was the only person. For two years, I got no support for anything of that product or that label. No support from Motown with their artists coming over, nothing. Just the product going out. Then, at the end of two years, the contract is up for renewal, and of course EMI come along, whoosh, gone. What do EMI do? Put out

Mary Wells, 'My Guy', the song's a hit. I've done all the groundwork, all the BBC, everyone knows about it. For the last two years I've been shouting: Motown. They come along and said: Thanks, John. Thanks, Oriole. Thanks, guys. You've done a great promotion job for us. They had nothing to do but put the records out and make bloody money.

£££

DAVID ARDEN,
Manager

Andrew Oldham, I vaguely remember as a kid. I remember seeing him once but I always remember my dad talking about him, 'cause he really liked this kid. And what I remember was Andrew's always been very stylish you know with his fashion and, poor bugger it seemed he has to wear his dad's overcoat, big old Crombie overcoat 'cause Andy used to buy old-fashioned clothes out of the, I suppose out of the charity shops before it became the done thing. So the old man always used to, he was in dire need but he loved his, and this is again a true story, he used to promote, do the publicity for the Little Richard, Sam Cooke, Jet Harris tour, and I think he was at Doncaster when it opened up, and in at the second house, well it was almost a riot in the first house 'cause he wasn't singing rock'n'roll, and then in the second house he started off singing his Baptist music and then burst into rock'n'roll. I mean the police arrive... I wasn't there, but the police erupted. Andrew put the story out on all the local papers: And there's gonna be a riot, they're gonna rip the seats up, they're gonna this that and the other, and the head of Granada, I can't remember the name, they were brothers that owned Granada, Jewish brothers. And he said to the old man: You know we can't have this. What is this? What is this man doing? He said: Oh no I'm sorry about, you know, don't worry there won't be riots. He said: I don't want this kind of publicity surrounding any of my theatres, you better change your publicity agent or the show's not going on, and he literally had to give Andrew the sack and he was desperately unhappy about having to do it but he did, he had to otherwise.

BILL LEADER, Record Producer

Our only recordings were mono, so how many mics do you need for mono? One in the right place. If it was stereo, two in the right place. It's acoustic music; it's got a balance of its own; all it needed was to find where the microphone that's going to hear that balance, and that's it. Once you start using amplifiers and stuff like that, and things that have got very unequal levels, then you need to be able to control – you need a mixer; but you can record 99% of the world's music on two mics if you want it in stereo, or one mic if you're happy with mono. I recorded Bert Jansch and John Renbourn because they could be put in my little room in Camden Square and do their guitar duets and it cost peanuts to produce. Something that's still selling on whatever label it is on now.

JEFF JARRETT, Abbey Road

It was a very old-fashioned process where it was divided into sections. For example, I got sent home one day for not wearing a tie. You had to dress in a certain way. The technical guys, what they called the technical engineers, used to put all the microphones out. As a tape op, you were literally doing that, just operating the tape machines, getting the tea if you needed to get the tea, and keep everybody happy. A bit like what they call a runner these days, isn't it? Then there was the balance engineer, who had, obviously, the job of sorting all the sounds out. But if something needed changing, like a microphone, or something needed to be changed on the patch bay they used, they have to call the technical man to come and do that. Which actually for me was very good, because one of the things they never asked me in my interview was what did I know about the technical side of things. Had they asked me that, I'd have to be honest, I knew nothing. All I knew is that I absolutely loved music and had a passion for music, always have, from when I was a little kid. The idea of getting to somewhere where recording was being done was my ideal position to be in.

After a couple of years, things changed, and the tape operators would set the sessions up rather than the technical guys. The balance engineer would do a much more hands-on job. The balance engineer always would say where the microphones would have to be, obviously. If he felt that it should be changed, originally, then the technical guy would come down and move that. But as I say, after a couple of years, it became much more relaxed, and the balance engineer would go and move his own mic, or the tape op would go and move the mic. I started on £8 a week, which was not very much, even in 1966. That was unimportant to me, because I was actually doing something I really wanted to do. Once I started doing sessions as a tape op, and then as an engineer, it worked out something like, once you got to five-thirty, after five-thirty you got extra half pay, or something. By the time it got to after nine o'clock, I think you were on double pay, something like that. Working the inordinate amount of hours we used to do in a week, by the time you then added on your half time, your double time, you were getting paid for a hundred odd hours a week or something. Even if your basic wage was quite low, you ended up with quite a nice pay packet.

JOHN LECKIE,
Studio Engineer

We didn't wear white coats at Abbey Road; that was just a bit before my time. But I probably got the job because I was the long-haired hippie. I had long hair and bell-bottom jeans, got my clothes at Kensington Market kind of thing. I realised that everyone else was in suits and ties; really it was suit and tie smart dress really, even the young guys my age kind of thing. And I had long hair – there was Nick Webb and one or two other people had long hair but everyone else was very clean cut at Abbey Road. I always remember if you worked on a Saturday at Abbey Road you'd see all these guys walking around with their polo neck jumper, or their cravat; they wouldn't be wearing a tie. On a Saturday they'd be a bit more casual; have a sports jacket on, or a little roll neck or something. It was funny times.

I suppose I was lucky at Abbey Road because it was, you could say, the birth of multi-track recording. At the time the studios were 8-track; most of the sessions were 8-track. A lot of the sessions were 4-track still. And we had these big 3M 8-track machines, one in each studio, and you had to squeeze everything onto 8-tracks. We were always running out of tracks even when we went 16 and then 24-track. Between the period I suppose 1970 to 1975, it did go from 4-track to 8-track to 16-track to 24-track, which really expanded the creativity. Whether it made it any better I don't know. I think it did. I think 16 and one 24-track was a good way of working. Another interesting thing about the old days is we never had small speakers. You go into studios these days, or the last twenty years and one's got the S10, the little speakers with the white cones, what they call near field monitors – small speakers – all studios use them now and that's what you use. But in those days we only had the big speakers and we used to monitor quite loud, to drive the room as you used to say, crank it up. But you spent hours pretty close to deafening music in the control room. It was loud. And until the Eighties you never had small speakers or even think of playing it on a small speaker. Which is very odd actually because all those classic albums, all the great albums done in the Sixties and Seventies were all monitored on big speakers.

LG WOOD,
Chairman, EMI Records

I think George Martin thought his salary was too low. Although if you leave aside for the moment what EMI was getting out of the record business, leave that aside for the moment, what we paid our artists' managers, including George Martin, were reasonable figures at the time. And he wanted to get some sort of producer's royalty, which was entirely new to our concept. I remember discussing it with Lockwood as the Chairman as it was entirely new, and he felt it would be utterly wrong to give him the royalty; but we did improve their pension arrangements, all of them, but George of course was the youngest of the four and the improved pension arrangements in 1965 didn't appeal to him over much.

So he decided that the time had come when he would leave the company and set up in business on his own at the time when we still hadn't signed the second agreement, and at the time when it was quite obvious that he was the one man that we would have to retain for future Beatle recordings. So what I finally negotiated with him was that he would go off and set up his new company called AIR Limited I think, but it was AIR, that at our request we would continue to handle on an A&R basis certain artists that he had previously handled, and that he would make himself available to us, if both The Beatles and we wished him to make or continue to make recordings with The Beatles. In return for that I had to agree to pay him a producer's royalty on all records in future which he had any hand in. I think a producer royalty started in America. It was an entirely new concept for us here in the United Kingdom but I don't think it was all that novel in the States.

CHRIS THOMAS, Producer

In the mid-Sixties, basically what would happen for instance, I mean like my mentors, the people who gave me my first opportunity were AIR London Productions before the studio was built. So that was George Martin and Ron Richardson who did The Hollies. I mean Ron was very kind, he invited me down to all The Hollies sessions. John Burgess was there. Peter Sullivan who did Tom Jones and Engelbert, I went down to all the sessions and saw how they worked and basically the A&R man would find a song, so the music publishers would come around, he'd find a song for the artist, he'd then find an arranger to do the music, book the studio where the studios were just sort of set up and everything was done. It was like a sort of factory in a way because with musicians, when you've got session musicians there, they are very expensive. So you'd do three, you'd do three tracks in a session, in a three-hour session, you know. So everything just sort of went through bang bang bang. You'd never find a producer touching the board, and it was really watching The Beatles; actually Paul was a huge influence on me in that way; because The Beatles were, it would become hands-on. The engineers hated it obviously because it was like going over the, you know, going over the line.

I started off going to the Beatle sessions right at the beginning of the *White* album and the whole idea was the same as going down to Ron Richard's sessions with The Hollies; just to sort of sit in the back and just watch what went on. The *White* album started to go really, really slowly to the point they were only doing like one song a week or something, it was really beginning to drag and I started to get a bit bored quite frankly going down there because it was just really going so slowly. I came back from holiday, I think at the beginning of September something like that and George Martin went off on holiday and left me a note on my desk. It said, Chris, hope you had a nice holiday, I'm off on mine. Make yourself available to The Beatles. Neil and Mal know you're coming down. So I thought: Oh, I'll just sit at the back as usual with my tie on and the suit you know, and watching.

111

First one through the door was Paul, and he looks at me and said: What are you doing here? And I thought: Cor, this is a bit weird. Because obviously George must have said something to him about the fact that, like it's OK if Chris sort of still comes down. I said: Well didn't George say anything? Paul just said: Well if you want to produce us you can produce us and if you're no good we'll just tell you to fuck off. I walked down into the studio, down into number two. And I just sort of went like: Produce? What are you talking about? And I just became absolutely catatonic. It was like: What is going on? I just didn't know, I sat next to Ken Scott and they just asked Ken: What do you think of that Ken, how's that Ken, like I wasn't there. This was really getting excruciating. I just wanted the ground to sort of open up. Anyway, after about four, five hours something like that they had their usual sort of break about seven o'clock where they'd normally roll up a spliff and they'd been talking about the prospects of Apple because of course they were managing themselves then. So I was wandering around downstairs and I could hear them and they were sort of chatting and I heard John say something like: Well he's not really doing his bit, is he? For all I know he was talking about one of their mates that came down from Liverpool and was working in the office. I took it personally straight away.

When we started recording again they made a mistake, on one of these takes. And I interrupted them, because suddenly I thought: Shit, I don't want to lose my job with George Martin. Suddenly I didn't care who they were. The only thing that was important to me like, the fact that I was on trial with George and like, I wasn't going to lose this for anything. The only way you could interrupt them in those days from what I remember was there was a button, they had a claxon in the studio. They were going: What's that! Because nobody used to sort of interrupt them and say do it again. That's what I did, you know. They went: No it wasn't. They all came up the stairs one by one to listen to the tape and I thought: Oh, what happens if I've just sort of hallucinated this? It was just so horrible, anyway we played it, you could hear the mistake, they went: Alright, and they all went downstairs and they started doing it again. About half an hour later you know there was another mistake, I interrupted them again and they just didn't come up and check it this time, they just went: OK, we'll try it again. And that's about the long and short of what happened that first night. Except that when Paul left who was the last one to go I turned round, I said: What happens about tomorrow? He said: Oh, if you want to come down that's fine. I went: You didn't say fuck off! Fantastic. So that's how it started and I just carried on, I just ended up working on it, I played on various things and after a few weeks George Martin came back and we'd done I think seven new songs compared to the average of about one a week so he was really, really surprised. And I just stayed on board then right through till the end.

DAVID STARK,
Apple Scruff

I was still at school, July 1968 just coming up to the school holidays, I remember skiving off with a pal, let's just go up to see the premiere of *Yellow Submarine*, see everybody arriving. So we get there in the afternoon, crowds forming and milling around, we were just standing there and not expecting to do much, except I just happened to see a door at the side of the London Pavilion, now the Trocadero, I wonder if that door is open, and it was, and right inside was a lift. So we took the lift up to the top floor and we ended up on the roof of the cinema which a few other people had also done. We all spent about three or four hours up there looking at the crowds forming down below until it is thousands of people. Must have been forty, fifty thousand people there, this is the last big Beatlemania event where they are all turning up, we could see all the cars arriving with the guests. As it was getting to time for the premiere to start, seven, seven-thirty OK let's go back inside. We got into the top-circle and got stopped immediately by an usherette, where is your ticket? Oh we gave them in downstairs. You should not have done that, you should have hung on to them. She called the manager and my pal and I were just shitting ourselves, what was going to happen? The manager comes over, how are you supposed to be here, who invited you? Well actually it was Clive Epstein, Brian's brother. Well actually I had met him in Torquay several years earlier but I had not been in touch with him since. So I said, we had better go and find him in the foyer. I thought, what am I going to do if I do?

So we were traipsing around the cinema, I can see The Who, Status Quo all coming in and we are just walking straight past them. Luckily I cannot see Clive Epstein but then I saw a familiar bald head and glasses, being Dick James who I have never met in my life, so I went up to him and just like that said, excuse me do you know if Clive is here tonight? Oh no he rang me this afternoon, he is held up in Liverpool and will not make it tonight. And the manager says, OK I can see you know people here, you are OK. So thank you Dick forever!!

So we were in, we had no tickets and we were standing at the back of the Grand Circle where all the VIPs were, and suddenly all pandemonium breaks loose and all. The Beatles and wives arrive and literally start walking past us down the centre aisle to their seats right at the front. It is complete chaos, flash bulbs everything. So as it kind of subsided I saw a couple of spare seats right behind John and Paul, second row, centre aisle, come on, let's go down there. Third seat along is Keith Richards with Anita and I said anyone sitting here? No, Mick and Marianne but they are in New York, you are alright here mate. So I sat down, two hours in the cinema behind The Beatles. Every time a new song came on, I'm leaning over to Paul saying, that's a good one. Oh thank you. When the film finished they were completely trapped there, everybody trying to get to them, no-body could move and I am just standing there chatting to George.

JEFF JARRETT,
Abbey Road

I'd done a couple of sessions, and we did the backing track of something, which was the first time that I heard it. It was just a beautiful tune with George. At the end of the session he said: I'm going to do a session tomorrow night with Billy Preston and Eric Clapton. Will you engineer it for me? Yes please. It was one of the most amazing sessions I've ever done. Eric Clapton had been my hero anyway. They had recorded the backing track with, I think it was Eric Clapton, Keith Richards, Billy Preston, and Ginger Baker at Olympic Studios. They brought the tape in, and we were going to overdub Eric Clapton and Billy Preston, and Doris Troy, and Madeline Bell onto this tape they were bringing in. It was one of the most amazing sessions. They were playing off of each other on these solo parts. With Eric, he just makes such a beautiful sound anyway that you just have to make sure that the microphone was in the right place. There was nothing to do in the control room, because he just creates this fantastic sound. Likewise, with Billy Preston on the organ, he just got this magical sound. Microphones there, pull the fader up, and you've got your sound.

Sent the tape down to them, and on the first run through, it was amazing. Just magical. About two or three hours later, we're still doing it. We'd run out of tracks, we had what we call BTR tape machines, they were just stereo tape machines. We were having to synchronise the multi-track with these BTR machines, because we didn't have enough tracks left to do all these various takes. We had these stereo tapes running with lots and lots of different takes on them. It was quite difficult getting everything to synchronise, but musically, it was the most amazing evening in my life. Hearing these two guys just playing, saying: Yeah, we can do that a little bit better all the time. I think we actually ended up with a take early on in the evening, but that didn't matter, because we just had an amazing night of great music with two of the best musicians ever. 'That's the Way God Planned It', which was the title track of an album that Billy Preston did. That was truly amazing.

JOHN BAGNALL,
Tony Brainsby PR

One of the strangest things I recall was when the phone rang and Tony Brainsby answered it, was talking and then put the phone down looking a little bit shell-shocked and said something amazing has just happened, or we are being wound up absolutely royally, but that was Paul McCartney, he wants to go back on the road. This was just after he played the surprise gigs turning up at universities, and he wants PR for it and is coming to the office at two o'clock tomorrow to talk about it. And come two o'clock there was a knock on the door and one of the girls answered it and there was Paul McCartney, an ex-Beatle, the man who had broken up The Beatles and wasn't everybody's favourite person then by any means, standing there with Linda and obviously as nervous and as unsure of his situation as we were. He came and sat down and had a cup of tea and told us about his plans, made arrangements for me to interview him and Denny Laine and the rest of the band he was putting together, so I ended up almost by default writing a Paul McCartney tour programme. The six months or so we worked with McCartney was just magic strange stuff.

Tony had a very strict ethos that today's headlines were tomorrow's chip papers, so we kept the cuttings because those went off to the managers with the invoices, but it was all about we have got that one in the book, what is the next one we are setting up? It was a fantastic ethic to take forward about a year later to EMI which came about because one of the clients we had at Brainsby's was Don Arden and I never asked too many questions about the politics of The Move and the break-up of The Move and the setting up of Wizzard, ELO and all those relationships. Don Arden being Don Arden, you just did not ask too many questions. I met him quite a few times and I can honestly say I never found him anything other than the perfect gentleman. It was fun going to the gigs and the TVs with Wizzard including the TOTP bar, which was staff only until you produced a bottle of Guinness for the man on the door. In fact I bumped into Eric Hall there who was working for EMI and he said that they were

116

probably going to be looking for someone, let him have a word, and the next day he got a phone call and so at the beginning of October 1973 I found myself as Pop press officer for EMI.

LESTER SMITH,
Abbey Road Technician

The technical group of engineers were mostly involved with studios, and making sure that whenever they were working – Saturday/ Sundays, sometimes late at night – there was always an engineer to put anything right if something went wrong. Whether it's a microphone going down and they'd change it, if it was a unit on the desk, they would change it. Just keep the session going. The session's the most important thing. It's the most expensive thing. With an orchestra, you can't have down-time.

After a couple of years, 1972, the management said: A lot of the equipment isn't getting fixed. The service engineers, who were on sessions and changed equipment, they never bothered to repair stuff when it went wrong. There was a huge mountain of broken microphones and outboard gear in the middle of what we called the amp room at that time. The management said: We'll form a new department, technical services. We'll have five people, two of them maintaining the EMI recording desks, one looking after all the tape machines in the building, which numbered over ninety, and one chap looking after all the microphones, which numbered about five hundred. They gave me the choice. They said: Would you like to join this department? I said: Yes. What would you like to look after? I said: The microphones. Tape recorders, I'd got bored with those. Microphones, no one knew anything about them, so I thought: That's interesting and I started from scratch. No notebooks, nothing, just started from scratch.

In 1975, we had the first non-EMI desk come to Abbey Road. Our chief engineer – Mike Bachelor was a very, very clever and thorough engineer. He and other engineers had been to sample the commercial desks. At that time, there wasn't great choice of desks available: Calrec, Neve, SSL, a few others, not many. We liked the Neve, they liked the Neve desk. That came to Abbey Road in number three studio in early 1975. They said: Lester, will you look after that desk? It was totally different to anybody else's experience, and mine as well, because I hadn't been involved with desks. For eleven years, the whole time it was in number three studio, I was the one who went in there every morning, made sure everything worked fine on that desk. Pink Floyd used it, and many artists, obviously. It was a good desk. It's got quite a reputation, even today.

John Lennon was always wanting to stretch the boundaries, luckily, George Martin was so acute to change, and very thoughtful about how to do it. We had a technical team here, like Ken Townsend, he was on the technical team at that time. They would ask him: Can you make this reverb last a bit longer? Or this fade away not deck so abruptly? Can you do this? My boss, Len Page, would take that bit of equipment away – for instance, the Altec compressors – and put a little capacitor in somewhere and the resistor in, and measure it as he went, so he could see what he was doing. That's the thing with these chief engineers, they would measure everything before and after they did anything, and then give it back to The Beatles in the morning and Paul or John would say: That's just what we want, thanks. A lot was done in-house, modifying equipment that was made by EMI, or by other people like Altec, from America.

Bernard Speight was quite a clever engineer, and he would build equipment to new projects. The new project was reverberation and gimmicks. Gimmicks were very much in the Seventies. He would build this piece of equipment, which Pink Floyd used, and we've been looking for it ever since. I was a hoarder of equipment, when the valve equipment went out and transistor came in, I would put away some of the old valve stuff, because it was interesting to me. It was locked away. We were searching through that, because whatever Bernard built was valve-oriented. We never got any further with that. There were several other names for inventions. Azimuth, I think The Beatles used that. Just go off azimuth gives you this lovely effect. You swing in and out. You can do it by hand with your hand on the record head altering it, the azimuth. Bernard built a machine that would do that automatically, and you could vary the amount of in and out of phase. Wouldn't go completely out, but it would go almost out.

JEFF JARRETT, Abbey Road

Floyd was amazing. I had done a few sessions as a tape op, and then the chap, called Francis Dillnut, who used to walk around with a little board in his hand and mark off who was doing what session, came up to me. Mr Jarrett, he said. We have a new band coming in. He said: Can you do these sessions? There was a whole list of sessions. I said: Great, I'd love to. What is it? He said: it's a group called Pink Floyd. I checked out who Pink Floyd might be, and found that they were performing down at the Regent Polytechnic, and went down there one evening to see them play. I was absolutely knocked out. I'd never seen anything like it. By the time they came in the studio, I knew what they were about. It was a fantastic experience. That first album was brilliant. Syd Barrett was a genius in this fresh way of presenting a music style. I got on quite well with him. I don't know, you just had an automatic thing with somebody, and we always got on well. I was only the tape op, but we used to get on great. He fascinated me, because he was invariably walking around on tiptoe. Nearly always. He'd take his shoes off and he'd walk around on tiptoe.

It was just great to be in that environment where you see some new kind of music. People coming and developing and creating. Norman Smith who produced that first album, the engineer was a guy called Peter Bown. They normally were booked in – we're going back a long time – but I think they were normally booked to start about two o'clock or two-thirty. Then they might turn up close to that, but not quite. I don't remember them really turning up on the dot. But there had been bands much worse than them for turning up late. They were pretty well organised. They had very good management with Peter Jenner and Andrew King, who kept them on their toes and kept track of what they were doing. They came to quite a few sessions. Great guys. Very nice guys. Again, it was great to have Norman producing that, because as an ex-engineer, he knew how everything worked. There are some people that you get to work with who have no idea what's going on, which can be a little frustrating. It doesn't happen that often, but when it does… Which was one of the reasons that I later on wanted to transfer to being a producer, because there were various sessions where the producer doesn't have much idea of what's going on, and you don't take over, but you are doing very much what the producer should be doing.

DAVID STOPPS,
Promoter,
Friars Aylesbury

We had done a couple of shows at the Dunstable Queensway Hall which was a much bigger venue, 1,000 capacity. We had done Pink Floyd there which was a total sell out and which actually subsidised Aylesbury for about six or seven months. That one gig, we made so much money, well a lot of money compared with what we had done before. I was not a very good business man, I was much more music driven so I just loved putting the bands on that I liked you know and hoped everyone else did as well. Generally speaking it tended to work and people went along with our rather eclectic taste. February 1970 for example, we put on Black Sabbath, paid them £25 just three days after they released their first album. Genesis, paid them £10 the first time in April 1970, then £15, then £25, then £75, I think I was the first person on earth to pay them £100 and Peter Gabriel came out on stage shook my hand and announced to the audience that I was the first person on earth that had ever paid them £100. We were very involved with Genesis in those early years and Mott The Hoople were the other band, we put them on in December 1969 the first time, I think it was the third gig they had ever done, and the first two gigs had not done that well but suddenly at Aylesbury it caught fire, the crowd absolutely went mad for them and they suddenly realised that they could do it and something was going to happen. They said after that, we knew we were on the way.

What I would always do as a music fan was try and get the band to do encores and as many as possible you know. Whereas other promoters would be pleased to see the back of them and they could just take the money and get home to the TV, I would try and get the gig to go on as long as possible and to get a great audience reaction. I remember Chicken Shack did seven encores, the atmosphere just built and built through these seven encores so everyone was going absolutely mad. I remember talking to Arthur Lee of Love, and said, will you do another one and he looked at me strangely and said why would I want to do that? And I said because they are all out there screaming and shouting. He said you want me to do another one? I said, I do but more importantly, they do. He said, I guess I can then and he went and did it. I had the same thing with Lou Reed and I guess, being American they thought they would not get paid unless they did what I said!

RICHARD EVANS, International Dept., Decca Records

I went on tour with the Moody Blues, very straight-laced Decca, and when I went abroad I had to go upstairs and get my travellers cheques from an accounts office like an old fashioned bank with a grill in and some old scrote who looked like they had been there since the old king died. The second time I went up there I got some Dymo tape and put 'please do not feed the animals' and I stuck it on the front of the cage. I have to tell you it was still there the day I left, stuck on the front. Anyway I went on tour with the Moody Blues, I think it was supposed to be their farewell tour but that did not work out. We started out in Copenhagen, and in Copenhagen then they were having this sexual renaissance, live strip shows and live sex shows and the whole tour was artists from the Moody's label, so there were forty-eight of us on tour. We stayed in this hotel next door to one which had just burnt down killing six people, and Ray Thomas and I found ourselves being accosted by the police the first night as he had bent down to pick up some flowers that he thought were for the Moodys, and they weren't and we were both arm locked by the cops, and that night we all went out on the town, forty-eight of us to live sex shows. You can imagine can't you, and these live sex shows did not sell alcohol so you had one of those human chains round to the bar round the corner passing beers along in the street. We went from one country to another like that, I had no idea what I was doing there, not a clue what my job was, fantastic. I think it was to buy Graham Edge and Ray Thomas drinks, and laugh.

Anyway when I got back after about three or four weeks and I've got expenses in God knows how many currencies, loads and loads of money all screwed up and sweaty and beery and that stayed in a drawer until one day I thought, I've got to do my expenses. So I got the expenses form out and I started going through the receipts and I found a receipt and it said 'The Spunk Bar' or 'The Bar Spunk' and the logo was a great big erect penis and it was for beer for about ten quid which was a fortune because we were all earning about thirty quid weren't we, a fortune. So I put that receipt on one side and I did my expenses with some alacrity and enthusiasm and I gave them to Marcel, my boss, to sign and he gave it back to me and the secretary said shall I take it up to the accounts department? No, I'll do it, don't worry. So I got the Spunk Bar receipt and clipped it to the very front and took it up to the accountant: Just in case you are wondering what I have been doing with the company's money, all your suspicions have been proved true.

I did International for Decca and I was finding myself travelling the world with lunatics who I can match. I went to Hamburg twelve time in one year with Thin Lizzy. One day I had been away with them, I don't know where we had been but we had been away for a number of days, and I got back off the plane in the morning with them and I said: God I am knackered, I could do with going home and going to bed but I have to go into the office. So I got to the office and I had been there about fifteen minutes when the alarm bell went off and the Tannoy said: Everybody Clear The Building, Clear The Building and Go Home – Bomb Scare. So I got home, I had been there about ten minutes and the phone rang and Phil Lynott's Irish voice says: Are you'se enjoying your day off?

JON HISEMAN, Musician

I had been with Graham Bond for a year, Georgie Fame for six months and then I went to John Mayall and I came to the conclusion that there was nobody to play with, I was stuck. Nobody was running a singing band where the singer would ask me to play for them because my style had become kind of set in a very busy kind of area which was sort of tricky. So I went on holiday with Barbara to Rome, to Italy, she had a cousin there, and I stood on the Palatine Hill overlooking the Forum and I said, I am going to back to England and I am going to form a band and call it Colosseum, there was the Colosseum laid out in front of me. I got back to the UK and I phoned Dick Heckstall-Smith and said I am going to form this mythical band of ours. Now while we were with Graham Bond together, we had often sat in the back of the vehicle travelling, saying wouldn't it be wonderful to have a band where there were no drug addicts, no crazies, no mad men because Graham was driving us crazy. I rang him up and said, you wanna form that band? I phoned the rest of the guys who were subsequently to become members of the band. We held auditions for a guitarist because there was not an obvious one. The band was formed and we did our first gig in Scarborough where they had to winch the organ into the gig because the only way in for the organ was half way up the side of this building.

ROBIN BLACK,
Studio Engineer

Black Sabbath – after Morgan Studios I was on tour and did the sound for Jethro Tull, I bumped into Black Sabbath in Los Angeles, like you do, walking through a hotel foyer and they said: Oh can you come and have a chat with us, you know. So they asked me to do an album which became called *Technical Ecstasy* and we did that in Miami. We stayed in a place called Thunderbird Motel which was full of quite old women looking for very young men. So we were all rather popular and a bit scary, but it was great fun doing the album. Ozzy was fantastic, I really like Ozzy, such a funny man, but there was always a bit of tension, the slightest thing could trigger off the end of the day's recording. I remember Ozzy said something, Bill was sitting at the drums, whatever Ozzy had said had slightly upset Bill and Bill decided to pick his kit up and throw it across the room and just walked out without saying anything to anybody. And as he walked out Ozzy just said, have I upset someone or something? And that was the end of the day's recording.

One of the first times I experienced bands not getting on with each other but with a smile, well the first one was with the Bonzo Dog Doo-Dah Band and they were making one of their crazy records, all quite off the wall, and two of the musicians had upset each other. The other musician who felt he had been hard done by went out. He came back half an hour later with a sandwich and said, no hard feelings, have half of my sandwich. The guy looked at him thinking crikey, you know that is really nice because we were having an argument half a hour ago, and just as he lifted up the sandwich a load of maggots just fell out of the sandwich. He had gone to the fishing shop and refilled a sandwich with maggots. Another strange time was on an Alice Cooper session, again two of the musicians were not really talking to each other. I had just been to get a coffee and one of the guitarists had just bought two beers. I watched him walk into the loo, he still had his guitar round his neck he poured half of one of the pints away and proceeded to top it up with his pee. He walked into the control room and gave the glass to the person he was having the argument with and said, no hard feelings mate, here is a pint. I was a pretty nervous engineer and you just shut up and watched this stuff going on you know. It was just part and parcel of what used to go on in studios in those days.

GINGER BAKER, Musician

The late Fifties and early Sixties was a period where I was really playing jazz and playing with big bands as well. This all started happening in 1962 with Alexis at the Marquee gig on Oxford Street. I couldn't believe there was so many people there. The way the band went down, it was a great experience. I thought: Wow, this is really cool. I was a jazz player. I was listening to Duke Ellington, and Charlie Parker, and Max Roach, and these people. I wasn't really aware of what was happening with the blues guys. I found playing with them was great, because blues and jazz is so close together. You can't really divide them. Eric's a great jazz player – he'd never admit it, but he is – through the blues. That period in London, 1960-1963, was an amazing period. It really was. It was really until 1963 that we started actually earning some money out of it, but then it wasn't much by today's thing. The Graham Bond, we were going out for £40 a gig in the clubs, and £70-£80 a gig in the universities. When I started Cream, I made them ask for £45. The guy said No, no, no. They'll never go for it. I said: Do it. Only one club refused to pay it. That was the Black Prince in Bexley. Cream never played there – their loss.

NORMAN BEAKER,
Musician

The system of music in Manchester at the time for blues was mainly soul clubs in this area. So to play blues we had to get a gig we used to say we were a soul band. In fact we had a blues band called The Soul Set to get the gigs, and then we played a couple of John Mayall tunes and people would think I am not quite sure what this is and it was as Alexis Korner once said, it is a great way to learn because nobody wants to listen. So quite often you would do the gig and there would be eighty people and they would all have gone by the end of the night because they don't know what you are playing. So you got loads of time to practise which does not happen now, you know, if you are just starting off a new band, you have got to have a CD out, you've got to be selling it, but you have got no back up. So when we started to play with other musicians we did it mainly to get our foot on the ladder, 'cause we could not get enough audiences in to see our band. We'd invite people to play with us and we would pay them, like Graham Bond and people like this. So we would get fantastic experience, becoming more or less the house band for musicians, again a bit like Alexis and Chris Barber did with Big Bill Broonzy, Muddy Waters, these sorts of people when they came over, The Yardbirds with Sonny Boy Williams I think. So there was plenty of experience for British musicians playing with Americans because they obviously could not afford to bring their own musicians, it was not feasible.

VICTOR BROX, Musician

When it comes to Jimi Hendrix an awful lot has been said and I am not sure that there are too many people left who played with Hendrix and could give an indication of what it was like. Certainly all the members of his trio are dead but I am the only person who can say I had Jimi Hendrix accompany my vocals on guitar as he refused to sing, whenever he played with us he would say, you are the singer, I play guitar. It was a great compliment. He was a very mild mannered man, with musicians that he admired anyway, and he would sit all night long with half a pint of beer at The Speakeasy, which was his favourite club. When we played at Steve Paul's Scene club in Greenwich Village he came down and brought Janis Joplin with him. When we walked into the club early, there was this big tall guy in a huge long black overcoat talking to himself, walking round the club which was deserted, looking at the photos. It turned out to be Leonard Cohen and also who came in was this guy with no teeth, black guy with no teeth, turned out to be Richie Havens and we had all four of them on stage singing 'Rock Me Baby', so that was quite a night and I don't think you could ever repeat it. Well obviously you couldn't because many of them have passed away. It was one of the greatest thrills of my life playing with Hendrix, Hendrix is a phenomenal bass player. He would quite often play bass and our bass player would take his guitar and play guitar. He played bass like Alex Dmochowski played bass and Alex played guitar like Hendrix played guitar, so once again it was a seamless transposition one from the other. He would stand next to Aynsley playing bass and whisper how the rhythm was going to change and they would both change together because they both had incredible technique and they would go on for hours, it was wonderful. I am on a CD of the last bootlegged Janis Joplin concert and Hendrix is on it and I am down as 'unknown singer' and it is thought to be Jimi Hendrix on guitar. But I have never been able to get this CD, I have only ever heard it. It was a thing in a club we were playing in the South of France, tiny little place and we were packing up our gear and they were playing a tape and someone said, Victor who is that singing and I said it sounds like me. It does not just sound like you, it IS you.

I went off to see who it was and it was Janis Joplin and I never could get the CD, it was a bootleg, but I later saw it reviewed in *DownBeat* or something like that and it said on the track I was an 'unknown singer'. I have never been able to get it unfortunately but somewhere or other there is a track with me singing with Janis Joplin and Jimi Hendrix playing on guitar.

JON HISEMAN, Musician

You have got to remember when The Cream had their success you were in a unique three or four years in time when the media would play anything. The record companies and the media were controlled by people who had come through the Pat Boone and the Bing Crosby years. What was going on was completely new to them, most of them did not understand. The bosses of the record companies had not got a clue what was actually going on. The net result is they were signing artists whose music they did not have a personal affinity for and did not understand. The net result of that was that the media were listening to everything and playing everything and we got the kind of exposure on the radio. Colosseum would go into the BBC studios, play completely original material for half an hour, it would be broadcast on the Tuesday night on the John Peel show, we would go to Sheffield on the Thursday, announce a number that nobody had ever heard before but which had played on that show and get a huge round of applause before we had lifted a finger. This is inconceivable now because there is no exposure. So the point about this is that it was a different time and it was an open time. I was so lucky to be there, so was Graham Bond, so were The Cream, Pete Brown, Yes, Jethro Tull. So lucky to have been at the moment in time where people would actually seek you out if you were at all original. It was a very important moment and we probably had five years of it.

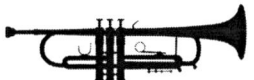

CHRIS BARBER, Musician

Nobody really bothered with that word at all but when Lonnie was in my band if he was going to do a number having done traditional jazz singing, playing the banjo, then he would say what about some skiffle numbers? It did not really catch on, the audiences did not say, what about some skiffle, they would occasionally say, what is that music there? We did our first LP in '54 Lonnie had been doing more songs, I played the bass on it which I did at college as well, it was just him and me really, occasionally Beryl Bryden played a washboard, she was a very kind hearted lady, her singing was pretty fair and she loved the blues. So we recorded 'Rock Island Line' we had a recording by Lead Belly the blues singer who I think had probably written it. Blues singers don't often turn out to have written many songs in a melodic sense, Lead Belly wrote 'Rock Island Line' and he also wrote 'Goodnight Irene' which is as well known a folk song as you can find. I do know that when 'Rock Island Line' came out here a certain element who was involved with getting folk artists, black and white in America looked after and recorded, came over here and went to the publishing company we had a connection with and said, listen I don't know who it belongs to really, put it down that I own it and we will split the money. The publisher said, no you won't, the money is going to go to Lead Belly or Lead Belly's widow for their child. So the self-important bloke was not accepted which was rather nice.

We did the number and it was a great success, the interesting part being that Decca Records only recorded us because a friend of mine used to work for them, Hugh Mendel, and he got us a chance to play there in the first place. He said, record this, record that, so we did. The record was immediately played on the radio and the head of Decca did not see it and they did not put it out as a single for twelve months which was very nice for us because our jazz band got into millions of people's homes who would have bought a single of 'Rock Island Line' if there had been one, but they bought it by buying our first LP. Rather nice of them I thought, rather handy, any inefficiencies were not worth worrying about as it got us a great step up with the trade. I think we had a royalty but it wasn't much for the LP. We did two more tracks 'Wabash Cannonball' and 'Nobody's Child' and they never did issue those. Lonnie Donegan was quite fun sometimes but very difficult. He had very strong opinions about certain things, you had to do a certain way or he could not understand why something was like that.

NICK SIMPER,
Musician

When we saw Lonnie on the television, I thought: Oh, I want to do that. My sister used to go to this club, Ken Colyer's club. She used to tell me that all these people came in and they had a jam session. I said: What's that mean? What's a jam session? She said: Well, they all just set up and play. You know, I didn't quite grasp what it meant. She made a tea-chest bass for me, with the old broom, and a box, and a bit of string. I had no musical knowledge at all, my sister played the violin pretty badly, but we came from quite a musical family. My granddad, he played all the wind instruments for the army band. He could play trombone, trumpet, the whole nine yards. We just made a racket. What we used to do was the put the Lonnie Donegan records on, and then we'd play along to it, and cavort about, and shout in there.

Then one Christmas, I got a ukulele, it was only a plastic one. I was a bit disappointed when I saw it. I saw a picture of Lonnie Donegan's guitar, and it was actually kind of red, like an orangey colour on the top, because you'd only seen it grey on the TV. I wanted to paint the ukulele, but I couldn't find any orange paint. Nobody knew how to tune it up, but I still used to bang away on this thing. Of course, then when the musical tastes changed, other stuff started coming in. My sister brought home Everly Brothers, the first 45 record ever came into our house. Everly Brothers 'Dream' and 'Claudette'. What a sound. Never heard anything like it.

One Christmas, my sister came home with 'Great Balls of Fire' by Jerry Lee Lewis. Oh, dear oh dear. The thing that did it for me, seeing Buddy Holly on *Sunday Night at the London Palladium.* We all wanted a guitar that was kind of vaguely the same shape with the hole in the middle. There's Buddy Holly with something that came from out of space. That's not a guitar, that's crazy! Pretty hard, in the black and white TV, to really see it in perspective. Then we found out, from some friends of mine, that there was a shop up in Charing Cross Road called Lew Davies, and they actually had a Stratocaster in the window. We'd go all the way up to the town from Hayes, where we all lived, just to gaze through the window at this thing. As it happened, I knew the lead guitarist with Cliff Bennett and the Rebel Rousers, and he was the assistant manager in Lew Davies. He would let us actually hold these things. They had a Gretsch White Falcon. He said: That's the most expensive guitar in the world. It was just incredible.

MIKE HURST,
Musician

'Silver Threads and Golden Needles' turned out to be a country record, and that's why of course it was a hit in the States. They thought we were American; and they were totally upset when we got to Nashville and realised we weren't. Really. You could see it in their faces – shock. Now, we waited to go onto Grand Ole Opry, next door, in the bar; we were booked. And do you know, they didn't want us on there because we weren't American. They didn't want us on. We were in Tootsie's next door; we even signed the wall alongside the Webb Pierces, the Hank Williams, everybody; we signed the wall, and they still didn't want us on that show. And then in a way I'm not surprised because when we were recording in Nashville, Tom used to say, in the studio, he said, I think we ought to sing pinching our noses. I said, what? He said yeah, we'll sound more country. Seriously. And we sang at least three tracks like that. I could see the other people's faces, the Americans, thinking these people are shit. I could really see it going through their heads, I could! But that's what we did. It was unbelievable. I think they were flabbergasted because 'Silver Threads' was in the Top Twenty; we got to New York as they say.

We went to Nashville before anybody else from this country. On our sessions we had Jerry Reed – Jerry Reed! – Bill Black! I looked at this guy – the other two, Tom and Dusty, couldn't understand it because I kept saying, that's Bill Black, and they'd say, who? I said, he's Elvis's bass player! I mean, please! We had these guys; I was just blown away at the playing, I mean, they did it by numbers, because even then it was a machine. They did it by numbers but it was still good. And so those were the recording sessions; we were there for three weeks making a record. I met Johnny Cash, his brother Tommy; I met lots of faces. And it was, again, sorry to repeat myself, you're nineteen; you take all this in. And afterwards people would say to me, God you must have been... and I'd go, no, it's fine.

And yet it was right around the corner with The Beatles. It was all going to happen. This is now end of 1962, and of course end of '62 we're back here in England and win the NME Poll Winners Award, which is there – that beaten up tin cup. Top British group you see. Top British group! And that year at Wembley when we performed, the Best Newcomers were The Beatles. We'd already met them; we met them in Liverpool at the Cavern, and in fact John Lennon made us honorary members of The Beatles Fan Club. So we knew how good they were; there was no argument, we knew it. So that was all just around the corner. That was all going to change – marketing, everything else, directed very much at America. It was all about to happen. We were the trial; I always felt that way; we were the guinea pigs. By luck we had that hit, but we didn't know how to follow it up.

NORMAN JOPLING,
Journalist, Record Mirror

We got sent a paper called *Mersey Beat* and I had just done another of my articles about the funny group names in Liverpool and said it sounded like the rocking it place in Britain. Then I noticed that this group The Beatles were topping the bill over Bruce Channel. Then I saw a picture of them, well I had been going part-time to Hornsey College of Art, a weekend thing, I was into art school, mod bohemian fashion thing, and at that time about 90% of the art students were still under the visual influence of Elvis Presley. I saw a picture of The Beatles and they actually looked like the hip kids looked, the business was way behind, I thought they are going to be big just by the way they looked. Then 'Love Me Do' came out, it was OK, a bit cautious but OK. I remember I was in the back room of the office at *RM* and Jimmy said I have got Sid on the phone, the EMI press officer, apparently he has got this group The Beatles, does anyone want to talk to them? I said, yeah I do, I want to talk to them. So later Paul and Brian Epstein came up, Brian blushing, and I just got talking about rhythm & blues with Paul. So I did this article, not the first in London, but it was a very early one. Probably for about the next few months I spoke to them a lot on the phone, I certainly spoke to John two or three times and Paul again and then they got so huge that it was all the editors that wanted to interview them and I was just the lowly eighteen year old who had first hipped onto them.

ADRIAN KERRIDGE,
Studio Engineer

We were sent from Keith Prowse Music groups for doing demos. That was the big thing. They were all looking, because the skiffle – this is the period from late Fifties, 1961, 1962. There was a group came down from Keith Prowse music called the Dave Clark Five, and I did a demo and I thought, this group's pretty good. They were obviously green as heck, you know; so was I. I was only a kid in short trousers almost. And I said to them, this is great; have you got a record deal? They said, nope. So I introduced them to the EMI A&R department, they signed a contract and it went from there. We did something like nearly 100 million records worldwide over a ten-year period. I don't think Keith Prowse took the group up – well, obviously he didn't, and I said to Dave, we've got a studio, let's do a deal. That was my responsibility because by then Joe Meek had left. And the reason he left, walked out, because he was always pestering Dennis Preston to record his 'artists'; and when you're on a session where the producer is concentrating on Afro-Cuban band jazz, you don't need an engineer pestering you. Dennis used to have Mach 1, Mach 2 and Mach 3, in anger, and I think he had a Mach 3 with Joe, and Joe walked out.

During my time at Lansdowne with him he'd work all night; he was fanatical. I was quite naive in those days; he used to give me 2/6d and say, go down the chemist and buy Preludin. I didn't know what they were; they were slimming pills but they gave him a high, kept him working. I only learnt that later when I spoke to somebody about it; I had no idea what it was. But he didn't do anything harder than that. And of course then Joe set up his own flat locally, then he moved to Holloway Road, and of course 'Telstar' was a big hit and he had other hits. I never visited the Holloway Road studio, Joe and I kind of didn't really talk after that, which wasn't my fault; it was very difficult.

LG WOOD,
Chairman, EMI Records

We had an arrangement with Capitol Records, as indeed Capitol had with us, that they had first option to release in America, any record which we released in England. But whilst they didn't like this over much, I also had arranged that if they turned something down, we would then be free to endeavour to license whatever they turned down to somebody else. And the somebody else was generally one of the American companies we already had a licensing deal with to handle their product, and whoever were those various companies naturally we were saying we're giving you the product, you've got some good product, why don't you let us have some of that? So if Capitol turned something down then as I say we tried to license elsewhere, and we had a lawyer in New York who was a great help to us in this regard; we paid him a retaining fee and he was a good man at that job at that time, and that was Paul Marshall.

Capitol turned down The Beatles and eventually Paul Marshall helped us to get a licensing deal, an outward licensing deal, with a company called Vee-Jay Records, who were in Chicago, from whom we had a licensing deal inwards anyway. So towards the summer of 1963, Vee-Jay got into difficulties, financial difficulties, and Paul Marshall got in touch with us and explained that they were financially unsound and we'd better be careful about the money that was due to us. He issued a document, or he issued a letter on our behalf to Vee-Jay to say that if the money due to us were not paid in so many days, say thirty-one days, the contract would be terminated.

The money was not forthcoming, so Marshall terminates the contract verbally in America and then rings through to me to tell me what he had done. He didn't get me, he got my personal assistant who was Roland Rennie, and sitting opposite Roland Rennie at the time that the phone call came through was David Dexter of Capitol, Dave Dexter who was partly responsible for turning down The Beatles in the first place. Rennie takes this phone call and when he's finished he says to Dexter, well our deal with Vee-Jay is at an end; Marshall has just told me we're cancelling it, so we've got two artists you can have: Frank Ifield and The Beatles. He said, I'll have Frank Ifield, I don't want The Beatles. That was in the summer of 1963. Later on in that year we licensed a single Beatles record to a company called Swan Records. Subsequently to that, George Martin came in to see me and said you, know – words to the effect – it's quite obvious that we've got a major act on our hands here and it's ridiculous I think that we haven't got a contract – only this company Swan in America handle any Beatles material at all now that Vee-Jay have gone; Capitol have turned them down. He said, why don't you go to CBS and get CBS to license The Beatles. I said we ought to go to Capitol if the act is as good as we all think it is; obviously it should be kept in the family, it should be with Capitol.

£££

PETER JENNER,
Artist Manager

Harvest was very frustrating because they didn't have their American releases together. This was a big issue. And that was the thing, you couldn't get your records released in America because they were on EMI so none of the other majors would take it. The little labels like Seymour Stein and so on wanted to get people like Kevin Ayers and wanted to sign some of our acts, it was always very difficult to get them to sign a deal with EMI because EMI would be very rightly suspicious that they wouldn't pay. Now what was interesting is that what really pissed me off was that Capitol were putting out all these bands from Island. So Artie Mogull would sign these bands from Island Records. They were signing things like If and Bronco who were not, to say the least, very successful and we couldn't get Edgar Broughton and Kevin Ayers released because they'd filled up their schedule. The answer was that Artie Mogull would sign these bands from Island because he would have to pay out money to sign them. So that was good because then he had ownership on them and that meant that he would get points if they were successful.

More important however, I discovered later, was that he would get a kick-back. If he took up an EMI record he got no kick-back, it didn't cost the company any money, but I think also he didn't get any money 'cause it just went on the intercompany account. So he got no benefit from it. Now Artie had a serious gambling problem and that was the problem. He needed to feed his gambling problem, that also was the sort of thing which led to the endless string of mafia people who ran Capitol. I mean these are serious men of honour, you know.

I think really it's an inability to cope with North America. They coped with Canada; a lot of the bands did well out of Canada. It did alright in Australia and New Zealand. It did alright sort of around the place. Did alright in Europe you know, 'cause EMI bought up companies and it worked, but they couldn't work in America. I think it's a way of doing business and they're so money oriented. If it makes money no questions are asked. I mean an idea of their being restrained by legalities; the only thing which will restrain you would be by being caught you know. Can I get away with this? If I can get away with this and it sells records I'll do it. Also really important in America, they don't audit the manufacturing plants. The plants are not audited by their MCPS equivalent; there's no such thing. So all of them run, or used to run, midnight shifts. In the big booms they were running midnight shifts and this was just a huge money laundering operation. So you'd have your shifts running, your two shifts in the day, and your midnight shift would have trucks rolling in and rolling out.

CHARLIE WATKINS, WEM PAs

Most of the groups we were supporting with PAs was because they already used our gear. It all went in with their stuff, with what we could get in our big Commer van. A big sound in those days, I mean 5000 watts hadn't been reached. I knew I could do it. Or thought I could do it. But the biggest we'd done was 500w – 1000w. You could get that in a Commer. We used to put our gear in with them and often more likely than not there'd be somebody else on with the group – everybody had a WEM PA – and all the support groups would pitch in with their stuff, and then you'd finish up with a pretty big sound system. Lovely. You just had to watch you didn't get the cheap speakers from the support groups, rather than the Axiom 301 that we had in our pro stuff, they would have the Axiom 201, which is small magnet, and that would affect the sound of the others so we didn't get them. But apart from that everything matched; just slave to slave; as long as the slave were unearthed you could do it. Yeah. Loved it. There was one big tour; it had The Move, The Nice. There was Hendrix, Floyd. Twelve bob. All those groups for twelve bob. I needed a bit of belief in what I was making and here it was a big cellar packed; everybody jiving, everybody could hear it, no problem with the foldback because we had the foldback going. And that's what we did.

BOB FISHER,
Fan

I saw The Beatles at De Montfort Halls in Leicester in one those Arthur Howe's type package shows and then I very swiftly moved on to American folk blues festivals. I was weirdly observed by friends because I could quite enjoy Sister Rosetta Tharpe at the same time as Gerry and the Pacemakers which was kind of unusual. They were very odd those shows, I can remember walking to the De Montfort Hall to see one of the shows and there was Willie Dixon and somebody else walking down the road towards you. Oh Hello Sir, and of course they were just made up by someone calling them sir and treating them like human beings. That is why they all came over to Europe like that. I went and saw Sonny Boy Williamson in the something Drill Hall in Leicester, quite a big venue and he had a phenomenal turn out and he was fan-tastic. He used to wear these check board suits so that half would be black and that half brown, and the trousers would be that half brown and that half black. He used to reverse them round half way through the show. I can remember watching him and thinking this was fantastic and then it was the intermission, guys we will be back in fifteen minutes. I go to the loo and there is Sonny Boy Williamson, no changing room, in the biggest boxer short I have ever seen in my life standing changing his suit round and talking to people. Leicester was quite lucky then because we had the El Rondo Club which was on the circuit. I saw the Rolling Stones there probably around the time they signed to Decca. The club carried on the blues thing because of Fleetwood Mac, I saw Howling Wolf, Lowell Fulson, Otis Spann, George Smith, all those people were coming over doing tours particularly if they were dealing with Mike Vernon as he was dealing with the tours. Then I eventually got slightly into promoting some shows, there was the Leicestershire Blues Appreciation Society which I joined and took up co-promoting gigs for them. We never made any money out of it, but we did not lose any either so that made it good.

James King and the Farinas were the big act that we followed in Leicester and they evolved in to Family. Roger Chapman used to hang out at the same record shop that I went to, Advance Records in the Leicester Market Place. My mother had gone back to work and used to work with Roger's mother at Parker Plant. Those guys were dangerous, I vividly remember being in the El Rondo one night and Roger was chucking beer glasses off the balcony not the sort of thing you wanted to be involved with. There was a huge party at the Holiday Inn in Leicester for Family that John Peel came to, and Jon Lord came as well. He and I hid in a broom cupboard because it got to the point where everybody was being thrown in the pool and Jon Lord said to me: I ain't going in the pool, this suit cost me a hundred quid.

MERVYN CONN,
Promoter

PJ Proby had been warned. Three times he split the trousers; these velvet trousers, and they split. And if you don't wear underpants you're going to be in trouble, aren't you. I can remember quite clearly that night, there was Joe Collins, John, or whoever it was, from Granada, Cissie Williams from Moss Empires, Stan Fisherman from Rank, and some guy from ABCs. They were the guys that controlled all the theatres. So I went to his apartment with his agent, a fellow called Tony Lewis; and Tony Lewis worked for John Hayman. And John Hayman – it was a secondary thing in his office because he managed Elizabeth Taylor and Richard Burton so he wasn't particularly interested that much in PJ Proby; and now Proby was becoming a bit of a thorn in his agency's side. So we got there at eleven o'clock; at twelve thirty he eventually came down, bottle of Chivas Regal in one hand and some bird in the other. Hi Mervyn, great to see you, great show. I said, yeah. And I'm sitting like this in the room and he comes in and he says, well I said great show. I said yeah, it was a great show, but tonight will be the last show for you, because if you do it again tonight you will be out of the business. Oh no, no; I promise you – this that and the other. We come to the show, he does exactly the same thing again. Not only did they drop the curtain but in the theatres at that time they had an iron curtain and they dropped that on him as well. He never performed again really for years after that. At that time Tom Jones had just got in the charts and he was number three then; 'It's Not Unusual' I think was the first major hit he had. We put him on, he was good but it was a bit early days.

DEREK GREEN, MD, Rondor Music

A&M Records asked David Betteridge at Island Records to look out for someone to start an English operation for them for their publishing company and David contacted me. Rondor Music was the publishing company, Ron being Jerry Moss's son and Dore is Herb's son and they put £10,000 in the bank account in the UK and said off you go. Then I got really lucky with that job, the first six months were fantastic, I met with Brian Lane who was managing a group called Yes and because I was interested in that whole progressive rock scene, I just knew that this band just had to happen. Brian was just shopping their publishing for the best money he could get, he said: I have been offered seven and a half and I said: I will give you ten. That is the best I can do, I have not got any more. So I signed their publishing for the *Close To The Edge* and the *Yes* album for Europe and offered them to America who passed.

The second deal was getting Bob Marley through Johnny Nash, well before Island Records. My job as part of the deal was to get them a record contract and the only thing they said to me was you can take it to every record label in England apart from Island because Bob Marley was very suspicious of Island for some reason. Consequently I did the rounds with all the record labels and got 'No's everywhere, people weren't ready for reggae, they were not ready for Bob Marley. I went back to CBS because Dave Margereson was in A&R and was someone I got into the music business and he owed me a big favour. He convinced his boss to sign the package, Johnny Nash, Marley, Rabbit and the Sons Of The Jungle group that Marley was recording under. We will take anything, Johnny Nash recorded 'Stir It Up', Bob Marley's song and we had a Top Ten record. We expected the Bob Marley recordings to go out on CBS but they refused and they refused to release him from contract. So they wouldn't do either. They re-auditioned him in the most humiliating way, they would not even give him studio time, they gave him the disc cutting room upstairs and these men in suits stood the other side of the glass and did not understand it. That is when Chris Blackwell came into the picture, however he did it, made a deal with CBS and acquired the rights to Marley who left Johnny and Danny Sims and there the big story starts.

TONY HALL,
Record Promoter

Straight Ahead Productions with Denny Cordell and Tony Visconti, I used to promote all their things. I discovered Joe Cocker. A schoolteacher in Sheffield came down to London to see me about my newspaper column, and brought with him a demo of this gas work fitter called Joe Cocker. I thought he was amazing, so I took him to Denny Cordell and I said this guy is amazing and you ought to sign him. I was appalled that Cordell took a week to come back to me, having asked everybody in the world whether they thought Cocker had any talent, before he agreed to sign him. I got blown out of it; Chris Blackwell wanted a piece, everybody wanted a piece, and I ended up being given a very small override by David Platz Productions.

Chas Chandler called me up and said, come down to the Scotch of St James, I want you to hear this American guitarist I brought over. There was a very top table hidden away in a corner of the gloom of the Scotch. Dick Katz was there, I was there, I can't remember who else was. And we heard this absolutely amazing guitarist who literally blew us all totally away. We'd never heard anything like it, and he looked fantastic. I went into Decca the following morning and said I've just heard the greatest guitarist in the world, but I thought totally uncommercial; God knows how you make a hit single with him.

JEFF DEXTER, Disc Jockey

I think 1967 the Summer of Love, went right through to the summer of 1968. It seemed to be one continuous trip for me, everything was happening and had grown, Middle Earth club had taken on and turned what UFO did into a much more professional thing. UFO at the Roundhouse unfortunately they couldn't handle, there was a small group of people and in order for it to survive one needed paying customers that would come in and help the budget. Because as the budgets grew you had to have paying customers in order to pay everyone's wages. There were people that did work for nothing or for very little, but by that time the psychedelic bands were going out on the road and actually getting paid, so why would they play UFO for less money? Although they wanted to be part of it, they all had managers and some of them began to have wives too, who also wanted to see part of the money. In some ways it may have ended but I don't think it ended like that. I don't think it really ended until the end of 1970 fully. I think a lot of us carried on trying to make things better but trying to make it work in a way that it would pay for itself to keep the whole thing going.

Middle Earth became a huge success until the spring of 1968 when Middle Earth was crushed by a police raid and then the market porters coming in to trash the whole joint. Middle Earth flew the flag for a good while after that, when it moved to the Roundhouse too and did manage to make it work. Other promoters had come in, some chancers, some greedy, some who really cared and there were wonderful things beginning to happen beyond that, in some ways a better way, but obviously without that unique shell that UFO had created. When something is new it always has a founding feel about it, but in order for it to work you can't have a club running on just a few friends that all know each other, you have to make it pay.

After the raids on *International Times* and all the trouble that was going on with the police of course they needed some funds. I think Hoppy had initiated the idea of putting together *The Fourteen Hour Technicolor Dream*, following on from something that had happened in January that year put together by a guy called Dave Howson who ran a company then called DICA Productions, they had an event called, *Freak Out Ethel!* at Seymour Hall. Many people have the idea that it was a wonderful event in terms of how many people came, but it didn't pay for itself. In fact they were a little untogether on the box office and many people didn't pay, and those people that had sold tickets apart from the real honest ones in the bookshop didn't send the money back for the tickets they had sold. So in the end *The Fourteen Hour Technicolor Dream*, in spite of it being a wonderful happening, was a bit of a disaster financially and rather than helping *International Times* out, it drained their resources even more.

**JOHN KNOWLES,
Sales Manager,
Island Records**

In those days there were not many accountants and we did things by feel and it was fantastic. And working for a company like Island where 90% of the staff were stoned, all the EMI guys had suits and ties and smart cars, we were all ripped jeans, yeah, but we had the best fucking music so it was easy for us. Great days. Chris Blackwell, a man with impeccable taste, musical taste, fantastic eye for photography and artwork. Brilliant. Brilliant. I remember going into the studio and he was mixing a Marley album and he had the biggest fucking spliff and he said we could have some of his stuff, so I took about three puffs. I was just off my trolley. And then he starts to question me. I'm fucked. Just didn't know what, I was just all over the place. But he was for me next to Ahmed Ertegun I should think, the number one A&R / music man that I ever came across. I'll tell you what a guy he was. Well Island Records signed a deal with Stiff. It was Elvis Costello's first gig at Dingwalls. Jake was a lunatic then. All the Press at Dingwalls and Jake, his favourite tipple was speed and cider and we just signed the deal. I was at the bar and he was screaming and shouting and abusing everybody and I said: Jake, for God's sake shut up. At that point he tipped a pint of beer over my head and I bashed him. He's on the floor. Matthew Kaufman from Beserkley, to cause a diversion, got his cock out and pissed on the bar. It was absolute chaos. I left Jake for dead, I went round to David Betteridge's house who was the MD and I said I think: David, I think I'm in shit. He said: Why? and I said: Because I just knocked out Jake. He went: Fantastic. Fantastic. Absolutely brilliant.

I went in the office the next day and Blackwell called and he said: Can I speak to Rocky? I said: What are you talking about? He said: John. I said: Yeah. He said: I want to speak to Rocky. I said: OK. He said: What happened. I told him exactly what happened and he said: Best fucking thing you could have done. Jake had complained to Chris that I'd broken his teeth and his dentist was in LA and he had to be flown first class to LA to have his teeth fixed. So Chris saw him and said: What I suggest you do is you go and see him now, let him do it properly and I'll pay, I'll pay your fare. And I thought I was gonna be in deep shit but Blackwell just fucking loved it. It was great. And to this day I see Jake and he sort of goes: Hello. Hello. Hello. Right, what else?

PHILL BROWN, Studio Engineer

I started at Olympic in Barnes in November 1967. I was out of school, sixteen years old, or just seventeen. It was 4-track. I basically trained with people like Eddie Kramer and Glyn Johns. George Chkiantz, who was an amazing assistant, really, he was always classed as assistant. He was behind the tape phasing for 'Itchycoo Park', he did all the phasing on the Family's *Music in a Doll's House*. He worked with me on the Stones doing 'Jumping Jack Flash'. He was a mentor to me, really. He was only twenty years old. You'd think of him more like a thirty year old, but he was twenty years old, I was seventeen. I was there for a year. It would be interesting to know if *Music in a Doll's House*, was mixed in a mono form, because a lot of the effects are extreme panning, and things that are out of phase that come out behind you. In mono, that would all disappear anyway. I remember them working on that at Olympic. I wasn't on at those sessions, but I remember George, I'm just trying to think who else, maybe Alan O'Duffy, but I remember these guys. It was pretty revolutionary at the time: the hard editing, and the tape phasing, and the effects. You know, you had no plug-in effects. Everything had to be manufactured. If it was an echo thing, a reverb thing, tape delays, or putting a speaker in a corridor, it was all pretty much thought up on the spot, which also made it exciting, but hard to repeat.

I think whatever happened at Olympic for that year had a huge effect on the way I worked after that. I think it might have been learning from these guys who were doing things on 4-track, and actually committing things to tape, and not worrying about sorting out later. Then the 8-track thing. Just the ease with which sessions happened. I worked with Traffic. Everyone would just sit around on the floor. They had their friends in from Berkshire. It was very hippy, very trippy, and easy. You're making these amazing records, but not with all that daytime or daylight pressure. The Stones' thing. The Small Faces, I mean, that was just like being at a party. They just messed about for three weeks, made this brilliant record. Every day, it was kind of fun. You were pushing all this basic gear to the limit, but

146

not in this pressured thing that happened in the Eighties you know, when all the gear came out in the Eighties, and the digital stuff, and everyone's 48-track, and Mitsubishis, and everything synced with sound. That was always stressful. This was a completely different era. This was just, you know, perhaps a spliff, set it up, low lighting, run the 8-track, and party.

That stayed with me. It's hard to have a specific. I suppose Traffic was a big influence on me, doing *Mr. Fantasy*, which was my first rock session. I think doing some of the *Beggars Banquet*. Obviously, 'Sympathy for the Devil'. I liked the whole 'Street Fighting Man', where Keith Richards brought in this early wowy cassette home demo. Because they couldn't really recapture what it was about, they dumped the cassette onto the 8-track and then added things. I remember that, just because it seemed so crazy and off the wall. Moments like that are just crazy in a sense, with this wow flutter and no great hi-fi, but made a great record. The Stones' *Beggars Banquet*, at the time, I think it took six weeks. That was a phenomenal amount of time to make a record, because we made records in three or four days. I mean, records were made in a day. I have memories of 'Sympathy for the Devil', just because of how long it took to really nail it, different versions. Some songs were really songs and were very together, other things were very experimental, 'Sympathy for the Devil' was one of those really.

The Small Faces, *Ogdens' Nut Gone Flake*, I think just for the fun of working with those guys. Every day was a bit of a party. Because they wanted different sounds, we used the corridors a lot, we used the toilets. Steve Marriott and Ronnie Lane were like two West End urchins on a stage show. They were always dancing about, and coming up to the mic, and doing all these just crazy bad acting routines, and then breaking up in laughter. The whole thing was brilliant. It's hard, in a way, to marry against some of today's sessions, or even sessions since the Eighties. It became a business. I think back then, we were all pretty naive, even the bands. Small Faces were a great example of not really making money out of their career, thanks to a manager. Yeah, it was a freedom and a naivety, but great stuff came out of it.

MUFF WINWOOD, Musician

Down in South London we played at a couple of the Kray twin's clubs and those clubs were amazing. I tell you what, we got ripped off by a few people, we never ever got ripped off by the Krays right? They paid cash on the nail right the moment you walked off stage. No problems at all. It's wonderful innit? You go to some places round the country and some guy will say: Don't worry, I'm sending the cheque to your agent, of course it never ever came you know. And there's the wonderful Krays, their business was impeccable. There was never any problem. Problems. Gigs were extraordinary then in the early Sixties. I mean you used to get a lot of violence in these places, mainly kind of sort of mods and rockers type punch ups. I mean we did Margate on Bank Holiday and all that stuff, and driving our van down the front and there's thousands of rockers pouring down on bikes and thousands of mods pouring down on scooters and you think: Bloody hell, what's going to happen to us in the middle of all this, and you play the Dreamland Ballroom in Margate and they'd all turned up. There was fights and punch-ups all the time. We never had proper security, we had one road manager. And we used to get out of these problems if they attacked us, usually the perpetrators would push one of their mates to come up and confront the band and laugh at it: Hey! Go on, you tell them, you tell them Larry, you tell them how crap they are. So this guy would come on stage, all you know, the lads are down below going: Go on! Get them. And he'd come on and we'd go – and we'd worked this out – and we'd go: He wants to sing. And of course all his mates right, who'd sent him up to wallop us are going: Yeah, yeah, let him. And we could play anything. Steve of course could play anything to start with and we would say: What do you wanna sing? And some guy, some evil looking heathen, actually said: I wanna sing 'Lipstick on Your Collar'. And I remember we played 'Lipstick on Your Collar' and the guys in the front were falling about and we found that that was the only way.

I always remember coming to Elgin in north Scotland and when we got to the venue there was a great fence up in front of the stage right, and we kind of get there four o'clock in the afternoon or whatever to set up and everything, and you walk in and you think: What do they need this for? Who is gonna come to this gig? And of course when you start the gig you realise they're a bunch of completely stoned out drunken out people and this was their local monthly dance and they were out to lose it. And they were frightening experiences but you had to deal with these things because you couldn't kind of run away and call security. There was no such thing.

DEREK NICOL, Promoter

We used to do the ten-day tour of Scotland with Ambrose Slade before they made it as Slade and all the big hits and such like. Did Robert Plant and his Band of Joy, ten days up in Scotland as well, going way, way back. There was a period of two years where I was in Dundee that we did a deal with the Isle of Arran Council, which is this island off Scotland that you might know, couple of thousand population; except during the summertime when all the students go on holiday, and it was round about 20,000 or something all working in hotels and whatever, or just basically being out there chilling out or whatever they did. And we used to run all the entertainment for the whole season. It might have been a six or eight-week season, I can't remember exactly, and there was three village halls four miles apart, Lamlash, Brodick and Whiting Bay; not necessarily in that order. And they all had their village hall that would take 500 or 600 people, so we would rotate entertainment each night – dancing tonight... I remember having The Kinks there; Kenny Ball and his Jazzmen as guests. I remember 'Waterloo Sunset' must have been one or two; it was really high on the current chart; I can remember watching the ferry, I'm on the Pier watching the ferry come in and Ray Davies leaning on the rail as it's coming in. We collect them and they spent the night, probably in Mrs Smith's Bed

& Breakfast. Great, great fun. Local Scottish bands and records; not a Disco because that wasn't invented, but playing the records for the dancing. Great, great fun.

The excitement of people queuing outside and trying to get in, creating a bit of a buzz doesn't exist any more because everybody's bought in advance. A walk-up business is negligible these days. So we toured and every single day was sold out. We were selling the dates and promoting the ones that we couldn't sell, and I always remember the Monday night, I couldn't shift – as you can imagine – can't shift the Monday night, nobody wanted it; I remember this new venue called the Electric Garden had just opened up in Glasgow at the bottom of Sauchiehall Street; big 1,300, 1,500, standing club basically. It was run by a guy called Frank Lynch who went on to manage Billy Connolly and some other acts. So I'd phoned him, never spoken to him in my life, Derek Nicol here, I've got this artist called Peter Sarstedt – this is like six weeks before or whatever – oh, never heard of him. Believe me it's going to be really big – did the usual sell. I said: How much do you want for me to hire the venue? Oh, he says, £60. OK, let's do it. We sold out – 1,300 people, probably about 6/6d a head, or whatever the ticket price was then. And the next morning he said, what else have you got? So following that we delivered David Bowie, Deep Purple, Elton John.

The first gig that Nazareth did was Dunstable Queensway Hall, supporting Mott the Hoople and Uriah Heep, and they travelled from their hometown in Dunfermline in Scotland all the way to Dunstable, played the gig and then travelled back again, for a fiver that's what it was like. OK we're going to play, the only way we're going to break it is to get out there and play, play, play.

David Bowie – can you imagine having David Bowie in the back of my Ford, with his guitar case doing a double from the Kinema Ballroom in Dunfermline to some Miners' Welfare Institute in Midlothian somewhere. I'm driving – the promoter – I'm driving, take him to the other one and he's in the back of this rickety old car. But that was the scene. And his backing group was Junior's Eyes at the time, in the early days. Alex Harvey, he and his wife used to share a flat with David Bowie, because Alex and David Bowie were managed by the same person at the time, and Alex Harvey was into all sorts; he had an absolutely amazing mind. You could discuss just about any subject under the sun with him; he was very intelligent and he knew lots of different things, and I think a lot of that he discussed with David Bowie. I think he got him into the whole space thing at one time, and all sorts of strange things.

DAVID STOPPS, Promoter, Friars Aylesbury

In September 1971 we put the first Bowie gig on which was very significant. It was the first time he had played *Hunky Dory* on stage. We had put Al Kooper on that summer and he had met David and told him what a great gig it was, so Bowie's manager, Tony Defries, contacted me and we put him on. For Bowie it was a very experimental gig, it was the first gig with Mick Ronson, Trevor Bolder and Woody Woodmansey. They were doing *Hunky Dory, The Man Who Sold The World*, the first time he had ever played it on stage, ever. He obviously did 'Space Oddity' which had been a hit the year before and I remember in the dressing room afterwards he said to the guys, look that was really great, let's do this properly. And they said, yeah alright we can do that. That was sort of where the band formed I suppose you can say in an official way. He had amazing charisma and came on in his Oxford bags, which looked like a dress from a distance but were actually very wide trousers and very long hair as on the cover of *Man Who Sold The World*. He then went and did one or two bits and pieces and then wrote and recorded *Ziggy Stardust*. We put him on again in January 1972 and he debuted *Ziggy Stardust* at Friars, it was just extraordinary. We expected him to do *Hunky Dory* because that had been released subsequently. It was not released when he did the first gig, he just played tracks from it 'Oh You Pretty Thing', 'Life On Mars'. It came out in December and went to number one in Aylesbury because of the gig, but not in the rest of Britain. So we were all geared up for him to do *Hunky Dory*, we

151

were going to have 'Queen Bitch' and all this stuff and it was going to be great. And he came on with this completely new material, we just had our mouths open, we had never seen anything like it. He came back again in July 1972; by that time the whole *Ziggy Stardust* show was completely developed and the production was developed, the show, the clothes and it was extraordinary. RCA Records flew in fifty American journalists just for our one gig, it was just unbelievable. That was just the most magic period because you just knew history was being created right in front of you, it was just extraordinary. When we became THE place to play, certain agents would put us at the top of their list and people like Jonathan Richman came over and did Friars, Hammersmith and then home, and that happened several times with American artists, we were considered to be THE key gig. That summer of 1972 three weeks running we had Bowie, we had Lou Reed and we had Roxy Music, three weeks in a row. Just an incredibly exciting musical period. Amazing. If I could go back, I could go back to that summer of 1972, that would be it. Amazing.

JOHN BAGNALL, Social Secretary

What really shaped me was going to Sussex University to read Economics and the year before I got there a couple of guys got together to start a blues club and when I arrived we managed to get a grant from the union of about £40 and we found a room above a pub called Jimmy's in Steine Street in Brighton and started putting on live gigs which we booked through a guy who ran a record shop in the town. More by luck than judgement, but also knowledge of the music we wanted to hear, I think the first band we put on was a then unknown band called Free who played for about £35. I think Jethro Tull was the week after and so on. Virtually every English band of the blues-rock progressive blues generation played at Jimmy's at one stage or another and it was an incredible two years to be running the Blues Club and getting involved with the bands that were playing there and starting to make contacts, all in inverse proportion to the amount of time I spent on Economics. We had built up a really nice bank balance of a couple of thousand pounds without trying but simply by running an honest operation putting on good music. I remember being in this record shop looking at the front page of *Melody Maker* with the headline 'Traffic to roar again' when the phone went and was asked would you be prepared to put Traffic on in two weeks time, free of charge, they have heard so much about Jimmy's and they want to build it into their tour. Oddly enough the Traffic gig wasn't a particularly good one, I think the venue was too small for what was effectively a supergroup and instead of the close intimacy that used to encourage Free to come back and play long after they had the hits, I think everyone was in awe of them and it had a very stilted atmosphere and it did not really happen.

The problem was that the Students Union itself carried on promoting concerts, badly, and losing money on them and getting more and more jealous of the success of the Blues Club as they saw it. So in the end we were hauled in front of the University Senate who conducted an enquiry as to whether we were making profits against the rules and the upshot was that they ordered us to close the club and to hand back the bank balance after a certain date in about a month's time with the cheque books and the accounts and such like. So we booked the University building ourselves and put on a concert at normal members' rate which was I think five shillings for members and 7/6d for non-members, and we put on The Who, The James Gang and Bonzo Dog Do-Dah Band supporting them and lost everything bar about £14/3/6d, and so we duly gave this back to the Union and that was it.

CHRIS BRIGGS,
Social Secretary

I think the first thing we did was the Nice, and it was Davy O'List's last gig. They fired him in the dressing room at Ewell Tech. Supported by Elmer Gantry's Velvet Opera and that's memorable, because Elmer was having a dispute with the drummer, who I think went on to play with The Strawbs, John Hudson. I think he crapped in his hat to make a point, if I remember. That was our first thing, we somehow got involved with Caravan as well. We put Caravan on a lot at Ewell Tech. They arrived, set up, sound checked. Dave Hitchcock, who was their producer, turned up with them. We just hit it off. We got involved in the social life with Caravan. Really nice people. Nigel Kerr is part of this gang. While we're promoting... though promoting is probably glamorising it somewhat. While we're putting on these shambolic gigs at Ewell Tech on a Saturday, on a Wednesday night, we go to the Toby Jug in Tolworth scouting. That's, on the surface, a blues club. It's the same guy who had the Black Prince, Bexley. I think the promoter was called Len Fletcher. He had a bouncer called Tiny, who wasn't. That was first line-up of Fleetwood Mac, Aynsley Dunbar Retaliation, Chicken Shack, Groundhogs. Then, as the blues thing was too narrow a format, it broadened out into Family, Spooky Tooth. I saw John Lee Hooker at the Toby Jug in Surrey. That is a photograph you'd want to have taken, John Lee Hooker at the bar of the Toby Jug waiting to go on with a Mackeson in front of him. That's a picture that I have in my head that I sadly didn't take. And the Star Hotel at West Croydon, the Star Hotel was down towards Broad Green, past the Top Rank. Captain Beefheart played there. We went there. It was a guy called John Pick promoted that for a bit. He was from Reigate, and was a David Arnott connection.

I went to a lot of things at the Greyhound. It was a very good area for live music. Toby's on Tolworth was a religion. We never missed Wednesday night at the Toby Jug. It was always at least, Paul, Lindsay, Bill, Nigel Kerr and myself, and John Lethbridge, actually. He used to do the light show in the spirit of the Fillmore East at Ewell Tech – on a bit more of a budget. It was like lens lights, that kind of thing. King

Crimson was the other. That was Mike Dolan saying you'd have Junior's Eyes on too, because he told you they were good as the support band. That's how it worked at colleges. You'd allow the agent a bit of a free hand with the support band. It was £50 to £75 for the support band, and £150 to £250 for the headliner. Sometimes you'd have two bands that were close to each other, so you'd double bill it with two bands that drew a bit. You'd have the Pretty Things with somebody else. The Pretty Things were fantastic. If the Pretty Things were on a co-headline, you always got a phone call from them saying: We've broken down. They'd be late, so they'd have to headline, they'd have to go on last. They were famous for doing that.

MAX HOLE,
Social Secretary

I was in bands at school and then when I went to university I realised I was shit. Suddenly it was bigger playing field, Steve Hillage was at my university and I saw him playing guitar one day and thought: Oh my god, it is over. So I got involved in organising, I was Social Secretary, booked bands like The Who for £1,000 and you could book Family for £500, you could book Led Zeppelin for £1200, it was an amazing time actually. I mentioned The Who, I think we made £50 profit, the ticket price was a quid. It was an amazing apprenticeship for a lot of our generation where you were allowed to promote concerts and if you lost money, the Union kind of picked up the balance.

I managed a university folk-rock group called Spyrogyra and negotiated a year off so that they could go and be a group and I could be their manager, I remember that my dad went mad and could not believe that the university would allow such a ludicrous thing. But I never went back, I met Sandy Roberton who was quite an influential producer at the time with Steeleye Span and people like that and he signed them. I met Geoff Jukes who had just left Chrysalis Artists and we started an agency called

Gemini Artists in 1972 representing Barclay James Harvest, Mungo Jerry, Martin Carthy and Plainsong with Ian Matthews and then we managed Camel, starting a record production company with the old Decca Record company at 9 Albert Embankment. Geoff was a very able booker, he was an agent, Geoff could sell ice cream to the Eskimos, he used to be a door-to-door encyclopaedia salesman before he became a music agent. We were enthusiasts, and fans, we took on artists because we liked them not really because we would think they would make any money. That was quite a steep learning curve because you realised that looking after Barclay James Harvest was a lot better than other bands because Barclay James Harvest made a lot of money on the road. Gemini Artists went bust in 1974 but as you did in those days, we just started again the next day as managers and the production company.

Camel were our calling card, we had managed them from the very beginning. Geoff somehow knew Peter Bardens and he brought them in and we got them a deal with MCA and their first album was on MCA, then MCA dropped them so we signed them to our own production company Gama, which was funded by Decca. Then we did their second album which was quite well known as the record cover was a Camel cigarette packet. We did not know it but we were one of the first people to do a sponsorship deal with the Camel Cigarette Company, we got a free supply of cigarettes and permission to use the image. That was about it except for all these guys in Switzerland saying, can you write a song called 'Twenty In A Pack' and the band did not think much of that. Their third album was 'Snow Goose' and they did a performance on *The Old Grey Whistle Test* of some of it and the album suddenly went in the top five. Our Decca guy at the time was Hugh Mendl who was a legend and a wonderful man, he signed Tommy Steele and I think Decca was going through a very bad time in the early Seventies, no hits and nothing contemporary and some of the American companies were starting to set up in Britain. I think they took a look at me and Geoff, we had really long hair and wore afghan coats and they must have thought we could be a good addition to the A&R department so they gave us a first look deal. But they took four or five artists from us, Michael Chapman, Martin Carthy, Camel and a complete failure called Coast Road Drive. I don't think we knew what a production deal was, I think they just offered us one and we said: Where do we sign?

BRIDGET ST. JOHN, Musician

The club that I remember most playing in was Cousins, or Lez Cousins, as some people called it. I always thought, having a French degree, it should be called Les Cousins, but nobody called it that, we just called it Cousins. It was this wonderful club downstairs, long before the days of any air conditioning in any room. Very, very deep with smoke then too. It was very steamy, and very smoky. You'd get very, very strong coffee in very thick workman-type mugs. A very small stage, just a little square of wood, maybe a foot off the floor. Everyone was so close to you. I remember, the first time I played there, John Martyn took me there, and I was terrified, because people were just up against my guitar almost, and I wasn't used to that, I was used to a little distance. That was my first experience there.

I got to really love playing there and I loved that place. It was sort of like a little home. After you played the gig, you'd go upstairs and eat. Big Andy was the guy that ran it, and then his father had the Greek restaurant upstairs. We always had wonderful moussaka that he put on for all the musicians. You shared the bill with people there. Often it was John Martyn's night. He played there a lot, because Big Andy was John's really close friend – him and Diane, his wife. John often was the one that would bring people in. One time, he had me and Nick Drake come down to play. I remember, it was a summer's night, so it must have been really hot downstairs. Both me and Nick went and just sat on the sidewalk, literally in the gutter, basically, outside one of the pubs. I don't remember the name of it. We weren't there to drink, we were just there to cool off. It was a sort of a silent communion between the two of us, because we're both really shy, and both really near the beginning. I think he had more experience than me, actually, but we were both very quiet people. We prepared for the gig there.

Nick Drake and I, I always thought were kindred spirits, and pretty silent people at that point. This was, what, 1969 onwards. We did a gig together at the Fairfield Halls. I remember watching him play, and I know I played, and then Fairport Convention played. I think Nick left as soon as he had played. At that stage of my life, I would look at reviews and wait for reviews to come out. I was just horrified, because the reviewer was Karl Dallas. He didn't mention us by name. He just said, the only thing I don't understand is why the promoters bothered with the first half. That was me and Nick Drake just dismissed, and it really destroyed me. I'm sure it did Nick too. It was just awful. Nick was around me at Cousins, and he was around me at Fairport Convention, but we never really had conversations, I would say. John Martyn is such a different kind of effusive, and buoyant, outward-going person. Nick was very, very quiet. At that point anyway, if I was around quiet people, that's exactly how I would be too. I was never pushy or trying to draw people out, because I felt the same way they did, I think.

KARL DALLAS, Journalist

When Dylan first came to London he went to most of the folk clubs, he was actually refused permission to sing at the Round House in Wardour Street, he sang at the Singers Club which was an incredible experience, you see we had all these American singers, many of whom had left America because of Joe McCarthy and the witch hunt. Wonderful performers, Jack Elliott for example, if you wanted a Woody Guthrie imitator for example, they don't come much better than Jack Elliott. Then Dylan turned up, he did not have the presence of Jack Elliott or the musical presence of Woodie himself and we were very offended by his 'hey, hey Woody Guthrie, I wrote you a song'. Well fuck you, who cares. So I had a very low opinion of Bob Dylan. I got *Another Side of Bob Dylan* to review for my magazine *Folk News*, I gave it to Sidney Carter to review because I could not be bothered with it you know, and of course I did not play it which was a big mistake. Anyhow I had a friend called Steve Sparks who was a Mod from East London and he was a photographer and a very influential person in my life. He came in one day and said, do you know how I can get in touch with Donovan? I said: Why? Because I want to kill him! Because Donovan had on his guitar 'This Machine Kills' and that was a rip off of what Woodie had written on his guitar which was 'This Machine Kills Fascists'. He said, yeah I am going to get a gun and kill him because he is ripping off Woodie Guthrie. Steve was not that into Woody Guthrie as such, his music was The Who. All these divisions between contemporary folkies, traditional folkies, mods, rockers was an invention.

He came into my flat one day and said: I have got something you have got to hear. So he put it on and it was 'Subterranean Homesick Blues'. I said that's Dylan, he said: Of course you know what it is based on? I said, No; because one of Steve's tasks in life was to broaden my musical horizons which he did all the time. He said, Chuck Berry. Well that pressed another button in my head because Chuck Berry and Bo Diddley were ripping off and commercialising the blues so I was not familiar with their work at all. It's Chuck's 'Too Much Monkey Business' so Steve being Steve, this was something I had to study up on and it changed my life. Rock'n'Roll became not a commercialised rip off, but as important to the music of the Sixties as say The Carter Family had been to the music of the Twenties and the Thirties and another illustration of the same phenomenon. All the musical compartments began breaking down to me, it is all popular music.

DIANA MATHEOU,
Les Cousins Club,
Soho

Soho was a very open the place, the girls were on the street, they were highly entertaining. There was such diversity, there were so many sorts of shops, lots of different people from all the way across Europe, loads of Italian and Greek families, this was before the Chinese families came in. It was exciting, vibrant, interesting and it was easy. And if you left one job you could always go and get another, and if you wanted to sing you could always make up for it by doing some cleaning or as often happened in the restaurant, Lucas would say if you peel some aubergines or do some washing up, I will feed you. He would help out a lot of people in that way.

FRANKIE LEIGH,
Personal Assistant

Later I became very friendly with Cat Stevens, and I used to go up to his mother's and father's restaurant just off New Oxford Street – it was a Greek restaurant. And downstairs was the restaurant, upstairs was the flat where they lived and he had a piano there and I used to go and hang out with him, and he used to sing to me and I was friendly with him for many years and I think in that time, you know it was so long ago that I can't remember but he landed up in the London Clinic and he was quite seriously ill. I'm sure it's marked down in history what he had but I remember going to the hospital and sitting with him, and he was really gravely ill you know, I didn't know whether we would lose him at one point.

MIKE HURST,
Record Producer

Bert Shallot sent me round this kid and this kid sat down and he played me another couple of songs, one being 'Here Comes My Baby'. And I said, phew, you're eighteen; he said yeah; I said, these are great, we'll do it. So we went into Pye studios, I made 'Here Comes My Baby', 'Smash Your Heart' and two others. Nothing. Bert Shallot couldn't get arrested with them; nothing. I had nothing; and I thought, I've got to go to America, I must go back to the States and I got a job at I think it was Vanguard Records; it was a semi-jazz label in San Francisco. They'd offered me the job as a staff producer. So my wife and I and the kids we were going to go, and a Saturday morning – I'd done everything, the green card, everything – and Saturday morning a couple of months before I was due to fly out with Marjorie, my wife, and everything else, the doorbell goes of the flat in London, which is Priory Road, which is near Abbey Road studios, and Steven Georgiou is standing there, who changed his name to Steven Adams, and he said he'd change his name again but he said it was a stupid name. I'm so confused now; he had three names. So I said, what's the current stupid name? Oh, he said, somebody called me Cat, so I've called myself Cat Stevens. I said – I really did, honestly – I said, that's a great name; don't lose it. So he said, are you still interested in me? I said, yeah.

He said, I've got this new song. So he plays me 'I Love My Dog'. And I listened and said, I really want to do that. He said, I've been to every record company in London; nobody wants to know. I said, well I do; I'll find some money; I don't have it but I'll find some money, we'll make the record. So I go into Decca, I go to Dick Rowe at Decca and say to Dick, I'm going to America – which was true – I said, I want to make one record myself, just as a parting gesture if you like, to the country of my birth. Not quite as theatrical as that. I said, can you give me some time. He looked at me and said yes, I'll give you three hours in number two at Decca, West Hampstead. I took Cat Stevens in there and I found a guy, an old friend of mine, Chris Brough, who was Peter Brough the ventriloquist's son. And Chris had put up the money for the musicians, and I had John Paul Jones, I had Andy White actually playing drums; and there were about twelve of them altogether, because I had one cello – I'd worked this out, I wanted a totally West Coast, off the wall, recording; really, I was so into that, like Left Banke 'Pretty Ballerina' stuff – I wanted one cello, one something else; I wanted a contra bass clarinet because Brian Wilson was using this sound, this horrible, wonderful growl so I wanted that. So I got an arranger in and said I want you to do this, I want it to sound like that; I do not want a drum beat through this record. And they all looked at me and said, you've got to have drums. I said no, all I want the drums to do is just snare and a hi-hat. I said, yeah, that's all I want it to do. So we go in the studios, Decca number two – a bit like going to America for me in 1962 – so there I am, this is 1966, I am in the studio with these musicians. We run through this arrangement; it sounded bloody awful. I was petrified; I thought, oh God; not only have I conned Decca Records, this is going to be such rubbish I'll die on my feet here. Second take, third take, fourth take; I'm starting to think, hmmm, it sounds quite good. We go on to six, and it sounded great to me; I loved it. So we made that. We're about ten minutes short of the three hours, and they were very strict on time, and I realised I hadn't got a B side so I said to Steve, what are we going to do, we've got nothing written; have you got anything? Oh yeah, he said, I've got this – I did it with Kim Fowley – I've got this 'Portobello Road' song. I said great, do it. Sat on a stool with his guitar, did 'Portobello Road'. I listened to it and thought, I love it; it's great.

Then I go back to Decca with an acetate, tell him the truth. Dick goes, you conned me. I said yeah, but you've got to listen to the record. Oh, he said, it's a disgrace that you can do something like that. I said, would you listen to the record? Puts the record on, listens to it, picks up the phone – doesn't say anything to me – put me through to Sir Edward's office. I thought, God, they're going to throw me out on my ear; I'm going to die here. Sir Edward Lewis, the Chairman of Decca, the legend of the record business, walks into the room, and Dick says, Sir Edward you want to listen to this and puts on 'I Love My Dog'; finishes. Sir Edward looks at me and absolutely – again, it's like Peter Sellers time – my boy, you're a genius! I sat there thinking, what? And he said, this record will be one of the records that launches our new label Deram. I said, blimey. And of course the pirates went nuts, Radio

London and Caroline, they played this. And it happened. It wasn't a huge hit – it was twenty-three or twenty-four in the charts – but it was enough because it was a very different record, and it hit people.

TONY HALL, Record Promoter

Cat Stevens was the second artist on the Deram label which I was very closely involved in. I had also at that time a very influential column in *Record Mirror*, called Hall Hears, and I used to get sent a lot of advanced copies of things in those days, including, *Revolver* by The Beatles. Then I got a bollocking from Sir Edward Lewis, who ran Decca and who owned *Record Mirror* – why was I publicising EMI artists, blah, blah, blah. Anyway, out of the blue in my mail came a record called 'Happy New Year' by an artist called Beverley, who I'd never heard of; and I just thought this was a terrific record. Anyway, eventually Deram, picked it up and it became their first release. But apparently it was a hoax, a joke played on me by a producer, Denny Cordell, who'd sent it to me. Beverley in fact turned out to be Beverley Martyn, married to John Martyn. Anyway, it became the first release on Deram. I thought it was a fantastic record, and we thought if we put it out in September – 'Happy New Year' it was called – people would maybe think it a bit quirkish, and quirky. But no, they didn't at all; again it didn't get any airplay. But it was a terrific record.

The second record was produced by Mike Hurst who was an ex-Springfield by the way. I thought he came up with some very innovative productions, and his first production 'I Love My Dog' was the first Cat Stevens single. But the secret of that record was the arrangement – a really off-kilter string arrangement, and I'm ashamed to say I've forgotten the guy's name but he was so talented and he did get a certain amount of recognition, and he did a lot of other records for Mike Hurst. Really talented guy.

DEREK NICOL,
Promoter

I'm trying to remember which record Cat Stevens had at the time, but it must have been earlier in his career and he was working with a ten or twelve-piece band at the time. It was in the days where you would do two shows in the same night but not in the same building, different venues. I remember we were in this venue; it was a Miners' Welfare venue, and the promoters there were basically 'the committee' and Cat Stevens took stage fright and refused to go on. We had a packed hall out there all waiting for Cat Stevens to come on and he wouldn't. I had to go to the committee men, and Big Mick, or whatever his name might have been, and say, I'm sorry, Cat Stevens can't go on. Oh, we'll see about that. So he went into the dressing room and said something like, I hear you're no going to go on laddie; or words to that effect. Eventually he did go on, and I believe that was the last performance of Cat Stevens before he disappeared. I'm not saying it was that particular event that caused that; it might have been a build-up and that could have been the last straw, or whatever.

JOHN COOPER,
Transatlantic Records

I'm going to see Pentangle who were musically one of the most fantastic bands, and although they are highly rated even now, they're underrated in terms of their real brilliance. They were playing the Colston Hall, Bristol, and as Transatlantic I was there and we took a very parental look at these people. Their manager was a guy called Jo Lustig who was this brash American, and I arrived to mumbling in the audience, went backstage. I could see the band sitting onstage, I could see the curtain closed,

I could hear mumbling going on, and I'm saying, what's going on? They're refusing to open the curtains. Who's refusing to open the curtains? The hall aren't going to open the curtains. Why? Because that guy there with the guitar is smoking. Yeah, they kind of do.

Well, they're not opening the curtains so I was trying to persuade Bert Jansch not to have a cigarette stuck in the end of his guitar because the rules said that you weren't allowed to smoke. And they were refusing to give way and the audience were getting more and more pissed off on the other side. I'm thinking, how does this work then? In the end I persuaded Bert that he should not smoke for a little while but maybe he could sneak one halfway through when it was too late, and that in fact is what happened. But that same evening, going to a club with them and Bert getting rather melancholy, which he did from time to time, and decided he didn't want to be with them and was going to leap over the balcony of this club.

The first time I ever worked with Anthea Joseph was actually when we were together at EMI, when she was Artists Relations there, but I'd come across her before at Transatlantic Records. The story is quite true that Dylan came over and slept on her floor and she kick-started his career; as she did Paul Simon's too. She was very much involved in the early days of their being. I mean, she was both the most strange and wonderful person. Strange in that she was an Amazonian figure in all sorts of ways; never sure of her sexuality but she seemed to enjoy whatever it was.

Ever since I knew her, she would start the morning with a heart-starter, and I mean any time of the morning, which was a double gin; that was it, simple, no debate. Breakfast was a double gin, end of story, no doubt that's what she died of in the end. Which is fine, she ended up her life doing... but she was just fantastic.

I used her as Artists Liaison once. I used to film Cambridge Folk Festival at one stage for Anglia Television, as it existed then; rather difficult thing to do using a non-music company to film an event like that, so I used Artists Liaison, and some of the artists were quite difficult, people like Queen Ida who was a zydeco player that we brought in for it, and she was a strange old American lady. Like a lot of them had only one idea in mind: if they were going to open their mouths, or in her case play the accordion and sing, she was going to have cash before she did, and Cambridge Folk Festival being Cambridge Folk Festival didn't understand that as a concept; nor for that matter did Anglia Television. So we had to use Anthea to kind of cajole her into allowing the cameras there, and I saw Artists Relations at its best. In the end she accompanied her onto the stage with her arm around her.

BRYAN MORRISON, Agent

The Pretty Things didn't go tour America however, about a month later if they'd listened to me they'd have had a number one record in America, because I found a song for them. Donovan was a great mate of mine who I was trying to manage; he was managed by Geoff Stephens I think and was publishing with Southern Music. But he was a mate of mine, and I said to him one day, I'm looking for a song for the Pretty Things. He said, I've got a great song; got his guitar out and sung a song and it went, 'Hey Pretty Tangerine Eyes, play a song for me, I'm so dadada, and I don't know where I'm going'. I could hear it, the guitar, 12-string; I said, that's the song; make a demo of it; go to Regent sound and make a demo. He said, yeah, alright. Next day I get a phone call from one of the publishers in Denmark Street, can you come and see me? I went to see him and he said, has Donovan played you a song? I said yeah, a great little song. And he said, have you ever heard of a fellow called Bob Dylan? I said no, who's he? He said he's an American folk singer. I said, so what? He said, listen to this and plays 'Hey Mr Tambourine Man, play a song for me'. Well I went fucking potty. I said, that's even better, that's the song – that is the song.

Now, the Pretty Things at this point had had a Top Ten record, and the Rolling Stones had had a Top Ten record. The Beatles were the clean boys, and the Stones and the Pretty Things were the long-haired gits. And I knew that the first one to a number one record, a major record, was the one that took over the world. Rushed back to the Pretty Things and I spent three weeks; and they wouldn't have it, it was crap. I said this is a giant song, do the cover. A month went by, a phone call from the publisher, went to see him, and he said Bryan, are your band doing that record? I said I'm trying. He said well, there's an American group that recorded it, but we can hold it because we'd rather the Pretty Things do it because they're already a band. I said, let me give it another try. Went back; two days later went back to him, I said no, you have to let the other band do it; what's their name by the way? He said The Byrds. It's a classic, a great, great song, and they didn't get it; they wouldn't have it. So their next record came out went to ten, and the Stones went to two or three.

MERVYN CONN, Promoter

The Beatles had two Press Officers, Tony Burrow and Derek Taylor, and I got friendly with both of them. As a matter of fact Tony did work for me on my first festival. But Derek Taylor left The Beatles and went to live in California. When I went to America on my very first trip, I went and met with Derek, because he was living in Los Angeles, and he said I want to take you and show you a group called The Byrds. They could have been called anything for all I knew. And we went to the Troubadour and saw this group. They were very good, and he said, I want you to take them to England. I said I can't take them to England, because it involved paying them a low fee, plus it was the airplane tickets, the hotel, the sound, the lighting; all the whole rigmarole that you have to do to put on a major production. And said, well I better have a word with Joe; so I phoned Joe the following morning in England and I told him; well he didn't know, they could have been called the Fairies for all he knew, or the Flowerpot Men. So I booked them, and of course by the time they got here they were number one with 'Mr Tambourine Man'.

TONY HALL,
Record Promoter

I mean The Byrds were absolutely amazing. I saw them once in LA, live, and I'd never heard anything like it. The first set was brilliant; second and third sets collapsed because the drugs had worn off, but the first set was amazing. And that was a trip in itself for me, because my first wife and I went over to stay with Phil Spector at his house, which was quite alarming. We arrived very late at night after a long trip and Phil sent one of his bodyguards in a clapped-out old Cadillac to meet us at LAX and took us back to his house, where he greeted us and then said, listen, I'll see you in a while. I don't think we saw him again for three or four days and there were so many rooms in his house, he used to hide from everybody there. It was very, very weird. And then he said, I'm going to take you on the town and show you LA, and we ended up, he took us to some dreadful fast-food place with garish lighting and oh, a nightmare. But I'd been heavily involved with Spector because again, I thought he was amazing. I thought his Wall of Sound was totally new, revolutionary, and I personally got involved with the promotion of all his records, all his acts; 'River Deep Mountain High' was especially important to me, because in America it had died at number 99, never got above 99. I said to Phil, listen, this is your best ever production; I'm going to get this to number one, and with the help of the pirate stations, thank God, I did.

MUFF WINWOOD, Musician

The first record I bought was I think Little Richard or something like that, an EP. Little Richard EP which I'd heard at the local boys' club because in those days you know you just went to boys' clubs, that was the only entertainment there was you know. You played football and you joined the football boys' club or the scouts and that was it. My younger brother Steve was already playing the piano and going to piano lessons. He started when he was about three or four and I was messing around playing a little bit, but my dad had found an old banjo in the shed and skiffle was going on and stuff like that and so I kind of got into a little skiffle group and then trad jazz came along and having a banjo was really useful, and so I was playing a banjo in these sort of trad jazz bands. And we used to again play all those boys' clubs and things like that. And then my brother joined in with me when he was about sixteen and just as his voice broke we were really into Ray Charles and all that kind of early rock'n'roll / rhythm & blues and as his child voice broke he moulded it into this wonderful kind of almost black sounding voice unconsciously really. So there he was, from a child you know, four weeks later when he had a man's voice, it sounded like Ray Charles; it was amazing.

Island Records when it starts there's four of us. Four or five, yeah. We started with Traffic. and then we signed – reasonably quickly – Jethro Tull through Terry Ellis and Free and Cat Stevens and, oh Fairport Convention who was brought in by their manager Joe Boyd, and those were the key early acts that really gave Island that feel and sound. 'Till about 1976 so I'd been there about seven or eight years. We'd struggled with Free, made a couple of albums with Free and we'd built them up on the road and they were doing very well on the road and they were a very well respected kind of blues band. Alexis Korner brought Free to us. And finally, on the third album, they cut 'All Right Now'. And the moment that we all heard it was like: Wow. This is a killer, killer record. So we made the record, and Muff, you know all those people up at the BBC, you take their record there and they're gonna love this.

169

I took the record up and the very first person I played it to said: We can't play this. And I said: Why? And he said: Listen to the words. It says on the second verse: We pay the fucking rent. And I said: Does it? He said: Yeah, listen. We played it back and 'we paid the fucking rent'. And I said: Oh my God, I didn't realise. So I went back and they said: No, here's the lyrics right. The second verse was about on the London street and at the time they'd just put in parking meters and what the verse was something about 'park your car and you pay the parking rate' but it sounded like 'you pay the fucking rent' but it was 'pay the parking rate'.

So emboldened I went back to the BBC and I said: Here's the words. I took them. Look, it's 'parking rate' right. They said: No, it's 'fucking rent'. So I went round every producer of all the Radio One shows and said: Listen to this record, it's fantastic. And they all said it: We can't play it, because it says 'fucking' in it. And I said: Honestly, here's the words. So I was walking out of Egton House which is where Radio One was, and coming from one of the end offices that I'd never ever been in before there was Miles Davis was blasting out and I'd had such a terrible day. I didn't know what I was gonna do. What was I gonna tell Chris? What was I gonna tell all the guys? The greatest record I'd ever heard and I can't get anybody to play it. So I wandered past this office and I kind of wandered in and I thought: I'll sit and listen to a bit of Miles Davis, that will calm me down. It was the office of the BBC Jazz Club, which ran on BBC Two or whatever it was. And the guy who was the producer of BBC Jazz Club was a guy called Teddy Warwick and he said: What's the matter with you? It looks as though somebody's died. And I said: I don't know what I'm gonna do. I said: I've got the best record I've ever had in my life and nobody will play it. I can't go back and tell them. I don't know what I'm gonna do. He said: Let's hear it. So the Miles Davis record came off the player and he stuck on 'All Right Now' and he said: It's unbelievable. It's fantastic. and I said: But what about the... He said: Leave it to me. Give me the lyrics, right, and just leave it to me, right. He said: I'll get this played for you. The rest is history right. Teddy Warwick who was head of jazz right, went round and battered all those guys in the pop end to play 'All Right Now' and the record became a monster hit. Those are the sort of things that happened on a daily basis that you didn't think meant anything at the time but were key moments.

PHILL BROWN, Studio Engineer

John Martyn, a remarkable guy, I love John very much, he was a good mate. He lived another village on. His kids, about three years older than mine, and they used to come babysit my kids. We really only worked on one proper album together, which was *One World*. Did other things from time to time, but that was the main album. It was done at Chris Blackwell's house near Theale, which is a big disused gravel pit, with the house almost in the middle of this. I'd been out there in '75/'76 with Robert Palmer. We used to take the mobile, go there, and do overdubs there. Mainly vocals. I was into doing vocals outdoors. We'd go and do that.

Then I think Chris, who saw what we were doing, liked some of the results. When he came to do John Martyn, it was particularly because of John Martyn's reputation and temperament, I think he thought the idea of John being at his house in Theale, with a recording studio, as it were, and a place to live, we knew where he was. It was a bit too far from London for him to go back after a session. There we could work at any time. I think it was started for perhaps those reasons, and then it just grew into recording outdoors.

A friend of mine, a guy called Hutch, who used to own a PA system, he was driving back to London from the West Country, and called in to see Blackwell on his way back. I know him, so we just got talking. He goes: I've got a great PA system in the truck. Do you want to borrow a PA system? It was like: Well, we're recording John. Well why don't I leave it here with you anyway? As soon as this was left, we went: Wow, we could set this up and blast it across the lake. It all just grew. It was not a big plan, but it turned out to be just stunning. We recorded at four o'clock in the morning, this track called 'Small Hours'. Basic drum machine in 1976, with John going through all his pedals. We were taking feeds from every pedal, so his guitar was probably on the eight channels or something. Then sending whatever he wanted of this to the PA system. It was just a great way to work.

John, he was adorable. I'd say I've seen all sides of John. He can be incredibly violent, or he could have been incredibly violent, incredibly rude, but was a sweetheart as well. Underneath, just this softest guy. How can anybody who wrote some of the songs he writes be a complete idiot? You know what I mean? He was pretty violent at times, depending on what he was on. Alcohol was probably his real demon. He dabbled in various things, but that was the one that, in a way, finished him off in the end as well. He went from somebody who was probably my kind of weight, and just got bigger, and bigger, and bigger. Not long before he died, he was like Orson Welles. Then he had a leg off. The last couple years of his life were horrific, really. A lovely guy, but vicious and dangerous. Could turn on a matchstick. I loved the guy.

I was always very good at, in a way, talking him down, or talking my way out of what might be next is a punch. You know what I mean? He never attacked me physically. He's fiddled around and toying with knives while he's talking to you in a pissed off way, but I've never ever thought that the guy was really a threat. Yeah, I loved working with him. He's really special. It's very sad. The first twenty years of his life, fantastic. The last twenty years, pretty hard. I saw him, he came into a Faithless session about fifteen years later. Sister Bliss from Faithless loves his voice, and said: John Martyn would be perfect in this. We phoned him up and he came in. He was on his best behaviour. He was looking good, before all the weight. He had one pint of beer, a toke on a joint, and did his bit. He was just Mr Charming. For him, the last twenty years of his life was a lot of regret, a lot of sadness. Unfortunately, also a lot of mad drinking and abuse.

DAVE COOPER,
Musician

I played keyboards in a seven-piece band called The Bunch in the Sixties, we were getting £60 or £80 per gig, going up on the A31 from the New Forest. We never made any money out of it but it was a great experience to meet everybody on the road, you used to meet them all there at the Blue Boar, the only motorway services, and we used to have three cups of tea between seven of us because we could not afford any more. You used to meet all the groups with their Ford Thames fifteen hundred-weight vans, we had an ambulance and we were known because it was a 1949 model and you had to double de-clutch it but it had a side door and you could get the females in. When all the gear went in we slept on mattresses on the top and we had a driver and a co-driver. When we left here they used to phone though to the next person, two rings on the phone to let them know you were on your way, I was the last, then four and a half hours up to London was a good run then, and set all the gear up ourselves.

We did the Flamingo and the Marquee a lot, we saw Pink Floyd in the early days when they had all these slides to project onto the walls. I said that band will never go anywhere, that is just a gimmick, they just want to make funny pictures on the back of the wall. The other one was, I thought what an idiot this bloke was playing his guitar with his teeth, what a prat – that's two I got hopelessly wrong.

In those days when a hit record was rising up the charts, they would get studio musicians to make a cover of it and they would put it out in Germany at or before the English release. At that time there was a song called 'Winchester Cathedral' by the New Vaudeville Band starting to creep up the charts. They had their session musicians' version and released it in Germany where it got to number four or five as John Smith and the New Sounds. Our agents needed someone with a brass section to do the TVs and they asked, would you be willing? So we learnt it and got to do the German equivalent of *Saturday Club*. We flew out all dishevelled and got met by Mercedes cars, wow this is the way to live, went to the studios, treated like royalty there because we had a record at number five. Driven around that night and the following night. Then of course flew back to Heathrow, zilch, no-one to meet us, but it was great to have your bit of glory there and the agents made some money.

£££

BRYAN MORRISON,
Agent

The year before Pink Floyd signed to me for agency they did twenty-two gigs I think it was, they did two hundred and thirty in the year they were with me; not necessarily the ones they would have liked to have done, and they would turn up at places that wanted to see the Ram Jam Band and they had Pink Floyd; or they'd turn up where people wanted to see who had been on *Ready Steady Go*, or whatever the pop show was at the time, and there's the Pink Floyd. But it taught them stagecraft. Then the split came with Syd, and Blackhill Enterprises who were the managers, decided they thought that Syd was the fountain of everything, and they wanted to manage Syd, so the boys came to me and said would I manage them? So I then became their manager. Steve O'Rourke and Tony Howard were two of my bookers and eventually, because I was just doing so much, I put Steve in charge. Steve was in charge of Pink Floyd and two or three other bands, Marc Bolan and two or three bands, etc., and latterly when I had my second ulcer and whatever, and I was advised to stop managing because it was killing me, Steve naturally took over and became their manager.

PETER WHITEHEAD, Film Maker

It was entirely due to Andrew Loog Oldham that I ever got into making any kind of film in those days, music promos and all that; it was entirely thanks to Andrew that I was dragged in to it. I had absolutely no intention, or no expectation really of getting involved with it. At the time I was working for Italian television, and Greek television here in London just as a newsreel cameraman; so that was my background. But then I did *Wholly Communion*, my first real film, and by a fluke it did very well. The event itself – the Beat poets at the Albert Hall, poetry incarnation, flower this, and goodness knows what else, and 7000 people turned up at the Albert Hall and 2000 were turned away and all this; and I just happened to be there with my camera, having gone to see Allen Ginsberg here, reading poetry, at Better Books.

Anyway, I made this film and it did very well and everyone was talking about it and the film went on and won the Gold Medal at Mannheim, so it in fact launched me, and it launched me into the same boat as Andrew Oldham and Tony Calder and an outfit called Immediate Records. I was in my flat in Soho; phone call, pick it up, and a voice says, this is Andrew Loog Oldham. I pause. Hi, this is Peter Lorrimer Whitehead. He says, great, you know who I am, of course? I said, well, I don't really; I know the name... made something up, because he was obviously very put out. He said, I am the manager of the Rolling Stones. I didn't want to say I wasn't quite sure who the Rolling Stones were either. Anyway, I said oh, that's very interesting. He said, I've heard you've just made this film, called *Wholly Communion*? I've heard you were filming and the camera was silent. Silent? Didn't make any noise? I said yeah, that's right. He said, you hold it on your shoulder? That's right. You don't need a tripod? I said, yeah. And he said, you made the whole film just like that? I said yeah, yeah. He said, I'd like to meet you actually and I'd like to talk about this; sounds very interesting. Can we meet? I'll send the car, shall I? What, now? That was how Andrew worked – Immediate Records.

175

Well I wasn't doing anything at the time; I said OK, fine, that's interesting. I gave him my address in the middle of Soho, very small street between Soho Square and Dean Street, and he said, yeah, I'll send my Cadillac. He had this massive big black Cadillac, with chauffeur. A *Sunset Boulevard* feeling about the whole thing actually. So he drives me to this office to Andrew Oldham. He was very friendly. I was sitting there in his office with his secretary – can't remember what her name was but she was with him for years and years; very nice clever female. So we chatted about the whole thing, then he had a little quick chat to his lady, then turned and said, how would you like to film the Rolling Stones? I hadn't by this time had a chance to answer the question which he hadn't asked, which was whether I liked the Rolling Stones, or believed in the Rolling Stones, or whatever. Like most people in London the only thing I knew about them was they got arrested for peeing in a garage, and that the saying was you don't allow your daughter to marry a Rolling Stone. That was literally the only thing that you knew about them if you were not into music. I was into music – I was into Bach, Rachmaninoff, Hayden; I had never, ever at that time listened to what one could call rock'n'roll or popular music, nothing. It wasn't my style.

This was a Monday or Tuesday. He said we're going to Ireland on Friday for two days. We've got a concert in Dublin and a concert in Belfast; just a two-day trip, and we thought it would be an interesting idea maybe to film it and I said I could just walk around and film. They said great, just what we want; what fun. It had never been done in England. I said Friday doesn't give me too much time. What do you have to do? I have to buy the film, get the tapes. So Friday morning I am told to be at his office, which is near Regents Park at eight am. It was a bit early for me; and I imagine for them. I arrive at the office at eight am and there's all these guys looking completely totally wrecked and Andrew introduces me to Mick Jagger. So I say, Hi Mick. Hi Man. And we all dragged downstairs into a bunch of cars and were driven off to Heathrow. Andrew didn't give any instructions; he said what do you want to film? I said I'll film the whole thing – arriving, going there, if there's any press thing, the concert, and so on. And I'd like to sit down and talk to them. Because by then, having said do you want to film the Rolling Stones, I had not told him I'd never listened to a Rolling Stones record ever in my life.

£££

BRYAN MORRISON, Manager

The A&R man was a guy called Jack Baverstock, an American, about forty-seven years-old I'd guess. Very languid speaker. And I got this message to go and see Jack Baverstock, not far from here, just in Hyde Park Place, Marble Arch. I went in to Jack Baverstock's office and he said, Bryan, I want to sign your band. He was American. I said, oh, great. And he got this contract, and I'm sitting over there, and he said, sign this. We didn't discuss the points, we didn't discuss advances – sign it; we didn't discuss anything. And do you know something, no lawyers, didn't look at the contract – I may have read it but there was no discussion because anything that was in it you signed or on your bike. Turned out it was three points, and that's how I signed the Pretty Things to Fontana. It was probably one of the first of a dozen deals where an artist got paid a royalty. Because I then met a couple of their artists there at the time, I met them in the tea room or whatever over the next few months, and they had all only got session fees for recording.

£££

GLORIA BRISTOW, PR, Philips Records

The A&R man at the Philips Record Company there who did the most in terms of success with groups was Jack Baverstock. He was the person most interested in those groups. He and I and someone else who worked closely with him on that label; on the Fontana label, came up here to Stoke-on-Trent and were the first people to see – I won't say discover because she was already very popular up here, and people on a local basis knew her – to find Kiki Dee. And we went back raving

177

about her but we said you know the only trouble is appearance-wise she leaves a lot to be desired and poor Kiki, I don't think she's ever forgiven me, 'cause in the end I was the person who had to sort of take her off to the dentist to get all her teeth done.

We were sent out like scouts for Philips to look for new talent and we... myself and the guy I was working with at that time in Philips, he was my on-the-road man actually, 'cause he did all the driving and I did drive, I was still driving at that point, but I didn't do the driving, he did all the driving; it was another John, can't remember his surname and we came up here for like forty-eight hours and our brief was: Stop anywhere where you think there might be something worth looking at and listening to and then head for Liverpool and see what you can dig out. And what we dug out were The Merseybeats and then of course we did Manchester and got Wayne Fontana. But that was all for Jack Baverstock.

DAVID SHRIMPTON, Production, Philips Records

In the Sixties I was looking after the production side for Philips, I don't mean the music production but the physical production of records. Making sure that they were all available by the release date, ordering enough to supply the demand but not too many whereby you had a warehouse full of stuff you could not get rid of. No computers, all we had was daily sales figures from our depots in the belief that if they started out with 152 in the morning and they ended up with 142 at the end of the day, they had probably sold 10. That was the only way that we could judge how many records had sold. If there was a delivery from the factory of 10,000 we would obviously take that into account and if we exported 1,000 to somewhere that would also be taken into account. It was just every single record arithmetically worked out in your head to produce these sales figures. We would have had the best part of a thousand titles at the time. With the slower selling items they would only do them monthly but all the hot ones like *West Side Story* and *My Fair Lady*, the Dusty albums and all the major singles that had recently been released were all done that way. There were also wholesalers around the country who would take chunks of maybe 1,000 at a time. Big hits like Dusty Springfield would sell hundreds of thousands of copies and I was involved with trying to work out how many records needed to be pressed and to do that each record needed labels and sleeves manufacturing in advance. No computers then, no print outs.

MIKE BERRY,
Musician

We did a gig at the Wimbledon Palais with Neil Christian and I remember it very clearly because they had a guy on drums Trevor Morais, Jimmy Page on lead guitar, Neil on vocals. I do remember Neil Christian introducing Jimmy Page as the best guitarist in the country if not the world at fifteen years old. It did not mean a light to me, I listened and thought he's not as good as our bloke. Initially we just travelled around in a Thames van which was freezing cold in the winter and roasting hot in the summer. The heater was a race, just a joke, so the old Thames van used to have the engine inside the van and the engine cover was in between the two front seats, you would just lift it off and there was the engine. So that was always warm and you sat on that, no safety belts so that was for three and then there would be one slung in the back, or two if it was The Outlaws. The lucky ones got the seats, Bobby Graham always drove for us so he got a seat, but if one of the band farted he stopped the van and got out so you could breathe. Chas Hodges was very guilty of that, he used to nearly kill us, and in the middle of winter it ain't a lot of laughs. I remember we had this old Thames van, white it was, and then we had an old sofa put in the back, a two-seater couch or something. You would sleep in the back as well and if you were unlucky enough you slept in the back with Chas and he would rest his worn out cowboy boot in your mouth occasionally. He was all arms and legs Chas, very gangly, he would throw his legs about while still asleep. It was not the lap of luxury we would all know about later when the luxury became a minibus with all seats and the gear in the back. We would drive from London to Scotland in the middle of winter with ice ruts in the road. It was like driving down a rocky mountain pass, there was no salt or snow ploughs. As soon as you got past Watford the snow would start to come and as soon as you got to Scotland the snow was appalling and the tyres on the vans were mostly remoulds and they were threadbare, you literally had the canvas coming through, there would be no tread on the tyre. You kept going until you had a puncture and when you did you stopped the van jacked it up and put the spare on or you repaired it in the middle of the road.

NEIL CHRISTIAN, Musician

The 2I's Coffee Bar, yeah. At the time when I started driving around at the beginning, the 2I's Coffee Bar was breaking big. Everybody was there on a weekend. That was it. We used to go down there. Get down there about midday and stay there all day, till the evening. It was really a fantastic place. You'd see everybody. Everybody would accumulate there, even if it was just for fifteen minutes. All the big stars of the day, like Adam Faith, Marty Wilde, remember Vince Taylor, he was a good friend of mine. He lived and died there. It was fabulous. It looked like a very small coffee bar from the outside, very small. Well it was very small. I mean, that was it, that's all it was. Tom Littlewood, who used to run it, had an idea, and he opened up the basement, which was even smaller than the upstairs. He used to put a group in, a trio, at one end. He used to charge people half a crown to go down and watch. I'm not kidding, you couldn't have got anybody more down there if you wanted to. It used to be steaming down there. There used to be queues outside, just for them to pay their half a crown to see something down at the 21's. No one could hear anything or anybody, because it was so condensed. You know what I mean? You couldn't hear anybody singing.

I remember one day, I was standing outside at about one o'clock talking to Taylor, Vince, that is, and all of a sudden, a big open truck pulled up. It was Billy Fury on the back, and a couple of others. The guy said: Got a bass player in the crowd there? The guy said: Yeah. On he gets, and up he went, plays the Kingston Granada. You know what I mean? It was fabulous. These sort of things went on all the time. Yeah, that was the 21's all right, Tom Littlewood days. Fabulous.

BIG JIM SULLIVAN, Musician

On the road what they used to do, they used to get these big packets of flour and put them in little packets so they could throw them. And they used to go past people and hurl these packets; they'd burst and they'd be covered in flour. There's one particular thing I remember; Chas Hodges was with them, out of Chas and Dave – there's Ritchie Blackmore and Chas, whoever else was in the band at the time, and they were going up North somewhere; they passed through this little town and there was this guy up this ladder painting his name on the front of the shop. So as they went passed they pelted him with these flour balls, and of course it got all over the paint and everywhere. They got the police out, the police chased them, fortunately didn't catch them, but on the way back they passed through the same village and who should be up the ladder? The same guy, painting over, and they got him again. The police did get them this time. Once the guy found out who it was, didn't bring any charges, but they could have got done for that. Yeah, they were hooligans; they were definitely on-the-road hooligans.

CHAS HODGES,
Musician

Me mum come home one day from shopping and she said, they have a sign in the sweet shop round the corner that the Horse Shoe Skiffle Group over the road, want a guitar player and a banjo player. She said, go and audition for it. I said I can't, they are all experienced musicians. You go and audition for it, she said. I went and found I was the best guitarist in the band, they were just mad on what I was playing, I had learnt from Lonnie Donegan and I was much better than I thought I was. I remember I just floated home on a cloud. The first or second gig was the hall over the top of the Britannia Pub in Edmonton. I remember just having the fantastic night of me life and then at the end of it someone came up and plonked ten shillings in me hand, like a ten bob note. What's that for? It's for tonight's show. I could not believe it, and I thought this is the life for me, enjoying meself and getting paid for it.

In 1959 there was a place called the Kings Head in Edmonton which every Friday night they had a different band on and I just used to go up there and whoever was playing I'd sit in with. Eventually there evolved a band I was asked to join called Billy Gray & The Stormers. I used to play an electric guitar with the notes tuned down to sound like a bass and it sort of sounded quite good so someone said why don't you get a real bass? I bought a bass guitar in 1959 and I was the first one in North London to have one. I was just so much in demand, nobody else had a bass in all those bands that played down there and I was like working, well not working, playing seven nights a week and earning a fortune in those days. I had a job, me one and only proper job I had, which was mending clocks in a jewellers shop, which I quite liked but I did not like the idea of getting up in the morning. Of course playing all these gigs I was turning up later and later. In the end I got the sack and we went to Butlins Filey as Billy Gray & The Stormers that season 1960. At the end of 1960 the band virtually split up, a couple of them got married and I got a knock on me front door about November time and this chap said, I have got a singer Mike Berry and I have just auditioned with him up at Joe Meek's. I didn't know who Joe Meek was then. He said he loves Mike Berry but he doesn't like the band, could you get your band back together? I said yeah, I'm up for it. He went round everybody's house 'cause I don't think anybody was on the phone in those days. We auditioned up at Joe Meek's, we passed the audition and we became Joe Meek's house band.

Joe was alright, very quietly spoken unless he lost his temper which he did for sort of unknown reasons at times. He named us The Outlaws and we were on the road all the time, a couple of gigs a week. Loads of gigs, good gigs in and around London in those days, also doing sessions up at Joe Meek's so I was doing alright money-wise. I had a little amp that I used to practise with indoors before I went on stage, I'd put records on and play along to them, all the kids used to stand round outside 'cause it had a great sound in your front room. This little amp and the bass. Come the day I remember I was going to do a gig at the Kings Head, not a vast big ballroom but it was pretty big. I remember plugging this in and it was like rattling and farting, it couldn't cope with it. I thought it sounds alright in me front room, I've gotta get a different amp. So I ended up buying a fantastic amplifier. I'd seen Cliff Richard and the Shadows with Jet Harris about six months before that at Walthamstow Granada and he had this great big solid bass amp that Wallace had made for him in Soho Street. It was a great, great sound but you could not carry it on your own, needed three people. He sold it to Johnny Rogers out of The Hunters and I bought it off him before I went to Butlins. £20 it cost me for the lot and it really was a good sound.

The Outlaws were auditioning for a guitar player and they could not find one. I said to Joe, we can't find a guitar player, everyone we audition I can play better than them. So why don't I go on guitar and we can audition for a bass player? Great Idea. I know a bass player he said, I know a lovely bass player. I said what is he like? Oh he is tall blond. I went: No, what does he play like, you know what I mean. It was Heinz. When he come down I just was not mad on him, I did not like his attitude, and he was not all that on the bass so I took the easy way out and instead of sacking him or saying I did not want him, 'cause I knew by then Joe was in love with him, I said I don't think I am up for playing the guitar really, I want to go back on the bass. OK well I am going to form another band around Heinz. Fair enough. With that we had an ad in the paper, the *Melody Maker*, for a guitar player and a drummer at the time and someone rung me up and see Clem Cattini and Alan Cady, who were ex-Johnny Kidd & The Pirates, are going to audition. So I rung up Joe and said I know them. He said: No, I am having them for my new band I am forming round Heinz. To this day Clem says I went up to audition for The Outlaws and I was choked when he said, no we want you in The Tornadoes, who? That was Joe, it was our ad that we paid for.

BOB HENRITT,
Musician

I had been to school with Unit 4+2 and I got a phone call from them asking me to do a session. They said come and listen to this and it was 'Concrete and Clay', we went to Nova Studios behind Marble Arch and as I recall Tommy Steele's drummer mixed it. It was supposed to be like The Drifters tempo but we played it differently. The guy who wrote it was a friend of mine and he was disappointed until the cheques started coming in. We got £5/15/6d that was session money.

One of the others that I did not play on was when I got a phone call, when we were knee deep in the Roulettes, Adam Faith's band.

We were working in Wimbledon Theatre doing a week in Variety. This American voice said, what are you doing on Friday? Why? Well we have got a session for you. Great. Where? IBC. OK what time? Usual time in the morning. So I said, Great, see you there. I had no idea what it was. He did not tell me what it was and it did not really enter into it.

Like a fool I said to Adam Faith, oh I have got a session on Friday. I don't know why because I did not have to say a thing. He said, you cannot do it. I said, Why, it is in the morning? He said, you might be late for the gig. I said, I won't Tel. He said, well you cannot do it, that is why you get a retainer. I could see the writing on the wall, so I had to phone the American voice back who turned out to be Shel Talmy who produced The Kinks and that was the session for 'You Really Got Me'. So Bobby Graham played on 'You Really Got Me' and I didn't. Years later when I joined the band, I didn't know that Dave knew this story and he said, you know what, if you had done the session you would have got the gig and you would have hated me twenty years earlier than you did.

DEL ROLL, Musician

I left school at fifteen and at sixteen went to work in a drum shop in Footes in the West End which was real education for a couple of years. It was the start of the golden era of the Sixties, we constantly had bands coming in with their Commers, Ford Thames vans, suddenly you would get Billy J Kramer coming in with their stage clothes on a lot of the time because they had come from *Top Of The Pops* on their way to a gig. There was a band called Nero & The Gladiators that came in and they were in their full regalia except for their Trojan helmets, it was ridiculous, to buy a pair of sticks and maybe a plectrum. I was curious about them and I went back upstairs to see their van and it was an old Commer or something and in the middle they had a paraffin heater. In the van they took turns to hold the paraffin heater upright when they went round corners, it always stuck in my mind. Anyway it was a good education, the band I was in ended up backing a couple of girl singers one of whom was called Jenny Scott in them days and her boyfriend was Barrie Marshall who became the promoter with Marshall Arts and went on to marry Jenny. He became our manager, do you want to go on the road with our band, yes of course it is better than working, so Friday the 30th July 1965 we all left our day jobs, I got on my motorbike and went to Catford and that was us turning professional. The night before funnily enough was Tom Jones and the Squires in this dodgy pub in Catford. We woke up Saturday morning, said goodbye to our mums and dads, who all gave us a suitcase full of food because they had heard bad stories and we drove up to Harwich and they actually craned our van onto the ferry, Hook of Holland and drove up to Essen to the Star Club. As you know the Star Club was in Hamburg primarily but they had a little chain of them. I was nineteen and a couple of the band had to go and get passports as they had never been abroad before.

BIG JIM SULLIVAN, Musician

I used to get on well with Joe Meek. There weren't too many guitar players that could play up to my standard at that time, so consequently I used to get in with Joe. We did all Michael Cox's stuff up there, with Joe Meek and I did things with all the other artists that Joe had. The Wildcats just used to go up there and record tracks, and the next thing you hear is the voice on the track and that was released under the auspices of Joe Meek. When Tom Jones first came in the studio he wasn't Tom Jones. As it happens I do remember the early stuff with Tom; I do remember him coming in with his winkle picker shoes and his big nose, and the way he could sing. There was very few people could sing like that. So he stuck out in particular, he recorded a couple of things with Joe. We used to actually just go up to Joe's place for a cup of tea. But we'd have our Bedford Dormobile out the front with all the gear in it, and there weren't any yellow lines at that time so we parked outside the studio.

The Bedford Dormobile was quite good. Brian did all the driving; then we got another guy, a roadie, called Hal Carter. He used to drive us about, sitting there in his sweatshirt and his braces; big old steaming Hal. They tried to kind of put the gigs into some kind of order. There was a cinema circuit called the Star Cinemas, and they were all over the North especially, and what they couldn't do, because some of the towns were near each other, they couldn't put us in this town here at the Star Cinema and then four miles away, and so-and-so, because they couldn't get the crowds; so they put us here, and they'd put us up in Liverpool, and then they'd put us back down in Birmingham. So there was always miles and miles to travel, every day, with all the gear, and Hal driving. I was lucky, being a big fella I always had the left seat. There was one night we were in Wales, had to find this club, where Marty was making an appearance. And you know what the fog was like then, we got caught in this fog and we drove and we drove and we thought we were on the right road, and this road became narrower and narrower; and I thought, where the hell are we? We stopped and got out of the car, and walked about ten feet in front and there was a sheer drop of 200 feet – we'd driven to the top of a coal slag in this mining village. If we hadn't of stopped we'd have gone; that would have been it.

DEL ROLL,
Musician

The sax player who owned the name The Riot Squad was looking for a new band and we were perfect and we got a few gigs. He came in one day and said we had got an audition with Joe Meek, he's looking for a new band, well we had all been in studios a few times but not above a ladies handbag shop in Holloway Road. It was an interesting era, I am sure we made seven records with him that were flops, but we got good exposure with him, Radio London, Radio Caroline, it got us a lot of work. At times it was fine and at times it was painful, you never knew which side of the bed he had got out of, but it opened a lot of doors, got us a lot of gigs. I do remember once we opened the door to the studio, it was a separate door to the shop, and a bass drum came rolling down the stairs, Joe had kicked the drum downstairs as he had had enough of whoever was playing there. Sadly we were on our way to a gig when we saw one of the newspaper placards, *Evening Standard* or something saying that Joe had killed himself, that is how we knew about it, which frankly kind of signalled the end of the Riot Squad as it was then.

We plodded on as a six piece and then split three and three, I stayed with Bob the sax player who had the name to the band so we started running auditions and had quite a few musicians. Ultimately Bob said, David Bowie is looking for a band because he wants to create more, he wants a band that is pliable, which we were. By now we had a massive coach with beds in it, well it seemed massive at the time, so David came along, smashing bloke, and he had these great ideas which included wearing make-up at one point, to be the first when flower power was coming in. We did rehearsals and we had gigs already booked. I am sure our first show was Basildon youth club, we did not really have enough numbers, but we did numbers we already knew and David just sang along. We had lots of great experiences and he taught us a lot, obviously he slept in the van with us guys, that was our hotel on wheels. It was always a done deal that he would move on, we got another singer and then we got an audition for *Opportunity Knocks*. We drove overnight from a gig in somewhere like Scarborough to the Odeon in the Kings Road, London, where you went upstairs into this ballroom. Hughie Green was there with his producers and there were ballroom dancers and jugglers everywhere. We got through our audition and they said, you've got three minutes. In that three minutes we wanted to get across to the audience a) we were the first band to wear makeup on telly, b) we had a new single coming out, c) we were a comedy band, d) we also did some soul music. All those four into three minutes, well it was always filmed in Manchester on a Saturday afternoon when if you were under fifty you were either at Old Trafford or Maine Road. So therefore all the audience was over sixty and when the curtains opened and they saw six monsters with makeup on, there was a gasp that you could hear on broadcast. We came last on the clapometer.

BOB SOLLY,
Musician, Songwriter

Davey Jones/Bowie wasn't the first to leave the Riot Squad, but we just couldn't sustain anything, first of all because we couldn't afford a new van. Equipment was all on HP, so we had to work to pay the HP, and of course if you don't have a van you can't work. So Wolf I think it was, our baritone player, he said, I'm going to get a job, that's it. So he went off and got a job, and then one of the others said the same thing and he went off, got a job, and Davey was way down the line really. So the band breaks up; I'd already started writing songs with Shel Talmy, so that's what I carried on doing for quite some time, writing songs. He was starting to record some of the things I'd written with my song writing partner Paul Rodriguez who was also a member of the band. We could both read and write music which was fortunate, so we were a good partnership. We'd demo, and then we gradually got more publishers.

We had Leeds Music, Flamingo Music, Carlin I think it was; all these different music publishers. Sometimes we had four or five different music publishers and we had to produce two songs a week for all of them, which is pretty good going. So I would go up on a Tuesday to Central Sound or Regent Sound with my guitar and make the acetates, one side of the acetate, of each song, and come back home, do the top line, and on the Thursday we'd go round all the publishers and we'd have a package with a sheet of music with the top line and the lyric and this acetate inside. The secretary in these places would just go under the desk and give us a little wage packet every week. So we did the rounds every week and we got a little wage packet. It was OK; didn't earn a lot of money, and you more or less gave away the copyright; by accepting the wage packet you gave away the copyright of the song, but who cares, you were earning enough money to go on.

Every song was contracted, so if I took two songs to Shel I would have a contract for each song; we'd be assigned a contract for each song. But we didn't have a blanket contract at all, but they expected you to write two songs a week, or within ten days. So what I used to do of course, if I'd taken Shel maybe a couple of ballads, and I'd taken Leeds Music a couple of fast numbers, I'd sort of swap them around the following week, change the lyrics and just dolly them up a bit differently, because it was like a production line. You had to alternate them like that. But it was good fun and no-one was too fussy in those days.

CLIVE SELWOOD,
Dandelion Records

At some point during this period while I was at Elektra, I was managing John Peel and John had this great reputation for finding new artists and sponsoring new artists. I said to John at some point, you are doing this for record companies, why don't you do this for us, you find the artists and I will raise the finance and run the company so that is what we did and we started Dandelion Records. John had his ear very much to the ground and he was told about this Australian band Python Lee Jackson who were playing at somewhere like the Ad Lib. He went to see them and was very impressed because the lead guitarist Mick Liber actually played until his fingers bled which in Peel's eyes was commitment. So we decided to record them, they had three songs at the time and we took them into a cheap studio in Wimbledon and they were terrific. But it was a mono studio and we had to have a better recording, so I booked them into CBS studios as we had a deal there, and they just got drunk and fell apart. We took them back to Wimbledon and they played again superbly, back to CBS again and they played very well indeed but the leader of the group, the keyboard player and the singer got very, very drunk, so drunk he was falling off his seat. We had no vocals so the manager of the band who was by trade I think, something like a scrap metal merchant, he said I know this bloke who has just got free of a deal and I could have him here in ten or fifteen minutes if you will give him a session fee and pay his cab fare. I said, for sure yeah.

So Rod Stewart turned up and he mastered the vocals in seconds, it was quite a remarkable performance, he put down three vocals, maybe two takes of each, maybe only one. Magnificent. At the end of the session the manager said, instead of a session fee is there anything you need for your car? Rod said something like I have got an old Armstrong Siddeley and I need a new differential for it. The guy said come round to my yard tomorrow and I give you a differential for your car. Part of the deal was that we were not allowed to use Rod Stewart's name, we released it twice, sold about three hundred copies the first time. The record was turned down by Elektra who were distributing Dandelion in America and by CBS who were distributing us in England at the time. They both of them said blues is passé, there is no future in blues. So I eventually leased it to Miki Dallon who released it and sold about 300 copies, I persuaded him to release it again and it sold a hundred and ninety copies and in the meantime Rod had signed with Mercury and released 'Maggie May' so we released it a third time and it sold about three or four hundred thousand copies, same record, no different. The amusing thing about that was that having been successful here Miki Dallon and his partner toured America trying to place the record and they went to Mercury

Records in America who then had a number one record in America with 'Maggie May' and they played him the record and he said I know that voice, I know that voice, play it again, got it: Johnny Ray. He is probably still there as head of A&R.

ALEX BROWN,
Fan

They had had a lot of bother with Rock 'n 'Roll concerts in the past you see, fights, Dundee was a rough place it was like Glasgow, always fights. Security had got their brains together and made some kind of system for this happening. Well sure enough it did, on the night Gene Vincent came out, did his thing, fantastic, brilliant. Eddie Cochran came out, he got about one and a half songs in and up it went, the local neds were waiting. Bang, Thud, have some of that, rearranging the furniture. So everybody was locked in, it was a lockdown as far as the stage was concerned and backstage. So I had been ready for it as well because I had seen all the carry-on, so I stood near there knowing that it was going to be a quick exit. I didna know I was going to be locked in. So I was backstage with them, fine, we all finished up in this dressing room. So here I am with Eddie Cochran and Gene Vincent and a couple of the guys, you know. It is hard when you are in these situations, when you are Joe Public, and all of a sudden you are touching these people. You go, this is fantastic, you are trying to re-adjust, twenty you know. Look at them, that's Eddie Cochran you know, 'Twenty Flight Rock', it's on the juke box just up the road. I tried to speak to Gene Vincent but he was a very withdrawn man, very withdrawn, I wasna too partial to him. Eddie Cochran was different, he was very gregarious you know, nice man, really nice guy. Only twenty-one, a year older than me. So he was sitting there and I was sitting on the arm of the chair yattering away like hell. Don't ask me what I asked or what we spoke about, don't know. It didna matter, we were just holding a nice conversation and I was excited, the adrenaline was flying. The time came when they had to abandon the show because they were still knocking hell out of each other. There was a big labyrinth of corridors underneath this hall, so we all get led out into this garage in one of the side streets and the time came for those guys to get in the limo and just as he was going he says, well Alex I thoroughly enjoyed the conversation. Good Luck Eddie, I said, it has been fantastic meeting you and away he went. It was just about six weeks later that he was killed.

JOHN LECKIE,
Fan

My mate's sister was going out with someone in the Quiet Five and they were playing this pub in Peckham, the Perseverance in Peckham, and, yeah, let's go over to this pub. I would have been, what, thirteen. Still had pints; well, half-pints I suppose, but yeah, thirteen. Then I saw The Yardbirds at the Marquee with Eric Clapton on my fifteenth birthday, which was in 1964, October 23rd, I went to see The Yardbirds, because we'd just bought the album *Five Live Yardbirds*. And then I forever went to gigs at Klooks Kleek in Hampstead on a Tuesday and Thursday night. We followed John Mayall with Eric Clapton anywhere where we could go around London. My mate would borrow his dad's car and anywhere like Edmonton, Cooks' Ferry, Burton's in Uxbridge; Klooks Kleek was our regular Tuesday night and Thursday night haunts. So there we would have seen John Mayall, Eric Clapton, Graham Bond Organisation, who was the best band I've ever seen I think, which was with Jack Bruce and Ginger Baker, Dick Heckstall-Smith and Graham Bond. We saw all sorts of bands. For instance, Tuesday night was 7/6d, which was for John Mayall and the Nice, Family, and Thursday night was cheap; I think it was like, 3/6d to get in, and they were the second-rate bands, which was like Mark Leeman Five, Chicken Shack with Christine Perfect, Christine McVie playing, and this shit band called Ten Years After and this guy used to play so fast. And of course *Woodstock* came out and we went to see the film and we went, bloody hell, there's that band that plays at Klooks Kleek you know, Ten Years After, with the red guitar. Klooks Kleek was our sort of meeting point really, for bands and stuff and the Marquee and Tiles down in Oxford Street; as I say, anywhere which was within driving distance of London, we'd be there.

Saw the second Cream gig, and saw Hendrix at the Roundhouse on a Wednesday night, which would have been in 1965 I think, November '65, it might have been '66, I need to get my dates right. 1966, 1967. It was great because I went back to the Roundhouse and I always remember it was a Wednesday night and I was still at school and it was like 2/6d to get in and when I went to the Roundhouse recently after it's all been done up there's some posters of old Roundhouse gigs, and there's the poster for the Hendrix gig on the Wednesday night that I went. It was freezing cold, there were no lights, and we used to wear big army overcoats and you needed it then. And it was really loud and reverb-y. It was funny about the WEM PA stuff, because my memory of gigs in those days was they were deafening. You'd go to school the next day and your ears were still ringing. You never get that now. I don't know whether it's health and safety, but I don't think I've been to any loud gigs since 1972 or something; the last time I was overcome with volume at a gig. But yeah, all those gigs were full on.

PAUL KING,
Social Secretary

I went to Eel Pie Island probably about half a dozen times, the great thing about Eel Pie was is it had a stage at each end. The reason that was great was it cut down the time between bands 'cause we went for the music we did not go just to hang out with our mates, we could do that at anytime, so we wanted to see as much music as we could in as short a space of time as possible, so the great thing about Eel Pie was the change-over time was a maximum of five or ten minutes. The two I remember seeing there most often were Stray and the Groundhogs and I managed to put both of those bands on at university subsequently, just for old times sake as much as anything. After that it was Wishbone Ash, Blodwyn Pig, Pink Fairies, Hawkwind, Edgar Broughton. This was around 1969 and '71, it was just when the flowery powery thing was coming through and the hippie bands were starting to make some kind of impact. Prior to that the guitar was king, very much. We used to go to gigs on the bus and buy records, that was all we did. The record that made the most impact on me ever and probably in my view at the time, the best money I ever spent was the first Led Zeppelin album. Having said that, when the second and the third albums came out they were an even greater joy as the band had done quite a bit on the packaging. That was the best money we ever spent, it absolutely was, you just had to have those records.

The best gig I ever, ever went to, and it is a million miles from anything I ever went to since, and I think it was 1971 and it was The Who at the Lyceum and I was right at the front. It was the most staggering thing I have ever seen, it was just wild, and nothing has ever got near it. There has never been another drummer like Keith Moon he was a star.

JONATHAN KING,
Record Producer

Clem Cattini said to me: Do you know, Jonathan, amongst all us session musicians, you were the greatest ever British record producer? Well, a) I almost had a heart attack, and then b) when I picked myself off the floor and wiped the Thai meal from my being, said: Clem, that's terribly sweet of you and I really appreciate it, but I have to tell you, that as someone who worked with Joe Meek, you're talking bollocks. I wish I had been the best record producer in Britain. Not only was I not the best, I was probably not in the top five. I would have been pushed to have made the Top Ten, in my opinion, but I did have a wonderful time with sessions. I then said to Clem: What makes you say that? He said: Because everybody loved doing your sessions. That was true, because about a year earlier, I had lunch with Clare Torry, who had said to me that everybody liked my sessions more than anything else. They were the most fun, without any doubt. Certainly, they were very different from a lot of people, like Joe Meek, who was, to me, far and away the greatest British record producer of all time, and he's up there, to me, with Phil Spector as probably the two greatest record producers of all time. I was lucky enough to be produced by Joe on a session, once, earlier on. Never saw the light of day. I do have the tapes of it, because somebody found them in a skip and sent them to me, a taxi driver. He was very, very odd indeed. Clem used to go: Oh my God, they were a nightmare. I'm sure sessions with someone like Joe were a nightmare, although I thought they were absolutely brilliant. I thoroughly enjoyed my session with Joe Meek, mainly because he was so brilliant at it – although the record was crap, by the way, but it's more my fault than his.

Clem was very sweet, and I'm sure my sessions were absolutely fun for them all. I used to work with all the best musicians, and singers, and everyone else. I used to go in with the entire track in my head. I knew how the tracks would sound. Originally, my first arranger was Arthur Greenslade, who was fantastic, who did my arrangements for my Hedgehoppers Anonymous tracks 'It's Good News Week', and a few others in those early days. I can't read or write a note of music, but I used to know what I wanted everyone to do. I'd get an arranger round, and I'd then play him my – which was me on the guitar, and I could only play three chords on the guitar very badly – I'd play him my demo of the song, and I'd say: Right, this is the song. I then go through how it was from start till finish. I'd say: The bass goes dum, dum, dum, dum, dum, dum, dum, dum, dum, and he'd write them down and all that. Then he'd go off and knit it all together into something that was vaguely right.

Clem said: I can tell you myself why I loved your sessions. Because you were so mad, but so different. He said: You used to let me set up my drum kit every time, which I did. Then you'd come down and say very politely: Clem, do you mind – I'd say: No, Jonathan, that's fine by me – if I take away the tin things? I'd then remove the hi-hat, the cymbal, all the tin things and put them somewhere else in the studio very carefully, because you know what drummers are like. I'd leave him there with his empty kit, and Clem would look at me. He said: It was so brilliant, because I knew – and this is why I did it, drummers can be very lazy with their right hand, or whatever, and can easily just use it going ch-ch-ch-ch-ch-ch. I hated that sound. It always interfered with everything else I was doing on my records – the string parts, the brass line. I didn't want something going ch-ch-ch-ch-ch-ch. Plus, if I freed up that hand, his fills, and everything else, would get much more inventive and clever. That's what I used to get. I used to get some great fills of the toms and the snare, brrr, and all this going on. Clem said it really used to amuse him.

My sessions all started at nine o'clock with my rhythm section, all the usual session people on it, and they were fucking brilliant, my session people. That was the rhythm section. We'd lay that down. Four tracks I did always between nine and twelve. Then at twelve, in would come the strings or the sweeteners. The strings and the brass twelve to three. Then in from three to six would come the backing vocals, and all the rest of it. Then at six o'clock, I'd put my vocals on, or my artists', or whatever, six to nine. Then from nine o'clock, I'd mix all the way through till we finished, usually at about six in the morning. I'd go home with four master tapes. That was how I always did it.

ALEX BROWN, Songwriter

If you have a good song, I mean you cannot make a good song out of a bad song you know, but if you have a good song and you start to record it and it builds up into something wonderful that is great. So we were doing this and I thought it was great. I was in the house this day and my brother was down on holiday and I had just written this song and he said, Alex that would do Roy Orbison. I thought, yeah, and I was singing anyway and I could sing in Orbison's range. I said, that's a good idea David. Fortuitously he was on at Talk Of The Town that month so I said let's push it to him. We were all, great, yeah, so we met at Leicester Square, my writing partner Pat, the recording engineer and our manager and I was humping this recorder round. So we were trying to get a strategy on how to see Roy Orbison. It was just exciting, it really was exciting to do these things. We could not decide on anything, we were Joe Nobody on the street. We went the obvious route to the stage door. Can we see Mr Orbison please? That was the first line and we got the bums rush. So we sat in a wee restaurant, the ifs, the buts, the maybes, the what-could-have-beens. So this girl, she intervened, I don't mean to be nosey, she said, but I could not help overhearing you talking, are you trying to get a song to Roy Orbison. I said, yeah. She said, well I am one of the dancers in the show, if you like I will go and ask him. Thank you very much, fantastic! So away she went, Maive that was her name. She went away and came back saying, he wants to see you.

Right OK, off we went past the Stage Door Keeper, we went up opened the door and there was Big O sitting there, one of my heroes, a huge star. Very unassuming man sitting there smoking away, he says I believe you have a song for me. Well for Roy Orbison to say that, phew. I was ready I had a plug on the machine, took a bulb out and stuck it in. To sit there watching Roy Orbison listening to you singing your song – that was great. To his great credit and the gentleman he was, and the songwriter that he was, he listened to the very end, the very end. Lesser mortals did not listen to four bars. I think he knew how it felt, I honestly do, he could relate to the song writer who hadna made it yet. He gets up and he says, I like that, I LIKE that. Leave the song with me. I was glad I had about four sets of lyrics, copies, I got him to sign one of the copies, that is my testament that it actually happened, see. We came away, well if we thought we were charged up before, we could have started tractors with the way we were feeling. Then the girl came down to join us again, we had left her there, and she said he is going potty up there, potty, says he is on about going into the studio first thing in the morning, I am going to record this, I want to work on the song and record it.

The next day it was back to 'normality'. Did not hear anything for a fortnight, got on the tube, opened up the *Evening News*, the headline was 'Roy Orbison's Sons Killed In A Fire', he has been sedated and shipped off to the States. It was like losing the lottery ticket you had got for the first time, I was going to have been in the premier league of the song writing world, that is what it would have done. Then reality kicked in, look at Roy Orbison, life does not spare anybody no matter who they are, he has just lost two kids, shut it.

DAVE AMBROSE,
Music Publisher

I was at KPM when it was a very active publishing company and it was bought out at the same time that EMI took over Francis, Day & Hunter, the great Ronnie Beck was there, he signed Queen. He was a bit of a hero for me the man who signed Queen, I always admired him for that. Publishers had to be much braver people because there was no way you could put a record out, you just put your money down. He did a very good thing by signing Queen. KPM was a very old-fashioned publishing company with their own promotion people whose job was to work in tandem with the record companies. I never knew if anyone did everything but we always talked about it every week, it was very impressive. Publishers now are more bankers, they are the people who are always waiting for the record company to say, yes, maybe, and then they will come in with an offer. They are like radar operators, they make it their business to know A&R people and just get the word, they are always at the gigs and they know what is going on. In those days, it was much easier for a publisher to sign bands, it used to be for three years inclusive deals and the advance used to be not very large. They would get 50/50 deals and life of copyright, that seemed to be the norm in those days and then Virgin came along and Heath Levy came along, and they really beat up the industry in terms of publishing, they really shook the place up. They suddenly offered things like 75/25 and all the big publishers screamed, they really did not enjoy that.

ROD DUNCOMBE,
Bronze Publishing

I worked for Bronze running their publishing company which Sydney had set up many years ago. He was a great music publisher Sydney Bron, he knew where to find money like most music publishers should, he was proper Tin Pan Alley. What happened was that Motörhead became the star act at Bronze, much to everyone's surprise and because I got on with them so well they became my sort of personal thing to look after for the record company, and I was not working for the record company. I did a lot of touring with them, their first album for Bronze *Overkill* did OK, made the charts and got a bit of a tickle in France. Eventually after their third album they cracked it and they cracked Germany as well. They deserved it, they were hard working, always on time, never let anyone down, gave a good show, it was loud – like listening to road works at times, but I liked them, they were good folk. Lemmy's nickname was because it was always lenmmie a fiver, lemmie a tenner. He told me this story: Doug Smith was on the phone to the bank manager desperate to borrow two hundred quid, he was sweating on this money, he was desperate for it, he was on the phone to the bank manager for what must have been a good ten minutes and Lemmy came into the office sat in front of his desk, waited patiently while Doug was on this crawling exercise with the bank manager to get two hundred quid. Eventually he got it, put the phone down, calmed down a bit said, what do you want Lemmy? Can you lend me a tenner? You have just seen me talking to the bank manager, you know how difficult it is, where am I going to get that from? To which Lemmy said, can you ring him back and ask for two hundred and ten?

I was having lunch at that flash restaurant in Kensington Place in Notting Hill Gate with Simon Platz, independent music publisher son of David Platz, the father of modern music publishing who signed all the great artists, The Who, Black Sabbath, the Stones etc. So I was having lunch with Simon and a Dutch guy Paul Smith and Marianne Faithful walked past our table and I stopped her and said Marianne it's Rod, Rod Duncombe. Ehh? I said Marianne, do you remember when we worked at NEMS and we put out that album with Patrick? Those bastards. I said, yes. Could I introduce you please this is Paul Smith from Holland and this is Simon Platz, and she said and what do you do Simon? He said: I am your music publisher Marianne.

JOHN SCHROEDER,
Record Producer

There was a guy called Cyril Shane, Cyril Shane Music. He always wanted me to go down to his office to hear his new material, which I did. I went to lots of publishers' offices and they played me their material, instead of them coming to me. I used to go with Cyril. Cyril always used to be reliant on someone else's opinion at the same time as playing the material to me. Do you know who it was? It was his dog. He had a dog called Pedro. Pedro was a poodle. Pedro was with him day in and day out, all the time. If Pedro okayed the song, he would bark. I'll never forget, he was playing me these songs, and Pedro, not a murmur. I said: Doesn't he like it? He said: Well he's got his own preferences. Here's one song that Pedro really likes. I said: Oh yeah. He said: Yeah. I'll play that to you now. He puts it on, and he's sitting there, and suddenly Pedro goes, "Woof, woof, woof." He was barking it. John, he said, I'm telling you, that is a hit song. Pedro said so. He was right. I took the song, and it was a hit song.

Lots of the publishers, they were such characters. Yeah, such great people too. Of course, Christmas was the time that everybody was trying to, what's the word, get in the good books of the producers. We used to get baskets of fruit, and chicken, and hampers, and they're just thrown at us in those days, champagne. Because the publisher's earning power came from record producers. Hit records. That's what the whole industry was about, hit records. Without a hit record, forget it. The charts controlled the whole of the music industry for a whole number of years. If you didn't have a hit record you were nowhere. You didn't get work, you didn't get in.

ADRIAN KERRIDGE,
Studio Engineer

In the summer time, Joe Meek and I used to travel round the holiday camps doing shows for Radio Luxembourg with IBC Studios and in the winter we would visit all the Playhouses, the old theatres everywhere in the country. Joe was a very iconic, creative engineer, he upset everybody for his 'bent', shall we say. In those days to be a gay person, the word that was never used, was not legal. He was not liked for it by certain people in the management at IBC, but he had incredible talent. We travelled for a couple of years together on the road during the week or weekend to do shows for

Luxembourg, not all the time. Joe never approached me, we would go to the hotel have a meal, he would go out in the evening. In the morning he would roll in usually accompanied, 'this is my friend'. That was the way it was. Some of the people in that company took the mickey because of the way the law was. It would never happen today. I think certain people humiliated Joe and it was very sad to see, it upset Joe but he kept himself to himself. He had a boyfriend who was a chef, and when we worked at Conway Hall on shows, we would go to his café and get free food. He was very private in that respect. These days he is described as 'camp' and perhaps you could describe him as 'camp' but his talent was absolutely extraordinary and because of his talent and because he was in such great demand with artists there was jealousy in the IBC Studios.

£££

CHRIS PEERS, Agent, Manager

Chris Blackwell was going round selling records in Brixton, Birmingham, anywhere there was a large coloured population, with Jackie Edwards who a singer. I remember Chris saying, have a listen to this Jamaican record by Roy and Millie. She had this strange odd voice. We said, yes, well it's different. He said I will make some enquiries next time I go to Jamaica, and he did, as I remember him telephoning us from Jamaica and agreeing we should bring her over. So 'My Boy Lollipop' sold six million eventually. Recorded in the UK, Ernest Ranglin the Jamaican jazz guitarist did the arrangement I think. Harry Robinson had quite a tie up with Phonogram/Mercury and there was an A&R man there called Jack Baverstock which was why we formed a relationship with them. But we only licensed to them for the UK so that we could do where we wanted in other markets.

Chris Blackwell was in Birmingham because he had Millie on *Thank Your Lucky Stars* and so had to stay overnight. So he went to an R&B

club and heard this voice, young Stevie Winwood. He came back very excited, I have heard this young fourteen-fifteen year-old kid singing 'Georgia On My Mind', he plays guitar and piano.

BPR was almost a part-time company, we suddenly started to think why don't we have our own agency too? So Chris and myself started an agency with offices in Argyle Street almost next door to the Palladium. We had Millie, Spencer Davis and a couple of staff, George Webb and John Martin. George brought in Long John Baldry and we started the Steampacket with Rod Stewart, Brian Auger, Julie Driscoll who became huge on the R&B circuit. At that stage there was a very established R&B circuit and they were pulling in comparatively big money. Always after the act had done the gig, the following day the bookers would ring up the club owners and ask how they did, as maybe they were on a percentage of the door. Anyhow one of the gigs said he was a bit worried about Long John as he had some young boys with him, and almost from that day on the bookings started to dry up for the Steampacket.

GEOFF FROST, Recording Studio Owner

Maurice Levy sold Oriole Records and the studio to CBS in 1963 and they always seemed to get rid of the chief engineer when they bought a studio. So I went home, this was before I was married, and my mother said, why don't you start your own studio? I hadn't thought of that and I hadn't got any money. She said, I can mortgage the house and let's see if we can find a friendly bank who can lend us some money. We went to the branch she banked with and the manager said: What is a recording studio? Eventually we found a bank who said, oh yes this sounds fun, I will lend you three grand. So I said to John Wood who I was working with, we are going to start our own studio aren't we? Yes of course we are. It was agreed that John would stay on as he was earning a salary and I would leave and try and find somewhere to have our own studio. That took a long time. I spent every day driving round London looking for 'To Let' signs as obviously we could not afford to buy anywhere. I had given up but I suddenly found an advert in *The Evening Standard* for 1,000 square feet in 46a Old Church Street, Chelsea. It turned out to have been a cow shed, that had become a pottery but the pottery was not doing so well.

So we went up these wide stairs, I said these are wide: Yes they were for the cows and this was a milking parlour in Victorian times. It is only Victorians who would build a milking parlour on the first floor, but it was great because it had a sloping floor which is good for acoustics. We had some Polish builders take the centre part out of the floor and extend it but it took us about six months to build the control room. Because we had no money I had to build my own mixer, John Wood designed the aesthetics of the desk and I would build the electronics. We did a few test sessions which sounded fantastic, we sat there with nothing and then on a Friday evening about five o'clock, John and I were drinking our hundredth cup of coffee waiting for the phone to ring and it did. It was Frank Barber who used to arrange all John Schroeder's sessions and he said, I am looking for a studio for a client of mine but he needs three days a week for six months. I cannot find any studio in London that has three days a week for six months. Hang on a minute Frank, I will look at the diary. Which was of course empty. Yeah I think we can accommodate you here.

The word spread that if you wanted somewhere in London with fantastic sound, go to Sound Techniques. It did not take me long to realise that John Woods was a better engineer than I was and that is how it used to work at Sound Techniques so I started concentrated on building equipment and desks. We became best known for Folk-Rock and by the time we sold it to Olympic, that had become about 90% of what we did.

**FRED d'ALBERT,
Musician**

My group The Commanches got involved with this American A&R guy who worked for the music publisher Campbell Connelly who were in Denmark Street, Tin Pan Alley. So as a teenager I worked in the Trade Department of Campbell Connelly, so I was going up to Denmark Street every day. This was about the time we were recording our second single. I would be there sending out parcels of Beatles sheet music every day to music shops up and down the country. I was in there one day and Andrew Loog Oldham was recording something there under the name of the Andrew Loog Oldham Orchestra, and this American manager said Andrew Loog Oldham is recording something across the street and he wants to put on a guitar track. So he went and got a Stratocaster from Francis Day & Hunter in Charing Cross Road and I ended up playing on the track. Things like that happened all the time in Denmark Street, we were in and out of Regent Sound doing demos for the publisher and bits and bobs, it was really strange. Later on I got involved with Valley Music and Marty Wilde and his writing partner Ronnie Scott, not the tenor player, and I was in Marty's band and we used to do all the demos for the songs he had written. So we would go to the studio in Wimbledon and do in an afternoon 'Ice In the Sun', 'Jesamine', Lulu's 'I'm A Tiger', 'Down The Dustpipe' – £8 and we would have churned out I don't know how many songs that became big chart hits for Status Quo and the like. Marty would be singing and playing acoustic guitar with his big Jumbo Gibson. He would record his songs as demos and the songs would be farmed out to various artists to see if they could get them recorded. The publishers had songs which they punted around, anyone who had any talent for writing was there, that was where the money was in those days not in gigs.

DEREK GREEN,
Music Publisher

I am not entirely sure that I had ever left the country before but my first visit to America was flying to New York where my connections were Scotty English who was in the Brill Building and Kenny Young. It was thought that it would be a good idea if I went there and could buy up the publishing rights for RCA in Europe. I flew into New York and I remember it was like being a punk on the Kings Road in the Seventies. I walked out there in black patent leather shoes, my hair was long enough and as I walked along 54th people would stop and stare and point.

I went to the Brill Building to nurture my contacts but it was while I was there I realised that the music I most liked was coming from this place called Los Angeles. So I checked back home and said this and they said well go. I remember getting on the plane and I had a big afghan fur coat and was all dressed up as it was winter time, I was looking around me and everyone else was in T-shirts and the flight just went on and on. As we were coming in to land I was looking out the window and it was sunny and gorgeous, I really had no idea. Going to the head office of RCA, I thought it is a serious company and so I had my three-piece suit and black case, I could not get past the receptionist, they would not let me in, a complete waste of time. I came back to England and they had given my publishers job away, but I was able to move on to the record company.

TONY HILLER,
Songwriter

Irving and I would write songs, go down Denmark Street and sell our songs. And we sold many songs for £30 or £20 or if we were lucky £50. When I say sold, just advance royalty; you never sold the copyright. That's what we did. So that's how I became a writer, and Irving became a writer. We also became a double act, the Hiller Brothers and we worked with probably every major act of the period. In fact I became a London cab driver, and so did my brother Irving; it enabled us to be able to work at nights and go down Denmark Street. And that's really how we started. We worked in Germany as an artist; we worked in France. We worked all over the place, had a fabulous time. We worked with the biggest but we weren't big, but the getting there was just so exciting. My father and mother were always singing and harmonising; always. And I was, what song is that dad? And then as we got older we became very, very learned; we knew every record, every writer; we looked for the mechanicals. We knew everything – who the writer was, who the publisher was, who the arranger was, who the producer was, who the company was. So we had a lot of knowledge. So we used to go everyday and sell our songs, and we would meet all the other writers, and also the greats. We used to meet in Denmark Street and have our tea at the café. We'd see Dick James and see everybody. By going round and trying to sell, they knew. So we were getting a living out of it. We did well because I was a good harmoniser, and we really worked. We weren't nervous and we sold it, and we got £20 or £30 or whatever.

CHRIS SPEDDING, Musician

I suppose the Battered Ornaments were the first name band that I was to record with that you would have heard as a band. I'd been in various outfits before. I think the first record that I made as a guitar player was Frank Ricotti's Quartet which had Chris Laurence on bass, Bryan Spring on drums. That was the first time I was ever in the studio making a record which actually got put out. Before that I was doing demos. I would do demos in studios in Denmark Street for people you know, I remember being hired by Immediate Records, you know the Andrew Loog Oldham set up, to go in and do demos at Regent Sound in Denmark Street but none of that ever came out you know. We'd get around £3 for like a day's work or something. This is in the Sixties. Yeah. The Denmark Street circuit. It's pretty low on the totem pole really you know. It's a good grounding to start off learning to be a session man at the Denmark Street demo's thing I guess.

Although I never had any aspirations to be a session man because there was this sort of myth that you had to be a fantastic sight reader, and I didn't think that I was, it wasn't a thing that I did very easily. And I later found out that you didn't really need to be a sight reader as you probably realise talking to the guys like Jim Sullivan and people like that who were also brilliant fakers like me. Just never got found out. Could sort of read a little bit but you know if something really difficult was put in front of you you'd start panicking you know and I always used to dread the day I'd get found out, I never really got found out. I was always able to fake it because some of the other musicians were really great, someone like Herbie Flowers, the bass player, he'd maybe be sitting next to me and if I had something that was a complete jumble to me, I'd say: Can you sing me that phrase? And he'd sing me the phrase and I'd say: What, you mean like this? And I'd play it like rock'n'roll, full distortion. Producer would come rushing out and say: That's exactly what I wanted to hear, but I didn't know how to write it properly, but I can see that you can interpret this stuff really good. Book that man again.

I appeared on the session circuit around about the time that Jimmy Page left to form Led Zeppelin very successfully, and about the same time that Big Jim Sullivan left London to work in Las Vegas with Tom Jones, leaving a huge hole thank you very much Jimmy and Big Jim, and there was a need for another rock'n'roll session guy. And I fit the bill. So I was in the right place at the right time around about 1969 that's how I interpret it anyway.

MICK EVE,
Musician

We got a young guy who was a bass player on sessions who Joe Moretti and John McLaughlin were both very keen on. They said he is the best one, he can read and he's got a good feel, and he's got a Hammond organ at home. Sure enough I went up to Haverstock Hill where he lived and he'd got this lovely Hammond M. I'd got a Hammond L which was not the best Hammond organ by any means but he had the M which was a step up and that was John Paul Jones, John Baldwin to us. I remember moaning at McLaughlin one time and I said how come when we do 'Johnny B. Goode' you refuse to play the intro. Of course he wouldn't, he did not want to play it. On stage was a young boy playing with Shane Fenton and The Fentones, Jimmy Page, he was only about sixteen or seventeen and he was playing it really good. Why won't you do that? No, no, actually he is one of our pupils, we are teaching him because he can read music, we are teaching him to get in on the session scene because they needed a rock'n'roll guitarist to come in. Joe Moretti would do them but you would not ask McLaughlin to do a rock solo, he would not you know. He put me in my place, No we are teaching him, he said.

We knew Chas Chandler, he was always this lovely amiable man, I found, but he just had this great enthusiasm for Hendrix, you know, glowing. I met him in the Charing Cross Road, come and listen, he is going to be the next thing to come along. Strangely enough Jimi echoed what McLaughlin had been saying to me about how he was going to give up playing guitar. I said, what do you mean, give up guitar? No I want to play saxophone, I want to be like Sonny Rollins – he was looking for something a lot broader and bigger, he wanted the barrage of sound and he found it. I am not saying through Hendrix, but Hendrix pointed the direction. Fill it out more, you don't need anyone else in the band, just drums and bass. Anyway it was a sunny afternoon, I remember the sun shining and this racket coming out of a music shop, I was thinking, God what is going on there, and Chas was going, come and listen to Jimi in the shop but the whole of Charing Cross Road was already getting deafened.

We were playing the Speakeasy one night and Jimi wanted to play so we were offering him the guitar to come and have a play with us but no, I'd like to play the bass, he went, and he turned it upside down, left-handed whatever, and played lovely bass. Obviously he'd worked with The Isley Brothers and you had to be of a standard in America, you did not survive otherwise and he was well capable.

MARTIN NELSON,
TV Promotion Manager

Top of the Pops was the most powerful music show on television then. And as soon as it lost its Thursday evening slot the audience plummeted and that was really you know the beginning of the end which was really sad. And very bad news for the whole record industry when it changed. A lot of people just didn't understand it. A lot of people wanted to make their name by being the person that axed *Top of the Pops*. A great loss to everybody. I think everything came together, I mean people were stopping buying singles. The single wasn't as important as it was. *Top of the Pops* was based totally on the singles

211

chart and I think unfortunately there was a decline all round. But it was important on Thursday evening to the record industry because there were still two days left when the stores were open. When it moved to a Friday night there was you know just Saturday. A lot of people were busy on a Saturday so there wasn't much selling time left.

The first promo video I was involved in was Queen's 'Bohemian Rhapsody', which obviously got used everywhere. And from then on, promo videos were a varying degree of sophistication. But everybody then decided they had to have a film in order to promote their single, and it meant it could go all over the world so they didn't always have to travel everywhere because they could send a film of the performance. Well I was doing regional promotion then. And you know the band were doing the interviews so I'd take them out in my Cortina Estate and Brian, who had the longest legs always had to go in the back behind the back seat – you know, the dog bit – so the others could scrunch up in the rest of the car. It was great fun. We had a wonderful time.

So mid-Seventies with the beginnings of promo videos but a lot of people wanted the band in. They didn't want the promo video. And then the whole thing shifted, so through the Eighties it was the promo video. And so people would go in and do an interview and they would just show the promo video and not have the band performing, because don't forget the TV company still had to pay everybody in vision and everybody on the track if they had a band performing, so it made it very expensive, whereas they got a promo video for nothing. I mean TV companies realised that. They wanted to use the promo video 'cause it was free. I mean theoretically they had to pay VPL money. A lot of them didn't.

It was interesting with Wham! They had to have a promo video for every single and every promo video had to be better than the last. So for 'Wham Rap' it was pretty basic, but by the time they got to 'Club Tropicana' for example, which was the first time the company had spent quite a bit of money, they sent them to, oh was it Ibiza or somewhere to record this promo video. I remember having dinner with them after *Top of the Pops* when they'd come back from filming that promo video. It was interesting that they actually made it after release of the single, because singles took a long time to grow. So I was doing *Top of the Pops* before I actually had the promo video, and we sat down in an Indian restaurant near to the BBC Television Centre in

Shepherd's Bush and they told me what had happened, at the making of that promo video, and how annoyed they were that so many people were just hanging around, when they realised that it was actually their money that was being spent to make it, and it would all come back on the accounting. They were beginning to get very wise then as to what was happening and how much they were being ripped off.

Def Leppard were equally well organised. All the big rock acts were so well organised because they had to be. So whenever I wanted them to do a TV show or an interview, I knew all I had to do was arrange it with the manager and they would be there and we had enormous success with Def Leppard in this country during that time because once again people wanted to see them. I mean they were extremely popular, they were prepared to do TV shows like *Top of the Pops* and they just worked. We had one particular album where it went to number one in this country before it had actually taken off in America, so the manager decided to take some of us to America to actually show the Americans how to do it. Which was extremely funny. Very embarrassing for them but very funny at the time.

STEVE JENKINS, Regional Promotion

I know that the reputation of the Fewtrells in Birmingham is probably a little rough. They were tough guys. They were selling cars by the day and running night clubs in the evening. The one thing that you didn't do was mess with the Fewtrells. But I have to say, Chris and Eddie treated me well. I loved what I was doing. I was very passionate about working in the club, and working with the artists, and playing records. I think they took to me, and they helped me, really. I enjoyed it.

A little later I was working at another club the Rum Runner. The owners then started to develop Duran Duran, just as I was finishing

DJing. It took me a long time to finish. I'd go back and play a couple of gigs here and there. Duran Duran were around that time, all those guys really: UB40, Jeff Lynne, ELO. I knew Jeff Lynne via Keith Bertschin, who used to be Birmingham City centre forward. Keith and Jeff were friends, and so I got to know Jeff via Keith. Football and music in that area were the big escapes, I suppose. As you were growing up in the Midlands, if you could get into being a footballer or you could get into the music business, game on. I was at Joseph Leckie School in Walsall, and Noddy's probably four years/five years older than me. He was playing the clubs at the time I was at school. Everybody used to go and watch Ambrose Slade, because they were a great band.

Susan Buckler was the shop assistant at Graduate Records and she opened *Music Week*, which I'd never looked at apart from the chart before that. There is a job for a promotion man for an unnamed record company, she said: You should go and work for a record company, because you come in here every week, and some of the records you buy, we buy more copies of because we know other people are going to buy them. Anyway, I never thought too much about it. Ten days later, I go: You know what? I'll just write off for the job. I wrote off for the job, and I get called down for an interview, and I do the first interview, and I meet Rod Duncombe. It seems to go well. Then I go back home. Then two weeks later, I get invited for a further interview. The numbers involved in all of that was seventy-five people applied for the job. It got down to three, I think, for the second interview. At the end of the second interview, I'm offered the job as a promotion man for NEMS and Immediate Records. A month or so later, I was talking to Rod, and I said to Rod: How come I got the job, and the other seventy-five people didn't get the job? He said: Well your letter was really interesting. He said: Most people wrote and put all their qualifications, and whether they'd been to university, and all the rest of it. You just wrote about records. You wrote about records that you liked. I'd even put in the letter records that were going to be hits that weren't hits at that time. I think this is going to be a hit.

1974, I joined NEMS and was with NEMS for about a year before I went to Chrysalis, which was a much more professional outfit. From NEMS and Immediate Records to Chrysalis Records was a giant leap. Chrysalis Records was, you know, with Terry Ellis and Chris Wright. That was about touring bands, that basically played at universities and colleges, and then we got them on the radio, and they sold records from the back of it. It was basically about touring bands. When I went from NEMS and Immediate, which was basically about records, to Chrysalis, that was about bands, touring, and then obtaining interviews for those bands when they were in each town. If you were in Manchester and the band was playing in Manchester, then you'd organise interviews for that day on the radio to sell the gig and broaden their base. That led to a different kind of promotion, really. Yeah, there was Tull, Steeleye Span, Rory Gallagher, Split Enz – that went on to become Crowded House. They were just beginning to get into pop, because they knew Adam Faith, and he brought Leo Sayer to the label. Leo Sayer was probably one of the first pop acts that Chrysalis had. Chris and Terry were social secs at universities. They'd been booking bands into universities all those years when they were at university. Basically, Chrysalis Records came around on that social secretary mentality. Back in those days, in the Seventies, record labels grew and mushroomed for different reasons. They came around and were able to operate in what was a very big pool in very specific ways. When you went from one record label to another, it was a different philosophy. Back then, there was thought into what the record label represented, and what area it was attacking.

NEMS and Immediate was closing down, so I went down on a Friday, I got called to the office, and I got told by Peter Knight Jnr. that the record label was closing, and that, basically, I was out of work. But he said: Don't worry about it. I've got you another job, and it's at Chrysalis Records. Go and see Chris Stone. I was like: When? He went: Now. Jump in the car, go and see Chris Stone. You've got an appointment for three o'clock, and you'll be working for Chrysalis Records tonight. I had an interview at Chrysalis Records. That was on the Friday. On the Tuesday, I drove back to London, dropped the car at NEMS, and picked up a blue Ford Cortina Estate. Magnificent. I went from an Escort to a Ford Cortina Estate. I was in business. I started working for Chrysalis Records but it wasn't like a day-time job. Chrysalis Records was day and night. Wherever the bands were playing, you were expected to be there, and have serviced the radio station the day before, and acquired them interviews on the day before or the day of. With Chrysalis Records, you could stay in hotels. Fantastic. Nothing like a Holiday Inn in the Seventies, you've arrived.

ROD DUNCOMBE,
Chrysalis International

End of 1971 I had a year at Decca in an international position with Marcel Stellman who was a big influence on me I have to say. When you first go and work in an industry, you are only aware of your immediate surroundings, and one of the first things he said to me was you have to understand that 80% of world's record markets are outside of the UK. I became his sort of leg man as it were and I learnt an awful lot from him and from what I did in that year at Decca. I was fortunate enough to work with all the great Decca artists of the day, we were going through a purple patch with Gilbert O'Sullivan, Tom Jones, Lindsey de Paul. It was a good time to work at Decca as they were probably having their last hurrah, The Stones were about to leave to go to Warners, Ten Years After were about to leave to go to Chrysalis, Savoy Brown had just seen their last days as it were, Keef Hartley as well. You just felt that Decca were having their last days in the sun and I got offered a job at Chrysalis which was the hippest job at the time and I just snapped at it. I was Director of International Operations which sounds very grand but there were only five or six of us working at the record company at the time so everyone was a director of something or other. We had five acts while I was there, we had Ten Years After, Jethro Dull, Procol Harum, Steeleye Span and then we signed Leo Sayer. It was just a joy as they were all successful and you did not have to work that hard because they all created the success just by making another record. Jethro Tull were doing five nights at the Anaheim Center and doing massive schedules, Ten Years After were playing big open Atlanta Pop Festival, big open-air festivals in the southern states of America. Steeleye were very big but generally domestically, they did not crack it internationally, then Leo Sayer came along and he was very successful.

I did a bit of touring mainly with Procol Harum and Ten Years After because Jethro Tull were managed by Terry Ellis, part owner of Chrysalis and he virtually based himself in the States. Jethro Tull were sort of a race apart at Chrysalis but I enjoyed touring with Procol more than any of the others, they were jolly good to be on the road with. When you go out on the road with a rock band, certainly in those days, it was all done in a very relaxed manner. I think the unions in America were just becoming involved, the Teamsters Union, in setting up gear at the venues. You could go and play college venues and civic auditoriums and places like that without too much trouble or organisation. You could virtually turn up, set up the kit, play and then move on to the next one, all on a small budget with not too many people and just one or two small trucks. You would go on tour for three or four days to show the record company face and make sure the local company was doing their promotion and marketing bit for the current album that the band were promoting, 'cause that is how you did it in those days, they went on tour to promote the record. It was like being on holiday with your mates, travelling first class with five-star accommodation that someone else was paying for. I would come home and think this was absolutely wonderful and you did not do that much work. You saw the band perform every night and went out with them afterwards and got wasted and had a good time. They did it for forty days while you went back to the office, you saw a lot of the world and it was really rather nice. The thing that amazed me was that we were all amateurs, even the boys in the band were keen enthusiastic amateurs doing what we liked doing and it all got done. Even the dipshit roadie, way down at the bottom of the food chain, he did his job and under severe drug related conditions most of the time.

MARCEL STELLMAN,
Decca Records
International Manager

In those days, we had a couple of promotion boys at Decca. Tony Hall was with us as well. Nice chap Tony. We also had a lot of dealings with a situation when I spoke to my dear chairman, Mr Lewis. He wasn't Sir then. I said: I think we ought to start a publishing company. He said: Why? I said: Because there's a lot of items we've got that the publishers are having, and we don't get it. I said: Why should we have the B-side of this or that? He says: Jimmy Philips won't like it. I said: I know you're having lunch with him every day, but my bet is that if we don't do it, he will do one. You think so? I said: I think so. Two weeks later, he started a publishing company for EMI, Jimmy Phillips. I said to Lewis: Well? He says: We'd better start a publishing company. John Nice came in to organise it. I was given the great privilege of being a director of the publishing company. Not that it gave me any money, but it was the title that was given to me too, which I thanked him for profusely. Burlington-Palace. We had two companies. Burlington Music and Palace Music. He said: Good, we'll sit it out.

I do remember we had a big building on the Albert Embankment. I think it was a five-story building. Beautiful. I think it was on lease to us, we didn't own it. I remember somebody coming to my office saying: Where would you like your new office? I said: I don't mind. They gave me an office on the second or third floor in the front, with another one in another room for my secretary. I said: I've made it. I'm overlooking the Thames. At that time, we had another problem. Years ago, I think Harold Wilson was in charge, and you couldn't get a rise. Lewis called me up. He said: Stellman. I was never called by our first name, we were all called by our surname. Stellman, Rowe, Mendl. I said: Yes, sir. He said: You probably heard the news that nobody can have rises at the moment. He said: There's nothing I can do. I said: I understand. He said: Would you like a car? I said: Is it possible? He said: Yes. Go and talk to my accountant and see what you want, and you'll have a car. I said: Thank you. I went home, I

218

said to Jeanie: What did he say? I can have a car. I had a little car anyway. She said: What do you want? I said: I can't have a Bentley, because he's got one. She said: What would you like? Well, she says, don't be cheeky. I said: I'd like a Jag. I said: Can I have a Jaguar? He looked at me and said: Yes. I thought: The man who's going to hate my guts will be Townsley, because he only had the Rover. Of course, I could park as well. I came home, I said: Jeanie. She said: What have you got? I said: I got a Jag. She said: You bloody cheeky bugger. And I had the number 166, as well, with the letters. It was a red Jag with black top. Boy, was I proud. I thought: I must have something if I'm allowed to have a car. I don't think Hugh Mendl had one, he wanted his Bugatti, which was probably worth more than anything.

£££

DEREK NICOL, Manager

We decided we'd take on Alex Harvey, so we started off putting him out solo. I remember doing the first gig, I think was the Speakeasy in Margaret Street, and he was quite an unusual artist. There's only one Alex Harvey actually; very, very unusual. I always felt he was a genius, or bordering on that genius. And he had all these songs that were from the past that somebody had written or whatever, 'Soldier', and some really unusual songs. There was communication with an audience with him solo but it wasn't quite right, so we put two other members, a bass and drums, with him; and again I think we did the Speakeasy and a few places. It still wasn't quite right; in fact the members of the band, they were a Scottish band called Clouds from way back in the late Sixties, early Seventies, that didn't quite work, so from the Scottish days we were aware of the tour we did with Deep Purple in Scotland, I remember we had one of the local bands, Tear Gas, a Glasgow band, were on; a really good band, really quite aggressive as you might imagine from the name, so we linked up. We tried out Alex Harvey fronting Tear Gas, and, right, that was it; that's what we're going to do. They were all young guys and Alex was like the director – Uncle Alex or whatever, compared with the rest of the band. And effectively it developed from there. That worked.

I remember the Alex Harvey Band – I've got to give a name to this; and I gave it the name, Sensational, because by this time I could see the things they were doing and some of their music, sensational. It was a big risk; you call something sensational, you knew exactly what the press is going to say if they think the opposite. But fortunately most of the time the word, sensational, was generally used in the sense they really were sensational; so it really worked. I remember also in those days creating the logo for the Sensational Alex Harvey Band, and Nazareth. I remember giving somebody £15 for each of them – again I can't remember his name – to come up with these logos, which stood the test of time. That's how it was in those days; it was all do-it-yourself; nobody wanted to know.

JONH INGHAM,
Journalist, Sounds

I collapsed my lung, so I was in hospital, in a communal room of some kind there was a television. There was an announcement from the BBC: We're apologising. Earlier in the night, with this band, the Sex Pistols, blah, blah, blah. I was like: What? What happened there? What was that about? Then I'm in the ward, and the next morning they come around with all the newspapers on a cart. Everybody's going: I'll have *The Mirror*, I'll have *The Mail*, I'll have *The Express*, and da, da, da. I'm looking at this row of beds. It's like Sex Pistols, Sex Pistols, Sex Pistols. I'm thinking: What the hell happened? I asked everybody for their newspapers when it's over. Slowly, I see this bombshell has gone off on dinner time TV.

I'm sitting in hospital there. Slowly, I started thinking: It's kind of dumb that everybody's taking advantage of this situation. Miles Copeland's in like a rocket, and all the rest of it. I'm thinking: I kind of helped create all of this, it's kind of dumb if I don't try to take advantage of it myself. I have a good friend, Stewart Joseph, who's coming and visiting me. He comes to the ward, and I said: I'm thinking of starting a record company. He says: I'm thinking of managing a group. We agreed that we'd do both and that got me into 1977. As a journalist, you'd seen it all very close up with the most successful bands in the world. That looked like a good lifestyle. Out of all of that, Generation X were clearly, after The Clash, and the Pistols, and The Damned, they were the next ones that had any potential.

Then we went and saw a lawyer who said: You can't have a label and manage a band, because that's a conflict of interest. At the time, we knew nothing about things like Andrew Loog Oldham with the Stones, and all of these kind of license to production company, whatever. You didn't have manuals, you didn't have the internet to go and check, so we took it at face value. It was bad advice, really bad advice. That's when we thought: OK, we'll drop the label, we'll go for the band. Because we knew we could get an advance, and we knew we were going to make money off it. Then it was a case of which record label. We started thinking through: Who are the A&R guys? Who do we like? Who do we respect? Which labels do we like? We landed on a mutual friend, Chris Briggs, and we thought: Chrysalis, that's interesting. We started about a three or four-month courtship project without letting any of them know what we were up to. It was like: Let's draw up the plans for World War III and go.

221

CHRIS BRIGGS,
Chrysalis A&R

At Chrysalis it was the first time I realised that the bands you were looking for came in clumps and then there would be a pause for three or four years when not much happened. It was very frustrating, a lot happened all at once, I was not experienced, I didn't shout loud enough. I suddenly found myself going through a period. The way things get presented in the media you would think 1977 that was just punk, but the reality is that this is the period that Dire Straits and The Police came out of. The bands that are icons today all fizzled out very quickly with the exception of The Clash, there was not very much that made it to the third album. At Chrysalis, to suit a story, we were imbued with much more power than we really had, but I was in no position to sign anything, my only chance of getting things signed was to blag and convince the trio of Roy Eldridge who would then go and talk to Doug Darcy and then the three of us had to convince Chris Wright whose money it was. As far as I was concerned it looked as though it was coming out of his pocket because he struggled so much with parting with it. Generation X was the only band I got signed there.

That was one of the turning points with Chris Wright. I'd seen Squeeze. I had that first Police single. I had Police, Chelsea. Miles had done it. I can't remember what it was, the Miles Copeland Police single. I've got it somewhere in a cardboard box in the garage. I'd been chasing Squeeze, and Roy Eldridge really liked Squeeze. There was a Rock Garden gig where I thought: They're going to let me sign this. This is going to happen. Miles then steps in and goes: Well actually, what I really want is a bit of a label deal. If we're going to sign Squeeze, for not much more money, I'll chuck in Chelsea and the Police. This requires Chris Wright.

Chris Wright, Miles Copeland, and myself go for a posh Friday lunch. God, I was naive. What was the restaurant that Michael Caine, just off Piccadilly? Anyway, we go for posh Friday lunch – not something I'm allowed to do very often. I don't know Miles that well at the time, but he's on top form. Chris is playing it a bit too cool for my liking. At this point, I don't know much about The Police, because

I had been tracking Squeeze. They used to co-headline with Dire Straits in Deptford. I'd been tracking Dire Straits and Squeeze for some time, in the midst of everything else that was going on. Lunch ends, Chris's driver is driving us back to the office, and Chris Wright basically says to me: We won't be doing a deal with Miles Copeland, Briggsy. I'm like: Why ever not? He was always trouble when we were Wishbone Ash's agent. He still owes me for posters for the last tour. That was the end of that. I'm like: Oh, OK.

I had Dire Straits in my office. You do try and blag it a bit. They want me and Chris Wright. I'm not stupid. His brother wasn't there, I think I've got Mark and John Illsley in my office. I've told them. It's this thing where you actually have no power. You've delivered the band into the building. You need somebody who can sign a cheque to pick it up off you, and nobody really wants to. Richard Williams is in the conversation. The awkward silence conversation is about lawyers. I've gone out, had a piss, fled upstairs to Chris Wright's office, or to Doug D'Arcy's office, and said: Please at least meet them. All right, how about 'Sultans of Swing'? It was about seven minutes long. Who the fuck's going to buy that? Seven minutes long. Bye. Another one slips through your fingers.

SIMON DRAPER, MD, Virgin Records

I wished I'd signed The Damned. Jake Riviera was obviously originally one of the people involved and I had fallen out with him big time; but I don't think there were very many people who didn't, over nothing you know. He came to see me about something and I kept him waiting for half-an-hour in reception and he got so pissed off that he just came into my office. Actually after that I always got on OK with him but it was pretty loud. But in the punk era for us there were the sort of acts who would go to Stiff, who I don't think were paying much, but went there because they liked everything about Stiff and Dave Robinson. So I don't suppose we would have had a chance, if we'd been competing for Madness, or even the Damned maybe.

We were competing strongly with Chrysalis then, and to a lesser extent Island. Island really wanted XTC and nearly got them. Chrysalis got Generation X, we tried to sign them. The big companies were less competition because clearly we were so different, but on the other hand some of the punk bands preferred to be with CBS where they could see what they were getting really. What was deceptive about us, and I know bands like The Ruts told me they were deceived by it, is that they saw as a kind of anarchic bunch with no obvious hierarchies and scruffy offices and all that stuff; and they just thought well, these guys, it's a nice comfy place to be. And yet we had the toughest contracts. We had tougher contracts than the big majors. So when they found that we were actually quite good at the business side of it that came as a shock to some of them.

FRANK BRUNGER, Product Manager, CBS

After Harvest I was employed by CBS as product manager. I turned up and there were about six or seven product managers. We had, I don't know, about seven hundred acts between us. It was a massive situation. I sat down with Jerry Turner and he said: What acts would you like? I said: OK, well what have we got? I went through the catalogue, the bands that I wanted, from Aerosmith onward. The response to every one was: Well we've already got a product manager for that. Anyway, we got through every rock artist that I knew that was on the CBS catalogue, and everyone was allocated. I said: Hang on a minute, I came in on the basis you wanted someone who was going to market rock, but there are no rock acts. He said: Well there is one act. He said: Take a listen to this. He gave me a tape, and I went home in my car, in my lovely Ford Capri. Never got a decent car like that at EMI. I drove home in my Capri and I put this tape on. I had never heard anything like it. It was like: Yes, this is it. Got home, put it on the deck immediately for my wife. I said: What do you think of this, Kay? Isn't this just... She said: It's fantastic. She said: I really like that, and that.

I went back the next morning. I said: Yes, I'll take it. That's it. He said: Well that's good, because nobody else wants it. That turned out to be Meatloaf, *Bat Out Of Hell*. I found out that there were two other supporters of Meatloaf in the company. One was Judd Lander, who was head of promotions, and the other was Jonathan Morrish who was head of press. We worked this as a triumvirate. I guess because I was new, I managed to twist Jerry and Andrew's arms to give me a budget for this album, which they normally wouldn't have done, because this was an untried, untested band. It hadn't actually done brilliantly in America, so we were sticking our necks out.

What I wanted to do, what I'd sold on them was: What we want to do, we will do full page spreads in all the newspapers: *Melody Maker*, *Sounds*, *NME*, all of them. I said to them: What I want to do, I want people to hear this the way I heard it. I want all the punters to have the chance to hear this. I'd come across this company. I think it was the first time it had ever been used in the record business. You could record the music, and you'd have it on a telephone line. In the ads, I published this telephone number, and people could dial in and listen to this. We had 'Bat Out Of Hell', obviously, on there, and I think part of 'Paradise by the Dashboard Light' on there.

Judd managed to get the promotional film, which was incredible, and about eight minutes long, he got the whole of it on *The Old Grey Whistle Test*. The whole thing, eight minutes worth. I put these ads in the press to coincide with this promo film going on. The whole thing just started to explode. The next thing we knew, we had Meat coming on. Judd pulled off a live thing on *Whistle Test* with Meat and the lady who was, I think, the best of Meat's female accompaniments on the stage, was Karla DeVito – a fabulous name.

Through one of Judd's promo men, I wanted to have an escort for Meatloaf coming in from the airport. I wanted Hells Angels, because of obviously, the motor bikes. One of the promotion guys under Judd was associated with a group of Hells Angels, and next thing I knew, we had our group of Hells Angels, we had an escort, Jonathan got the press lined up, we had them filming them up Park Lane, we had them staying at the Swiss Cottage Holiday Inn, I think. My future at CBS was secured for a few years on the basis of that, because it just went from strength to strength. I'm just amazed that I got this landed in my lap. It just gave me the room to do what I wanted to do.

MIKE APPLETON,
Producer, OGWT

The Old Grey Whistle Test title came from the drummer of a band called Quintessence. It came via one of the producers on Late Night Line-Up called Gloria Wood, who lived with Jake. We were playing with various ideas, and we were down to two. One was The Old Grey Whistle Test, and the other one was the Florence Foster Jenkins Musical Emporium. I'm very pleased we stuck with Whistle Test, because Florence Foster Jenkins is a phenomenon, but would have grown, I think, quite tired, whereas The Old Grey Whistle Test was so enigmatic, people, all the way through, some of them didn't know what it was, so it had a certain freshness about it. I asked a guy called Roger Ferrin at BBC graphics for something, and he gave me something totally different, which was much better than what I asked for. That's why he's a graphic artist and I wasn't.

I chose Area Code 615 hoping it was going to run for a long while. I didn't think it was going to run for sixteen years, but I was hoping it was going to run for a long while. I wanted a piece of music that was recognisable, but not so whistleable that you would grow tired of it. In a way, rather like the title. It had to have longevity in it in some way. They were top session men, and it just seemed to me that this was a good piece of music to choose. It could have been a million other things, but it just was that.

We were the logical people to do *Live Aid*. It didn't have much time for it to be got together. We had a whole group of people who were used to doing rock'n'roll programmes and outside broadcasts. The BBC at that stage, they had their outside broadcast unit. We did a lot of *Whistle Test* specials and things with them, so we knew them, and we worked with them. We had people who were used to this sort of material. We had all the things that you'd think would be necessary. Above all, we had one thing which really decided it: we had a budget.

We'd been doing, for the previous two years, *Rock Around the Clock*, which now seems old fashioned, but it was really ground-breaking at the time, with phone-ins, and people choosing programmes that were eventually broadcast on the air. Nowadays, they do it on every other show, I think. When I heard about it, I was keeping track of it through Ferret and Spanner, what was going on there with the *Live Aid* project. I was able to go with Roger Laughton and get him to see Graham McDonald, who was the controller at BBC Two, and say: I think we should do this. What's more, I'm prepared – I'm prepared, it's his channel – to divert my budget for this year's *Rock Around the Clock*, which had been agreed, into this. You won't have to find more money. I'm sure that was one of the major decisions. I don't think it was a difficult decision for people to make, although nobody had any idea at that time how big it was going to be. Certainly, I think the final straw that broke the camel's resisting back was having a budget to offer. It was really, really weird, because everybody wanted to be part of it. As it got nearer to the day, you'd have taxi drivers who would deliver packages and not want to be paid. That never happens. It's crazy, producing a television programme. Much of the last days, I was having to clear the rights for people who had buckets on hillsides in tents, and play the things, and collect money. Nothing to do with television, all to do with getting the rights to collect money and have a performance going on. I've never worked so bloody hard in all my life, certainly.

It was just over six weeks, but in the middle of it, I was sent on a senior management course that had been booked down at Wood Norton. I was sitting in this room with lectures and things, with phone calls coming in: Should we do this? Should we do that? Only the BBC can do that. It's part of what I love about the BBC: totally eccentric, even to the day. It goes back to live programmes as opposed to recorded programmes. The downside of live programmes is you're never actually watching what's happening, you're watching what's coming up. You have a very different slant on things. Unless something goes wrong, and then everything stops. When The Who blew a fuse, then obviously, it all suddenly focused on the imminent and the moment. Most of the time, you're dealing with the director, who's getting on with that, and you're setting up the next thing so you can smoothly go into that. My memory of the day is of what's coming next, almost.

Then the end was weird, because we finished at three fifteen in the morning. We had the outside broadcast truck. We got out of it, and of course, the whole place was totally, totally deserted. Pitch black, and nothing there. Well, not pitch black. There were a few lamps, street lights and things. Not a sound. It was totally silent. We'd just come away from the nightclub in the West End, Legends. We walked out of this truck, and everything was going on in the truck and everything. Walked out and it's silent. Then I found that the production caravan had been locked up, so I couldn't get into the production caravan. My jacket was in there with the key to the car. I was stuck without a jacket, without a key to the car. I had to wander off down there, no money, my wallet was in my jacket in the caravan, and persuade them that I was a bona fide person at the hotel down there, and for them to let me have a room. It was a very strange ending to a magnificent day.

MARTIN MILLS, MD, Beggars Banquet

Beggar's Banquet in those days was a bit of a ragbag of taste to be perfectly honest, or lack of taste. My partner Nick Austin and I had very different tastes and it was all over the place. It took a while for us to kind of work out an identity. We survived, number one because we had Gary Numan, *Tubeway Army*, which was obviously an enormous series of records. At one time we had three albums in the Top Twenty at the same time which was pretty insane. So we had that much luck to get floated in the first place and before, actually between Gary's first and second album we were seriously going bust, we were bouncing salary cheques, we stretched the cash flow of the shops as far as it could be stretched to fund the record label and it was pretty much the end, and then we actually hired a consultant called John Cooper who used to work for Arista Records who got us an introduction to Warners to Dave Dee and to Mike Heap who was the sales guy at the time and they did a licence deal with us. We had a band called The Doll who had a hit with a song called 'Desire Me' who they thought were going to be huge. They didn't particularly see Gary Numan at the time, and they gave us a £100,000 advance which was absolutely insane as far as we were concerned. How on earth are we ever going to make that back; it's completely nuts. I mean £100,000 is a lot of money now, imagine what it was like then. But of course a few months after we did the deal, Gary Numan happened and they made it back within the first year I think.

Gary Numan walked into our shop in Ealing. Well actually he didn't, his now dead bass player Paul Gardiner walked in and we played a tape over the speakers as we always did. That was before we moved the office to Earl's Court actually, which was first beneath, then above another one of our shops, I think it was the luck of having Gary Numan early on, number one, and number two, being prudent really. Just kind of being you know the right kind of combination of being prudent but ambitious and I guess Stiff didn't survive because they were over ambitious, a derivation of Chiswick has survived but I

229

guess they were never that ambitious in terms of doing anything more than just mining the seams that they were lovingly mining.

We put out the first album of his which was called *Tubeway Army* and pretty much as soon as we put it out, and that was a kind of guitarry album, it was never really punk, it was more what became new wave than was punk, but he was doing it all intentionally for a purpose. And then as soon as he put out a first album he wanted to start making another one. He wanted to use synthesisers, he wanted a Moog, a Minimoog, which was something like £750 and we didn't have the money to buy it so we got it on hire purchase. And as soon as we got him that, he wanted a polymoog which was twice as much so we had to get that on hire purchase as well, so we were pretty mortgaged to Gary Numan. Then he went into I think Strawberry Studios and recorded the album that became *Replicas* and the single that became 'Are "Friends" Electric?'. I remember going down to the studio, he was in Portobello Road at that point, and hearing 'Are "Friends" Electric?' for the first time and thinking, that's gotta be a single. Doesn't sound like a single but it's gotta be a single. I thought it was amazing. By that time he had a reasonable following, reasonable support following, but we were licensed to Warners by that point and Warners had just released the first ever picture disc which I think was by The Cars, can't remember what the song was, and they offered us the opportunity to do the second one with 'Are "Friends" Electric?', and of course in those days people would buy every picture disc simply to collect them so it was a branch of chart hyping I suppose. We released it on picture disc and then in the same week we got him, or Warners got him I should say, *Top of the Pops* and *Old Grey Whistle Test* which nobody did. You were either one or the other, but not both, and it kicked off. Obviously records in those days didn't go straight to number one, it took like five weeks to get to number one, but it was unbelievable. A five-and-a-half minute song, no-one knew what it was about, but it was genius so it got to number one and that turned our lives upside down. I remember walking into Warners on chart morning, it was Tuesdays in those days, walking in and hearing we'd knock off Anita somebody 'Ring My Bell'.

DAVID MUNNS, EMI Records

It was all about Morrissey, and which label he was going to be on. I said I don't give a shit what label you're on. He said, well what labels have you got? So I went down to the factory, where you go in the picking lanes, and there was a lane for labels, where they pull them and stick them on when they squash the vinyl. So I went down the lane and I picked one of everything they ever had made – they never deleted anything – so there were rows of this stuff and I was just pulling them out of a big stack like this; I put them in a box, sent them round to Morrissey and said pick one of them. I didn't ask anybody. And of course he picked the HMV label. So the next thing I said, we're signing The Smiths and they're going to be on the HMV label. All the classical guys went nuts. you can't put that act on HMV – too late. Have you signed them? Yeah, that's the label. They're now on the HMV label, and they were. I'm not ringing them up and saying you can't have that one. So they all had to put up with it.

JOHN REED, RCA Records

When I was at RCA Records and nobody would ever believe me, and he would probably shoot himself, but Morrissey was responsible for Five Star's success. When Five Star were signed to the label, I was going round plugging, seeing the *Saturday Superstore* and *Wogan* and everybody was going, Yeah, well, like a poor man's Jackson Five. So they weren't really giving them a chance on TV, and there was a lady who was booking the music for *Wogan* called Sarah Lawrence, and I'd been plugging Sarah and saying: Come on, they're absolutely perfect for *Wogan*, they're slick, they're professional, it's a family, the kids love them, the mums and dads love them; perfect for your audience. Well. I wasn't getting that, OK, we'll have them, that definite thing, but I plugged it to death. One day I'm sitting in my office in Bedford Avenue when suddenly the phone rings. It's about midday, between twelve and one o'clock. Hi John, it's Sarah. Hello Sarah, how are you? She said: Where's Five Star? I said: Well they'll probably be at home in Romford.

She said: Well I've booked the Smiths and they're here, but Morrissey isn't here for the rehearsal, and nobody knows where he is and nobody will tell me where he is; so I've said to them, unless you tell me where he is and that he's going to be here in half-an-hour, you're off the show, because I ain't risking it live. I ain't risking my neck on the block. Well they weren't able to assure her that Morrissey was going to turn up, so she kicked them off the show, and she said to me: If you can get them to TV Centre by five o'clock, they're on tonight. I actually think they did have a couple of things in the can they could have got by with, or they could have just not had music on. So I phoned Buster up; Buster, where's the kids? They're in Romford. I said: You've got to get them NOW, and get all the stage gear, we're on *Wogan* tonight. Ooh man. So he's jumping in the little people wagon, I think it was a VW Kombi, so he's chasing around Romford High Street looking for the kids; and found them thankfully. We get to TV Centre, Shepherd's Bush Theatre, for five o'clock, they routine and everything, on they go on the show, and from that moment on, everybody wanted them; it was brilliant. That was down to Morrissey going AWOL.

£££

DOUG SMITH,
Clearwater Management

I don't know how it came about, but wouldn't it be a good idea to have Lemmy and Wendy O. Williams sing 'Stand By Your Man'? Because she had this fantastic voice that was like Mini Mouse in many ways, it was Wendy's voice. Then Lemmy had this blur, very gravelly voice that had been brought on by too much speed, and heavy alcohol, and hard living, and never going to bed. It was just a funny idea. I don't even know who was there. I can't even remember who was at the meeting at Bronze where this was decided. I think it had emanated from the fact that there'd been a photograph in one of the music papers with Lemmy and Wendy together singing at a club together, or something like that. That sort of started the conversation. Anyway, it was decided though they were going to do it, and Eddie was going to produce it. We worked out times that conflicted and we couldn't get it together. It just happened that they were in Toronto at the same time as Motörhead were going to be in Toronto doing a gig. I flew everybody out a few days earlier with our stable master, Rod: You'll keep them in order, won't you, Rod? Well he did, until they threw a riot. He called me and said: You'd better get out here. They're falling to pieces. Lemmy won't come out of his room, because he was working with the engineer. By that time, I think Eddie was actually quite instrumental in the production of Motörhead. He was working with an engineer, and the engineer was out there with him, and they would throw moodies, and smoke lots of drugs, and get really drunk, and just stay in their room and refuse to come out. Couldn't get them out of their rooms. This was going nowhere. In the end, I think Rod Swenson and Lemmy sat down and started making this record in the studio. They got the first mix of it. I can't remember exactly how, but obviously there was some very tight tension going on.

We did the gig in Toronto, it was very bad vibes. Some incredible bad vibes at this gig. They played fantastic, it was a good gig. The end of the show was over, and really bad vibes are still there. Eddie, in the dressing room with his engineer, and I think his engineer's

233

flying home the next day. They've got this mix of what Wendy, and Rod, and Lemmy had done in the studio with the backing. They get on the bus for an overnight to Montreal, which I'm travelling with them, and every now and again, Lemmy would play the track and listen to it. You'd just hear Eddie in the background going: Oh fucking cunt! Fucking how dumb are you? This fucking piece of shit sounds like Mickey and Minnie Mouse. There's a muttering going on the whole time.

$$$
JONH INGHAM,
Manager

At the end of 1977, I parted company with Generation X, because I found out that management is essentially looking after grown-up ten year olds. I didn't know enough about psychology at that point to be other than very straightforward. That was a band that had two basically unmanageable people within it, so we parted company. I went out to LA, where my mum lived, for Christmas. You know, it's Christmas, and it's 75 degrees, and sunny and beautiful. Then I come back here and it's misty, and 26 degrees Fahrenheit, and it's cold, and no-one's got central heating. I'm thinking: This is terrible. Why am I here? I went out to LA, and the punk scene was happening, booming over there. Then I'd realised a lot of girl groups were getting talked about in the press, whether it was The Slits, or The Raincoats, and there was some in New York, and so on and so forth. I made it a mission to go and see these groups and find what was going on. Clearly, it was being talked about, there was a reason that everyone's focusing on it. Let's find the right one.

Sure enough, in my own backyard, there was a group called The Go-Go's, who were very rough musically, but you could see that they had melodies, and there was something about it was working. I started managing them. I had a very old school friend, Paul Wexler, who was Jerry Wexler's son. Paul had musical chops, and he had production chops, and we worked on it together. We effectively taught them how to play. I mean, not in the sense of play your instruments, but how do you work as a group. Because they were like all punks that were starting from zero, except for Charlotte Caffey, who actually had a background to her, and she knew music inside out.

The interesting thing was that it became apparent very quickly they were ruthless. They would make a mistake once and never repeat it. You think, OK, that's interesting. Once they got the act together, the audience, it was exponential. It went from 50, to 100, to 300, to 700, to 1,000, to 1,500, until you go to the star world of the Whiskey and there'd be like 2,000 people. Then, of course, once you get 2,000 people, the guys who run the industry suddenly show up. Sure enough, my lawyer got a phone call from a lawyer, who said: I'm now representing the group that one of your clients manages. As we started to go through this at more length, my lawyer friend said to me: Do you know, there's a point when you're in these kind of situations where you've just got to accept you're going to lose? The interesting thing was, they never actually replaced me with a manager. This was an interesting point, I think, in the evolution of the music business. Here was a number one band, and they let their lawyer do the business management, and they took care internally of anything else.

SIMON DRAPER, MD, Virgin Records

I signed Phil Collins. All I could get was the UK but we paid a huge royalty, bigger royalty than we ever paid. We paid an advance which I thought we'd certainly get back but it was a high advance for one territory. And we had a meeting with the staff where we said there would be no salary increases until we had a platinum record; and thankfully the Phil Collins album was more than platinum. So that was a big turning point. It must have been 1981 that that came out. And then suddenly we were on a roll, because the Human League, when they saw all these economies were being practised, Nik Powell had tried to get me to drop them and I really dug my heels in, and luckily Richard backed me, and they came good. And Simple Minds came good and we signed Culture Club. I seem to remember looking at a figure where there was something like twenty million quid's worth of income from them over a period of years. But you think when *Kissing to Be Clever* came out, it didn't do that much. The last single from it was 'Do You Really Want to Hurt Me', which was the third single, which was a hit. And from there it took off. I remember that album selling at least two million copies. Then the 'Karma Chameleon' single and that album sold a million copies in Canada alone, that album. So what did it sell – ten million? Even *Tubular Bells*, then wouldn't have been that much, even over the long period.

We also found that – I think it was '81 or '82, maybe it was '84, but anyway it was one of those years – we suddenly found we'd been licensing all our hits to Ronco, and playing one off against the other, who did the best deals and that stuff; and I know it was Jon Webster's idea to call them up and, look, haven't you noticed, between us we've got enough hits to make a twenty-four track Christmas album, just without anybody else. Even if we haven't got twenty-four gold ones, we can license a few ourselves. So the meeting was convened in my office and Peter Jamieson came along and it all started to go. It took this leap of faith to actually cough up the £300,000 for the TV campaign. That was when Peter Jamieson was sitting opposite me at my desk and I had this poster behind my desk which Richard Branson had given me as a birthday present when he was wooing Joan, and Joan worked in this shop in Westbourne Grove which sold these sort of posters and he would go in as an excuse to talk to her and buy loads of them; and it was for the Danish marketing board for bacon I think, and it had the pig and 'that's what I call music'. And Peter Jamieson looked at it and said, that's what we should call the thing. I've still got it; it's in my office in London. And of course it worked spectacularly well, we made a fortune out of it.

MIKE THORNE,
Record Producer

Soft Cell were a really remarkable pair and they had come to the attention of Phonogram through Stevo scooping up just about all the acts at a New Music – Electronic Music Festival, call it what you like, and putting out a record which was a pretty spunky thing to do. Then they got signed to Phonogram along with B-Movie. I'd done a first single with B-Movie, again under Stevo's guidance, and I was doing a second one and it was suggested I just do the two back-to-back. I was in London doing a film score at that point and the phone went, and it seemed like a good idea so I thought: Well both of these groups need to get a little time off so they can get perspective on how the recording's going, so I'll just do them back-to-back which is fine for the groups, but it meant that I was putting in fifteen-hour days. But, *c'est la vie*. So B-Movie were getting going, 'Marilyn Dreams' was the single, and all of a sudden there's this presence in the back of the control room, seems to be a lot of that about, and it's two very suave looking people dressed in pork-pie hats and mackintoshes, and Stevo in his wisdom had thought it a good idea to introduce Soft Cell to the sessions of his other protégés. Not really a very tactful thing to do. But there they were, we said hello, and off we went.

We were due to record the following day having only discussed things on the phone. Not my ideal way but I was in the studio solidly and I couldn't make it up to Leeds. So we did it in one full day, two half days with each B-Movie and recorded 'Tainted Love'. The mixing went on till maybe four o'clock in the morning; lots of action particularly on the B-side which was 'Tainted Dub', which involved leaping around all over the control room trying to grab a knob in real time. This was before the days of fancy automation and computers. But at one point I noticed that the band who had been pressed into service turning knobs at the appropriate time, the engineer, the assistant and myself we were there and it was approaching the end of the mix, and I noticed that all of us were dancing in the control room without even thinking about it, but I just noticed that everybody was bobbing up and down. If ever there was a good signal that was it.

Anyway we got the mixes we needed and we were just sitting around afterwards and we were quite pleased with ourselves really and we said: Yeah that should become something of a cult hit, it'll probably make the seventy-five.

STEVE JENKINS, MD, Jive Records

It's the summer of 1989, and I've taken over Jive Records, and I'm canning a lot of artists that are on the label. Andrew Lauder is signing people like Brendan Croker and Loudon Wainwright. Music, really, I didn't know a lot about, to be perfectly honest. To me, it seems like it's 5,000 selling albums. I understood the philosophy of developing a label like that, with putting those artists on it. Anyway, so I go over, and I sit down and I have a meeting with Andrew. I go: Andrew, what have you got? What are you working on? I've got this group, Stone Roses. Yeah. John Leckie made the album, the album's out and we're selling a few. They're from Manchester. I took the album away, I listened to the album. To be honest, I listened to the album and I thought, this album is the songs that The Beatles threw away. I'm not sure about this. I could kind of see whatever it was, that flower power kind of thing that they had, but to me, the songs were OK, not great, and it certainly weren't The Beatles. Then I started to delve into how many records this album has sold, where is it selling, and starting to do the research on it. I was surprised to find out that the album, over a period of about six months, had sold 8,000 copies. A lot of them in Manchester and around the north-east and that, but it was starting to spread. I knew, because of the mathematics of the chart and Impulse, that if you could shift 8,000 records in five days, you could, on a good week, get in the Top Forty. 8,000 records in one week would give you a chart position of forty-two. 8,000 records another week, because of

238

the way the sales went, would give you a position of maybe thirty-six or thirty-seven. I'm like: Andrew, this is what I want to do. I want to issue a record, but I want to do it in such a way that I condense all those Stone Roses fans into a five-day piece so that we can get in the Top Forty and bring notoriety to the band.

Actually, I think with Andrew, I was talking Double Dutch. Andrew was like: Well, if you can get on the chart, get on the chart. I can't remember the exact things that we did, but we did a seven-inch, and an alternative seven-inch, and a twelve-inch, so we're selling the same thing three times, all to condense those sales into a five-day period. Basically, what happens is, the Stone Roses record goes on the chart at thirty-eight. It was a good week: 8,000 sales got you in the Top Forty. What then happened was, *Top of the Pops* at that time, were having the artists on that were higher up the chart, but for some reason, they developed a video piece that they would show twenty seconds of three videos, records that were between thirty and forty. All of a sudden, I'm thirty-eight on the chart – by the way, it plummeted like a stone the following week – but I'm thirty-eight on the chart, and I've got twenty seconds on *Top of the Pops*. The value of twenty seconds on *Top of the Pops* is seriously important. That album, after that one event of going in the charts at thirty-eight and the twenty seconds, that album goes from selling 8,000 copies to selling 30,000 within the matter of eight weeks. Now we've got a band that sold 30,000 records. I know, I'm game on. I know where the next record's going. 30,000 sales, I know where it's going. That was how we developed the Stone Roses.

TONY WADSWORTH,
Parlophone Records

It was a transition really. I went in as the marketing director, as the head of marketing, and the money act which had just broken through and was starting to launch its second album was Pet Shop Boys and so my timing going into there was great because I was right in the beginning of their, as Neil Tennant calls it, 'Imperial Period' where everything they released was number one and it was tremendous. They were very welcoming and you know, great people to work with and I think we had something like three or four number one singles between the September when I joined and Christmas, we had 'Always On My Mind', which is a track which wasn't on the album which was number one at Christmas, and 'It's A Sin' and they could do no wrong for probably about four or five years. A&R was, by that time I think was Nick Gatfield. Dave Ambrose was I think still there. Pet Shop Boys had been brought in by David Munns, because CBS had signed Pet Shop Boys, 'West End Girls' had been released on CBS and had failed, and so the contract was sold to EMI. David Munns picked it up and the rest as they say is *histoire*.

We also had a very interesting A&R relationship with Food Records at the time which was an independent label owned by David Balfe, ex-Teardrop Explodes. He had signed, well there were a few acts, but the two notable artists, Jesus Jones and Blur. I can't remember the day that we're talking about, but I think I'm thinking 1989. I remember going along just before we did the deal and the deal was a single deal for Blur, and seeing this band that was all ready, it was just larger than life, all ready you know you could see they had a front man who was bursting out of the Borderline which is where they were playing. You had a bass player who was like you know a caricature character. You had an amazing guitar player. The drummer was great, couldn't see him. And these songs that already were just really memorable and so I think what Food Records was doing to EMI at the time was actually bringing some real Indie heft if you like into EMI's culture, because EMI's culture didn't have it. The success of the previous two or three years had been with Duran Duran and Iron Maiden and you know that was world-wide success, not necessarily to my taste but you know pretty impressive. But not anything that in any way was Indie cred. But this is what the Food Records things was actually bringing

Food Records was a joint venture. All of the music, all of the A&R side was in theory done by Food and everything else was done by EMI, marketing, sales and so on. But what you found was there was a lot more interaction, I mean we were in and out of each others pockets all the time. Then eventually and not too long after EMI bought the whole thing and it became a wholly-owned label, but I think that EMI got a lot out of Food in that we learnt about how to deal with a certain type of artist, and that came in extremely handy for I suppose the next phase of my career when I eventually became managing director of Parlophone, because we, I suppose became the Indie label within a major and that was a lot thanks to what we'd learnt in the way that something like Food would operate, and from the artist that worked on there because of course you learn so much from artists. I mean the lessons from working with Pet Shop Boys were phenomenal because the innate understanding that they had of the way to do things, on the one hand with massive creativity and breaking down barriers, but also commercially, was a template really. And so there was a lot learnt there.

MAX HOLE,
A&R, Warner Records

My first job at WEA was to manage the musical career of Billy McKenzie, he had already kind of had a hit with 'Party Fears To' and then I did a record as his A&R man for the Associates called 'Perhaps' which I thought was going to be the biggest record ever in the whole world and of course it wasn't. He was a real challenge, an absolute charmer, real talent but a really odd character and I had jumped from leaving all the management madness behind to a different madness of trying to manage people's recording careers. I got lucky really early on because I got involved with Wah and they had a big hit with 'The Story Of The Blues' and the first thing I ever signed was a singles deal for Matt Bianco. That was a hit and went on to sell about two million copies in Europe.

The thing about Billy was that he spent money like water and eventually at Warners I was put under pressure for an artist roster clean-up. Billy's debit balance was hundreds of thousands of pounds, I always remember somebody saying to me, look Max you can be a fan, buy the record on another label and enjoy it at home but you have got to stop putting hundreds of thousands of pounds into this. So I had to drop Billy McKenzie, who up to that point I had thought was an undroppable artist. So I took him to lunch in Kensington and I told him in my best diplomatic way that I thought it was in his best interest and our best interest if we parted. But I was really quite upset about it, and Billy bless him, he said to me: Oh Max you look so sad and he cheered me up and said it is all fine, don't worry. So we had a nice lunch, at the very end of the lunch he said, could I ask you one small favour? I said, sure Billy anything. He said, could I just get a cab home? I said, absolutely fine. So we went back to the office in Kensington, got him a cab and he took it to Dundee in Scotland!!!

So many stories, dear reader, from the British music scene and all from those people who were actually real participants in the day. Their stories are as recounted first hand in the never-ending series of RockHistory interviews. It is now time to take a final bow – as indeed have some of our interviewees, such is the relentless march of time.

As before we have taken the liberty of editing out the obvious errors that have fallen out of people's mouths, did I really say *Abbey Road*? I am absolutely sure I said *Revolver*, that sort of thing. It was a very long time ago for all these folks and the memory is not always what it was any more, yet some memories remain vividly alive and I love to see the face sparkle as they tell it. Some have become embroidered with repeated telling, so let us assume that these memories were replayed with the best intentions and that your version of the truth is not always someone else's version of the truth. Treat it all as fiction if you will, but according to them, they were there, they did see it and these were the stories they recounted. But whether they remember events as someone else saw it is always a challenge. Nothing pleases me more than having two people tell me the same story, but from different perspectives – Lying bastard, this is what really happened...

RockHistory.co.uk is about collecting the British music stories and anecdotes while we are still *compos mentis* so an enormous thanks to everyone for taking part. We still love the music that was made all those moons ago, and you're such a lovely audience, we'd like to take you home with us...

Mark Rye

INDEX

Check out the RockHistory.co.uk website
for details of our series of CD releases

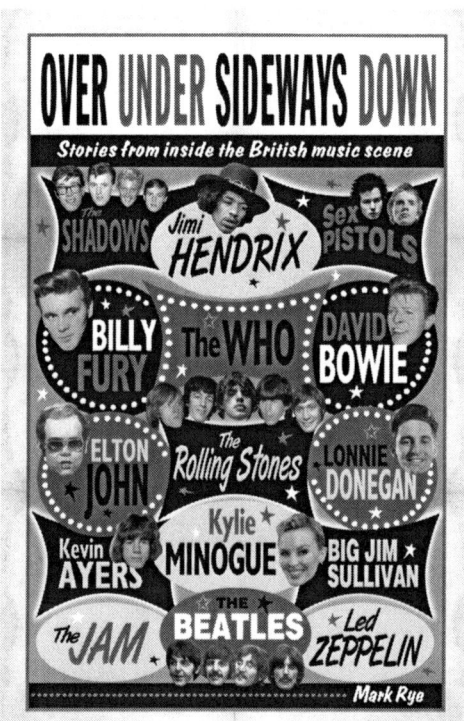

Also available by Mark Rye - **Over, Under, Sideways, Down** – RHBK01

The underbelly of the UK rock scene is laid bare and all major bases – The Beatles, The Stones, The Who, Floyd, Bowie, Bolan, Reg, Queen, etc. – are covered. Moreover, it's not just confined to Fifties, Sixties and Seventies music, as many of the principal movers and shakers from the Eighties and Nineties are given an equal share-of-voice.

The natural by-product of the RockHistory.co.uk body of work was a compilation of anecdotes in this first book – and here it is. It all makes for a compelling read, and at last you can hear – first hand – some of rock music's eternal myths and factoids either confirmed or quashed, by the people who were actually there when they happened.

Lightning Source UK Ltd.
Milton Keynes UK
UKOW02f1132021216

288964UK00001B/105/P